BY WILL DURANT

Heroes of History
The Story of Philosophy
Transition
The Pleasures of Philosophy
Adventures in Genius

BY WILL AND ARIEL DURANT

The Story of Civilization
    I.   *Our Oriental Heritage*
    II. *The Life of Greece*
    III. *Caesar and Christ*
    IV. *The Age of Faith*
    V.   *The Renaissance*
    VI. *The Reformation*
    VII. *The Age of Reason Begins*
    VIII. *The Age of Louis XIV*
    IX. *The Age of Voltaire*
    X.   *Rousseau and Revolution*
    XI. *The Age of Napoleon*

    Interpretations of Life
    The Lessons of History

Will Durant

HEROES
OF
HISTORY

A Brief History of Civilization

from Ancient Times to the

Dawn of the Modern Age

Simon & Schuster

NEW YORK LONDON TORONTO SYDNEY

SIMON & SCHUSTER
Rockefeller Center
1230 Avenue of the Americas
New York, NY 10020

SIMON & SCHUSTER and colophon are registered trademarks
of Simon & Schuster, Inc.

For information regarding special discounts for bulk purchases,
please contact Simon & Schuster Special Sales:
1-800-456-6798 or business@simonandschuster.com

Designed by Karolina Harris

Manufactured in the United States of America

10   9   8   7   6   5   4

Library of Congress Cataloging-in-Publication Data

Durant, Will, date.
    Heroes of history : a brief history of civilization from ancient times to the dawn of the
modern age / Will Durant.
        p. cm.
    Includes index.
        1. Civilization—History.   I. Title.
CB69.D87 2001
909—dc21   2001049361
ISBN 978-0-7432-3594-5

*To all those who seek to see their lives in total perspective;
who eschew dogma and prejudice and who desire the wisdom
to understand and the understanding to forgive.*

*To my parents, William T. Little and Corinne Little, who
instilled in me a love of literature, art, science, and
philosophy; thus sowing the seeds of appreciation for the life,
work, and message of Will Durant.*

*And to Alexandra, Christopher, and Sebastian; that they
might better understand the significance and richness of the
heritage that their great grandparents worked so hard to
transmit to them.*

—John Little

CONTENTS

HEROES
OF
HISTORY

INTRODUCTION

Four years before his death Pulitzer Prize–winning author Will Durant began work on what would prove to be his final book. The project grew out of a desire he shared with his wife and daughter to present an abbreviated version of his highly acclaimed book series *The Story of Civilization*. In that enterprise, which took some fifty years to complete, Durant (with his wife Ariel's assistance) presented an integrated overview of more than 110 centuries in eleven volumes.

Durant was keenly aware of the changing landscape unfolding in the world of mass media and communications. Audio recordings, television, and movies were all serious rivals for the attention of modern audiences. By contrast, in 1935, when the first volume of *The Story of Civilization* was published, literature's only competition was the motion picture and the comparatively new creation of the radio. In 1977, Durant's daughter, Ethel, in hope of broadening the audience for her parents' teachings, contacted Paramount Studios about creating a miniseries for television based upon *The Story of Civilization* and received encouraging news from the studio.

Even the face of publishing was changing; people who once preferred bigger books now wanted their information and entertainment in more concise form. The public found themselves with less time to devote to large books, viewing them more as daunting tasks than leisurely pleasures. With modern audiences seeking more efficient forms of entertainment and education, Will Durant decided to craft a series of "minitalks," i.e., audio lectures, that would focus on key figures and events in human history. Durant liked the idea, and Ethel arranged to have them recorded, but in a letter to his daughter on March 7, 1977, he expressed some trepidation—at the tender age of ninety-two—regarding his ability to complete the task:

I am looking soberly at the program I mapped out for a pair of intellectual kamikazes, [and] I perceive that it is beyond my physical capacity, even with Ariel's aid, to compose and recite so ambitious a
schedule; . . . I feel that the Reaper has at last found us, for he has
left his card in the form of fading memories, an uncertain stability in
walking and a novel stiffness in the legs. These intimations of mortality do not sadden me; I would be ashamed to outlive my usefulness. In any case I must not let you or Paramount invest energy or
money in my permanence.

Nevertheless, Durant formulated a tentative list of the figures from
history he thought would be of interest and benefit to a modern audience. His list ranged from Confucius and Li Po to Abraham Lincoln
and Walt Whitman. The concept would prove significant for reasons
extending beyond mere presentation; it would allow the average person to learn of achievements and lives of the greater men and women of
history directly from Will and Ariel Durant themselves. Via the magic
of audiocassette, one could listen to two of America's most decorated
historians expound on the profound significance of the poets, artists,
statesmen, and philosophers that peopled the landscape of human history. These tapes would prove to be, in effect, private lessons with the
Durants, lessons that could be attended over and over again, thus pro-
viding an ongoing means of education, in Durant's view (shared with
Lord Bolingbroke) that "history is philosophy teaching by examples."
    As Durant warmed to the task, a full creative wind caught his sail
and he found himself in one of the most creative and productive periods
of his life. By August of the following year he had created nineteen
scripts for the venture and had, together with Ariel, recorded a good
many of them onto audio tape. At this point the thought occurred to
him that, with a little refinement, the scripts of these audio lectures
could be developed into a very reader-friendly book.
    He wrote to his daughter on August 25, 1978:

Salt the enclosed away as "Talk XVIII." I have also completed typ-
ing, but not revising, Talk XLX. The Catholic Reformation:
1517–63, which will have 17 pages. As I intend these essays for a
book, HEROES OF HISTORY, rather than for television, I have let

myself spread out a bit more than in the earlier effusions. There [will] be about 23 in all.

There was now no question in Durant's mind; this was to be his final attempt at communicating his ethos of history as philosophy:

> To me history is a part of philosophy. Philosophy is an attempt to achieve a wide perspective, a large perspective of life and reality—a large perspective which will then determine your attitude toward any part of reality or life; for example, will it make you more understanding and forgiving? Now you can achieve a large perspective in at least two ways; one through science, by studying the various sciences that color all the aspects of external reality, but you can also achieve a large perspective by studying history; which is the study of events in time—rather than of things in space. I gave up the first kind, because I felt that it was too external and mathematical; it was unreal to the element of vitality that I found in myself and in other things. I said that I will study history to find out what man *is*—I can't find that out through science. So that history is the attempt to achieve philosophical perspective by a study of events in time. Consequently, if you will allow me to say it, I believe I am a philosopher writing history.

To this end Durant abridged certain sections from within *The Story of Civilization* series and crafted entirely new material for other sections. The finished book serves as a wonderful introduction to the subject of history, but it would (and should) serve to pique the interest of readers to pursue the "heroes" they found most compelling in the larger *Story of Civilization* series.

Durant at one time envisioned completing twenty-three chapters for the book, but fate had other plans. He would complete only twenty-one before his wife Ariel suffered a stroke. In late 1981, Durant himself would be hospitalized with heart problems.

Ariel, perhaps fearing this would be the trip from which her husband would not be returning, stopped eating. She died on October 25, 1981, at the age of eighty-three. The family decided to make a concerted effort to keep the news of his wife's death from reaching the philosopher. By all reports he had come through surgery fine and was on his way to a full recovery. However, Durant's granddaughter, Monica Mihell, believes Durant heard the news of the passing of his beloved wife as a result of a television report or newspaper that had—despite their efforts—found its way to him. Whatever the facts, Will Durant's heart stopped beating on November 7, 1981. He was ninety-six.

With the Durants' passing, their personal papers were dispersed; some went to relatives, others to collectors and archive houses. Among the papers was this manuscript, which would survive three moves and a major flood until I happened upon it in the winter of 2001—twenty years after Will Durant had finished it.

To find the last manuscript of a Pulitzer Prize–winning writer such as Will Durant is surely a bona fide literary event, not only to lovers of his prose but to students of history and philosophy the world over. For Durant was so much more than a highly decorated man of letters (he was also a recipient of the Medal of Freedom, the highest award the United States government can bestow on a private citizen); he was a philosopher who fought for clarity rather than reputation. Profoundly human, he was a man who wrote with dazzling and compelling prose, but who saw human beings as a species that could, when sufficiently inspired, rise to levels of greatness with the gods themselves.

Feeling with Nietzsche that "all philosophy has now fallen forfeit to history," Durant held that the best preparation for understanding the problems of the present is to study the past—for it is there where you will discover what the nature of humankind truly is. This attitude and this philosophy emanates from the pages of *Heroes of History*. The book reveals many of the lessons Durant believed history has to teach—from religion and politics to social issues such as the class war and even the more current debate regarding the viability of homosexuals in the military (you would, for example, be hard-pressed to find in history any indication that homosexuals are not fierce warriors; it was, as Durant reveals in Chapter Eight, a Theban army led by Epaminondas and 300 "Greek lovers" bound in homosexual attachment that routed the Spartans—the fiercest army in all of ancient Greece—at Leuctra in 371 B.C., and thereby ended Sparta's domination of Greece).

Heroes of History also reveals a more candid and personal Will Durant. Perhaps it was his age or a greater sense of freedom that comes with having spent over sixty years in the perfection of one's craft; whatever the reason, this is a refreshingly new Will Durant speaking openly, easily, and engagingly about issues such as sexuality, politics, and religion—always topics that most historians either shy away from or dress in excessively scientific nomenclature. In addition, Durant's use of the first-person narrative imparts a feeling of personal testament on subjects of deep meaning to him.

The motif of virtually all of Will Durant's writing was that civilizations have advanced certain ideas for the betterment of humankind and that the verdict on the efficacy of these ideas has already been rendered by the court of history—if we would but take the time to hear them. Rather than spending hours in theoretical abstraction regarding a philosophical issue—for example, whether or not wealth concentrated in the hands of the few should be redistributed among the general populace—our human heritage has concrete examples of whether or not such a principle engendered the desired result, or precipitated an unanticipated catastrophe.

This last book of Will Durant's is not merely a collection of dates, personalities, and events—nor simply a précis of his masterwork *The Story of Civilization*. It is the lessons of our heritage passed on for the edification and benefit of future generations. It is a keyhole through which we can spy, in Durant's words,

> . . . a celestial city, a special Country of the Mind, wherein a thousand saints, statesmen, inventors, scientists, poets, artists, musicians, lovers, and philosophers still live and speak, teach and carve and sing.

Heroes of History is Will Durant's last testament to the benediction offered by that "Country of the Mind" which he loved and dedicated so much of his life to revealing to us. Through the enchantment of his words, its borders are opened and our souls are beckoned in to visit for a while with people who are willing to walk with us and tell us tales of life, love, war, poetry, and thought, and offer to uplift us to a greater and nobler perspective of tolerance, wisdom, and a more avid love of a deepened life.

—John Little

Chapter One

꧁

WHAT IS CIVILIZATION?

Human history is a fragment of biology. Man is one of countless millions of species and, like all the rest, is subject to the struggle for existence and the competition of the fittest to survive. All psychology, philosophy, statesmanship, and utopias must make their peace with these biological laws. Man can be traced to about a million years before Christ. Agriculture can be traced no farther back than to 25,000 B.C. Man has lived forty times longer as a hunter than as a tiller of the soil in a settled life. In those 975,000 years his basic nature was formed and remains to challenge civilization every day.

In that hunting stage man was eagerly and greedily acquisitive, because he had to be. His food supply was uncertain, and when he caught his prey, he might, as like as not, eat it to the cubic capacity of his stomach, for the carcass would soon spoil; in many cases he ate it raw—"rare," as we say when he returns to the hunting stage in our profoundly masculine restaurants. Furthermore, in those thousand times a thousand years, man had to be pugnacious, always ready to fight—for his food, his mate, or his life. If he could, he took more mates than one, for hunting and fighting were mortally dangerous and left a surplus of women over men; so the male is still polygamous [or polygamous] by nature. He had little reason to contracept, for children became assets in the hut and later in the hunting pack. For these and other reasons acquisitiveness, pugnacity, and ready sexuality were virtues in the hunting stage—that is, they were qualities that made for survival.

They still form the basic character of the male. Even in civilization the chief function of the male is to go out and hunt for food for his family, or for something that might, in need, be exchanged for food. Brilliant though he may be, he is basically tributary to the female, who is the womb and mainstream of the race.

Probably it was woman who developed agriculture, which is the first soil of civilization. She had noted the sprouting of seeds that had fallen from fruits or trees; tentatively and patiently she planted seeds near the cave or hut while the man went off to hunt for animal food. When her experiment succeeded, her mate concluded that if he and other males could band together in mutual protection from outside attack, he might join his women in planting and reaping instead of risking his life and his food supply upon the uncertain fortunes of the chase, or of nomadic pasturage.

Century by century he reconciled himself to a home and settled life. Women had domesticated the sheep, the dog, the ass, and the pig; now she domesticated man. Man is woman's last domestic animal, only partially and reluctantly civilized. Slowly he learned from her the social qualities: family love, kindness (which is akin to kin), sobriety, cooperation, communal activity. Virtue now had to be redefined as any quality that made for the survival of the group. Such, I believe, was the beginning of civilization—i.e., of being civil citizens. But now, too, began the profound and continuing conflict between nature and civilization—between the individualistic instincts so deeply rooted in the long hunting stage of human history, and the social instincts more weakly developed by a recently settled life. Each settlement had to be protected by united action; cooperation among individuals became a tool of competition among groups—villages, tribes, classes, religions, races, states.

Most states are still in a state of nature—still in the hunting stage. Military expeditions correspond to hunting for food, or fuels, or raw materials; a successful war is a nation's way of eating. The state—which is ourselves and our impulses multiplied for organization and defense—expresses our old instincts of acquisition and pugnacity because, like primitive man, it feels insecure; its greed is a hedge against future needs and dearths. Only when it feels externally secure can it attend to its internal needs, and rise, as a halting welfare state, to the social impulses developed by civilization. Individuals became civilized when they were made secure by membership in an effectively protective communal group; states will become civilized when they are made secure by loyal membership in an effectively protective federated group.

How did civilization grow despite the inherent hunting nature of the male? It did not aim to stifle that nature; it recognized that no economic system can long maintain itself without appealing to acquisitive instincts and eliciting superior abilities by offering superior rewards. It knew that no individual or state can long survive without willingness to fight for self-preservation. It saw that no society or race or religion will last if it does not breed. But it realized that if acquisitiveness were not checked it would lead to retail theft, wholesale robbery, political corruption, and to such concentration of wealth as would invite revolution.

If pugnacity were not checked, it would lead to brawls at every corner, to domination of every neighborhood by its heaviest thug, to the division of every city by rival gangs. If sex were not controlled, it would leave every girl at the mercy of every seducer, every wife at the mercy of her husband's secret itching for the charms of variety and youth, and would make not only every park, but every street, unsafe for any woman. Those powerful instincts had to be controlled, or social order and communal life would have been impossible, and men would have remained savages.

The hunting-stage instincts were controlled partly by law and police, partly by a precarious general agreement called morality. The acquisitive impulses were checked by outlawing robbery and condemning greed and the disruptive concentration of wealth. The spirit of pugnacity was restrained by inflicting punishing injury to persons or property. The sexual impulses—only slightly less powerful than hunger—were disciplined to manageable order by banning their public excitation and by trying to channel them at an early age into responsible marriage.

How was that complex moral code—so uncongenial to our nature, so irritating with its "Thou shalt nots"—inculcated and maintained through five special institutions that are all in disrepair today: the family, the church, the school, the law, and the public opinion that these helped to form? The family, in the agricultural regime, taught the uses and comforts of association and mutual aid; the mother led and taught her daughters in the care of the home; the father led and taught his sons in the care of the soil; and this double leadership gave a strong economic base to parental authority. Religion buttressed the moral commandments by attributing them to an all-seeing, rewarding, and punishing God. Parents and teachers transmitted the divinely sanctioned code by precept and example; and their authority was strengthened, till our century, by this connection with religion. Law supported large parts of the code by the use and fear of organized force. Public opinion checked immorality with adjectives and contumely, and encouraged good behavior with praise, promotion, and power.

Under this protective umbrella of social order communal life expanded, literature flourished, philosophy adventured, the arts and sciences grew, and historians recorded the inspiring achievements of the nation and the race. Slowly men and women developed the moderation, the friendliness and courtesy, the moral conscience and esthetic sense, which are the intangible and precious graces of our heritage. Civilization is social order promoting cultural creation.

Now what if the forces that made for order and civilization are failing to preserve them? The family has been weakened by the disappearance of that united labor which held it together on the farm; by the individualism that scatters jobs and sons; and by the erosion of parental authority through the mental freedom, the utopian aspirations, and the natural rebelliousness of the young.

Religion has been weakened by the growth of wealth and cities; by the exciting developments of science and historiography; by the passage from fields proclaiming creative life to factories preaching physics, chemistry, and the glory of the machine; and by the replacement of heavenly hopes with perfect states. Our educational system is discouraged by class and race war, by armed minorities presenting "nonnegotiable demands," by the revolt of overburdened taxpayers and by the collapse of bridges between youth and age, between experiment and experience. Laws lose their edge by their multiplication and their bias, by the venality of legislators, by improvements in the means of escape and concealment, and by the difficulty of law enforcement in a population breeding beyond control. Public opinion loses force through division, fear, apathy, and the universal worship of wealth.

So the old instincts return unchained and untamed, and riot in crime, gambling, corruption, conscienceless moneymaking, and a sexual chaos in which love is sex—free for the male and dangerous for the race. Consultation gives way to confrontation; law yields to minority force; marriage becomes a short-term investment in diversified insecurities; reproduction is left to mishaps and misfits; and the fertility of incompetence breeds the race from the bottom while the sterility of intelligence lets the race wither at the top.

But the very excess of our present paganism may warrant some hope that it will not long endure; for usually excess generates its opposite. One of the most regular sequences in history is that a period of pagan license is followed by an age of puritan restraint and moral discipline. So the moral decay of ancient Rome under Nero and Commodus and later emperors was followed by the rise of Christianity, and its official adoption and protection by the emperor Constantine, as a saving source and buttress of order and decency.

The condottiere violence and sexual license of the Italian Renaissance under the Borgias led to the cleansing of the Church and the restoration of morality. The reckless ecstasy of Elizabethan England gave way to the Puritan domination under Cromwell, which led, by reaction, to the paganism of England under Charles II. The breakdown of government, marriage, and the family during the ten years of the French Revolution was ended by the restoration of law, discipline, and parental authority under Napoleon I; the romantic paganism of Byron and Shelley, and the dissolute conduct of the prince of Wales who became George IV, were followed by the public propriety of Victorian England. If these precedents may guide us, we may expect our children's grandchildren to be puritans.

But there are more pleasant prospects in history than this oscillation between excess and its opposite. I will not subscribe to the depressing conclusion of Voltaire and Gibbon that history is "the record of the crimes and follies of mankind." Of course it is partly that, and contains a hundred million tragedies—but it is also the saving sanity of the average family, the labor and love of men and women bearing the stream

of life over a thousand obstacles. It is the wisdom and courage of statesmen like Winston Churchill and Franklin Roosevelt, the latter dying
exhausted but fulfilled; it is the undiscourageable effort of scientists
and philosophers to understand the universe that envelops them; it is
the patience and skill of artists and poets giving lasting form to transient beauty, or an illuminating clarity to subtle significance; it is the
vision of prophets and saints challenging us to nobility.

On this turbulent and sullied river, hidden amid absurdity and suffering, there is a veritable City of God, in which the creative spirits of
the past, by the miracles of memory and tradition, still live and work,
carve and build and sing. Plato is there, playing philosophy with
Socrates; Shakespeare is there, bringing new treasures every day; Keats
is still listening to his nightingale, and Shelley is borne on the west
wind; Nietzsche is there, raving and revealing; Christ is there, calling
to us to come and share his bread. These and a thousand more, and the
gifts they gave, are the Incredible Legacy of the race, the golden strain
in the web of history.

We need not close our eyes to the evils that challenge us—we should
work undiscourageably to lessen them—but we may take strength
from the achievements of the past; the splendor of our inheritance. Let
us, varying Shakespeare's unhappy king, sit down and tell brave stories
of noble women and great men.

Chapter Two

꙼

CONFUCIUS AND THE
BANISHED ANGEL

It will not be news to you that Chinese civilization is as old as any known to us and that its history is alive with statesmen, sages, poets, artists, scientists, and saints, whose legacy can still enrich our understanding and deepen our humanity. "These peoples," Diderot wrote of the Chinese about 1750, "are superior to all other Asiatics in antiquity, art, intellect, wisdom, policy, and in their taste for philosophy; nay, in the judgment of certain authors, they dispute the palm, in these matters, with the most enlightened peoples of Europe." How revealing it is to find Confucius, some five hundred years before Christ, writing about "the wise men of antiquity"; the Chinese, apparently, had philosophers a thousand years before Confucius, before Buddha, Isaiah, Democritus, and Socrates.

The ancient Chinese, like our own ancestors, devised legends to explain origins. One tells us that P'an Ku, through eighteen thousand years of labor, hammered the universe into shape about 2,229,000 B.C. As he worked, "his breath became the wind and the clouds, his voice became the thunder, his veins the rivers, his flesh the earth, his hair the grass and trees, his sweat the rain; and the insects that clung to his body became the human race." At first, we are informed, "the people were like beasts, clothing themselves in skins, feeding on raw flesh, and knowing their mothers but not their fathers"—or, in our contemporary variation, they wore mink coats, liked rare steaks, and practiced love free for the male.

This wild freedom (the legend continues) was ended by a series of "celestial emperors," each of whom reigned eighteen thousand years, and helped turn P'an Ku's vermin into obedient citizens. The emperor Fu Hsi, about 2852 B.C., taught his people marriage, music, writing, painting, fishing with nets, domesticating animals and husbands, and persuading silkworms to secrete silk. His successor Shen Nung introduced agriculture, invented the plow, and developed the science of medicine from the curative values of plants. The emperor Huang-ti discovered the magnet, built an observatory, corrected the calendar, and redistributed the land—the earliest mention of governmental redistribution of (repeatedly concentrated) wealth. So legend, like Carlyle, saw history as a succession of heroes, and ascribed to a few outstanding individuals the laborious advances of many generations.

This imperial age was ended by the wickedness of the emperor Chou Hsin, who invented chopsticks and allowed his people to riot in licentiousness and violence; men and women, we are told, gamboled naked in the gardens of the queen. About 1123 B.C. a revolution overthrew Chou Hsin, and the Middle Kingdom, as the Chinese called their country, fell into a medley of semiduchies, whose semi-independence, as in eighteenth-century Germany, seems to have contributed to the development of poetry and philosophy, science and art. Confucius collected 305 poems of this feudal period into the *Shi-Ching,* or *Book of Odes.*

Most contemporary of them is the timeless lament of soldiers torn from their homes and dedicated to unintelligible death:

> *How free are the wild geese on their wings,*
> *And the rest they find on the bushy Yu trees!*
> *But we, ceaseless toilers in the king's services,*
> *Cannot even plant our millet and rice.*
>
> *What will our parents have to rely on?*
> *O thou distant and azure Heaven:*
> *When shall all this end? . . .*

What leaves have not turned purple?
What man is not torn from his wife?
Mercy be on us soldiers!—
Are we not also men?

One soldier returned, as we gather from the happiest of these odes, beautifully translated by Helen Waddell:

The morning-glory climbs above my head,
Pale flowers of white and purple, blue and red.
I am disquieted.

Down in the withered grasses something stirred;
I thought it was his footfall that I heard;
Then a grasshopper stirred.

I climbed the hill as the new moon showed;
I saw him coming on the southern road.
My heart lays down its heavy load.

To that feudal age belonged the first famous Chinese philosophers. Born about 604 B.C., Lao-tze—i.e., the "Old Master"—rejected the civilization of the rising cities of China, in a book known as *Tao-Te-Ching*—that is, *The Way and the Right.* It was almost a summary, twenty-three hundred years before them, of Jean-Jacques Rousseau and Thomas Jefferson. The Right Way, according to Lao, is to shun the works and tricks of the intellect, and lead a life of quiet rusticity in harmony with nature and ancient customs and ideas.

Unhampered by government, the spontaneous impulses of the people—their desires for bread and love—would move the wheels of life sufficiently in a simple and wholesome round. There would then be few inventions, for these merely add to the strength of the strong and the wealth of the rich. There should be no books and no industries, only village trades—and no foreign trade.

The Old Master draws as sharp a distinction between nature and civilization as Rousseau was to do in that gallery of echoes called modern thought. Nature is natural activity, the silent flow of traditional events, the majestic march and order of the seasons and the sky; it is the Tao (or Way) exemplified and embodied in every brook and rock and star; it is that impartial and impersonal, yet rational, law of things, to which the law of conduct must conform (as in Spinoza) if we desire to live in wisdom and peace. This law of things is the Tao, or Way, of the universe, just as the law of conduct is the Tao, or Way, of life. In Lao-tze both Taos are one; and human life, in its essential rhythms of birth and life and death, is part of the rhythm of the world.

> All things in nature work silently. They come into being and possess nothing. They fulfill their function and make no claim. All things alike do their work, and then we see them subside. When they have reached their bloom each returns to its origin. Returning to their origin means rest, or fulfillment of destiny. This reversion is an eternal law. To know that law is wisdom.

Quiescence, a kind of philosophical inaction, a refusal to interfere with the natural courses of things, is the mark of the wise man in every field. If the state is in disorder, the proper thing to do is not to reform it, but to make one's life an orderly performance of duty. If resistance is encountered, the wiser course is not to quarrel, fight, or make war, but to retire silently, and to win, if at all, through yielding and patience; passivity has its victories more often than action. Here, Lao-tze talks almost with the accents of Christ:

> If you do not quarrel, no one on earth will be able to quarrel with you. . . . Recompense injury with kindness. . . . To those who are good I am good, and to those who are not good I am good; thus all get to be good. To those who are sincere I am sincere, and to those who are not sincere I am also sincere, and thus all get to be sincere. . . . The softest thing in the world . . . overcomes the hardest.

All these doctrines culminate in Lao's conception of the sage. It is characteristic of Chinese thought that it speaks not of saints but of sages, not so much of goodness as of wisdom; to the Chinese the ideal is not the pious devotee but the mature and quiet mind. Even of the Tao and wisdom the wise man does not speak, for wisdom can never be transmitted by words, only by example and experience. If the wise man knows more than other men he tries to conceal it; "he will temper his brightness, and bring himself into agreement with the obscurity of others. He agrees with the simple rather than with the learned, and does not take hurt from the novice's contradiction." He attaches no importance to riches or power, but reduces his desires to an almost Buddhist minimum.

We can imagine how irritating this philosophy of retreat must have been to the ambitious young Confucius, who, at the immature age of thirty-five, sought out Lao-tze and asked his advice on some details of history. The Old Master, we are told, replied with harsh and cryptic brevity:

> Those about whom you inquire have molded with their bones into dust . . . Get rid of your pride and many ambitions, your affectation and your extravagant aims. Your character gains nothing at all from all these.

The Chinese historian relates that Confucius recognized the wisdom of these words and took no offense from them. He went forth with new resolve to fulfill his own mission and to become the most influential philosopher in history.

CONFUCIUS

Kung-fu-tze—"Kung the Master," as his pupils called him—was born about 551 B.C., in the feudal duchy, or kingdom, of Lu, now the province of Shantung. His father died when the boy was three. Confucius worked after school to help support his mother. He married at nineteen, divorced his wife at twenty-three, and does not seem to have married again. At twenty, he set up as a teacher, using his home as a schoolhouse, and charging whatever fee his pupils could pay. Like Socrates he taught by word of mouth rather than by books; we know his views chiefly by the unreliable reports of his disciples. He attacked no other thinker and wasted no time on refutations. He strongly desired fame and place, but he repeatedly refused appointment from rulers who seemed to him immoral or unjust.

His opportunity came when, about the year 501 B.C., he was made chief magistrate of the town of Chung-tu. According to a patriotic tradition, a veritable epidemic of honesty swept through the city; articles of value dropped in the street were left untouched or were returned to the owner. His subsequent appointment by Duke Ting of Lu to be minister of crime, we are told, sufficed of itself to end all lawlessness. "Dishonesty and dissoluteness," say Chinese records, "were ashamed, and hid their heads. Loyalty and good faith became the characteristics of the men, and chastity and docility of the women. Confucius became the idol of the people." This is too good to be true, and in any case proved too good to endure. Criminals put their heads together, and laid snares for the Master's feet. Neighboring states, say the historians, grew jealous of Lu, and fearful of its rising power. A wily minister suggested a stratagem to alienate the duke of Lu from Confucius; the duke of Ts'i sent to Duke Ting a bevy of pretty "sing-song girls," and 120 still-more-beautiful horses. The duke of Lu was captivated, ignored the protests of Confucius (who held that the first principle of government is good example), and scandalously neglected his ministers and affairs of state. Confucius resigned, and began thirteen years of wandering with his pupils. He remarked sadly that he had never "seen one who loved virtue as much as he loved beauty."

What was his basic philosophy? It was to restore morality and social order by spreading education. Two paragraphs in a book called *The Great Learning* were drawn up by his pupils to summarize his doctrine:

> The ancients who wished to illustrate the highest virtue throughout the empire first ordered well their own states. Wishing to order well their own states, they first regulated their families. Wishing to regulate their families, they first cultivated their own selves. Wishing to cultivate their own selves, they first rectified their hearts. Wishing to rectify their hearts, they first sought to be sincere in their thoughts. Wishing to be sincere in their thoughts, they first extended to the utmost their knowledge. Such extension of knowledge lay in the investigation of things.

Things being investigated, knowledge became complete. Their knowledge being complete, their thoughts were sincere. Their thoughts being sincere, their hearts were then rectified. Their hearts being rectified, their own selves were cultivated. Their own selves being cultivated, their families were regulated. Their families being regulated, their states were rightly governed. Their states being rightly governed, the whole empire was made tranquil and happy.

It is a counsel of perfection, and forgets that man is a trousered ape; but, like Christianity, it offers a goal to aim at, a ladder to climb. It is one of the golden texts of philosophy: Reform begins at home.

In the sixty-ninth year of Confucius, Duke Gae succeeded to the duchy of Lu, and sent three officers to the philosopher, bearing presents and an invitation to return to his native state. During the five remaining years of his life Confucius lived there in simplicity and honor. When the Duke of Shi sent inquiries about his health, he told his faithful pupil Tsze-loo to answer:

He is simply a man who, in his eager pursuit of knowledge, forgets his food; who, in his joy (of its attainment) forgets his sorrows; and who does not perceive that old age is coming on.

He died at the age of seventy-two. His students buried him with pomp and ceremony befitting their affection for him; some built huts by his grave and lived there for three years. When all the others had gone, Tsze-kung, who had loved him even beyond the rest, remained three years more, mourning alone by the Master's tomb.

꧁

Now put on your wings and leap across twelve centuries from 478 B.C. to A.D. 705.

One day, at the height of his reign, the emperor Ming Huang received ambassadors from Korea, who brought him important messages written in a dialect which none of his ministers could understand. "What!" he exclaimed, "among so many magistrates, so many scholars and warriors, cannot there be found a single one who knows enough to

relieve us of vexation in this affair? If in three days no one is able to de-
cipher this letter, every one of your commissions will be suspended."
For a day the ministers consulted and fretted, fearing for their offices
and their heads.

The Minister Ho Chi-chang approached the throne, and said:

> Your subject presumes to announce to your Majesty that there is a
> poet of great merit, called Li, at his house, who is profoundly ac-
> quainted with more than one science; command him to read this let-
> ter, for there is nothing of which he is not capable.

Li came and dictated a learned reply, which the emperor signed
without hesitation, almost believing what Minister Ho Chi-chang
whispered to him—that Li was an angel banished from heaven for
some impish deviltry. The story is probably one of Li's compositions.

On the night of his birth, his mother—of the family of Li—had
dreamt of Tai-po Hsing, the Great White Star, which in the West is
called Venus. So the child was named Li, meaning "plum," and sur-
named Tao-po, the White Star. At ten he had mastered all the books of
Confucius and was composing immortal poetry. He grew to health and
strength, practiced swordsmanship, and announced his abilities to the
world: "Though less than seven [Chinese] feet in height, I am strong
enough to meet 10,000 men." Then he wandered leisurely about the
earth, drinking the lore of love from varied lips. So he wrote:

> *Wine of the grapes,*
> *Goblets of gold—*
> *And a pretty maid of Wu.*
> *She comes on ponyback; she is fifteen.*
> *Blue-painted eyebrows—*
> *Shoes of pink brocade—*
> *But she sings bewitchingly well.*
> *So, feasting at the table*
> *Inlaid with tortoise shell,*
> *She gets drunk in my lap.*

Ah child, what caresses
Behind lily-broidered curtains!

He married, but earned so little money that his wife left him, taking the children with her. The emperor befriended him and showered him with gifts for singing the praises of Yang Ywei-fei, the royal mistress. But Lady Yang thought that the poet satirized her, and so persuaded the emperor, who presented Li Po with a purse and let him go.

We picture him wandering from city to city, much as Tsui Tsung-chi described him:

A knapsack on your back, filled with books, you go a thousand miles and more, a pilgrim. Under your sleeves there is a dagger, and in your pocket a collection of poems.

In these long ramblings his old friendship with nature gave him solace and a kind of rebel joy:

Why do I live among the green mountains?
I laugh and answer not; my soul is serene;
It dwells in another heaven and earth belonging to no man.
The peach trees are in flower, and the water flows on.

Or:

I saw the moonlight before my couch,
And wondered if it were not the frost on the ground.
I raised my head and looked out on the mountain-moon;
I bowed my head and thought of my far-off home.

Now, as his hair grew white, his heart was flooded with longing for the scenes of his youth. How many times, in the artificial life of the capital, he had pined for the natural simplicity of parentage and home!

In the land of Wu the mulberry leaves are green,
And thrice the silkworms have gone to sleep.
In East Lu, where my family stays,

I wonder who is sowing those fields of ours.
I cannot be back in time for the spring doings;
I can help nothing, traveling on the river.

The south wind, blowing, wafts my homesick spirit
And carries it up to the front of our familiar tavern.
There I see a peach-tree on the east side of the house,
With the thick leaves and branches waving in the blue mist.
It is the tree I planted before my parting three years ago.
The peach-tree has grown now as tall as the tavern roof,
While I have wandered about without returning.

Ping-yang, my pretty daughter, I see you stand
By the peach-tree and pluck a'flowering branch.
You pluck the flowers, but I am not there—
How your tears flow like a stream of water!
My little son, Po-chin, grown up to your sister's shoulders,
You come out with her under the peach-tree;
But who is there to put you on her back?

When I think of these things my senses fail,
And a sharp pain cuts my heart every day.
Now I tear off a piece of white silk to write this letter,
And send it to you with my love a long way up the river.

His last years were bitter, for he had never stooped to make money, and in the chaos of war and revolution he found no king to keep him from starvation. Gladly he accepted the offer of Li-ling, prince of Yung, to join his staff; but Li-ling revolted against the successor of Ming Huang, and when the revolt was suppressed, Li Po found himself in jail, condemned to death as a traitor. Then Kuo Tsi-i, the general who had put down the rebellion, begged that Li Po's life might be ransomed by the forfeit of his own military rank and title. The emperor commuted the sentence to banishment. Soon thereafter a general amnesty was declared, and the poet turned his faltering steps homeward. Three years later he sickened and died, and legend, discontent with an ordinary death for so rare a soul, told how he was drowned in a river while attempting, in hilarious intoxication, to embrace the water's reflection of the moon.

All in all, the thirty volumes of delicate and kindly verse which he left behind him warrant his reputation as the greatest poet of China. "He is the lofty peak of Tai," exclaims a Chinese critic, "towering above the thousand mountains and hills; he is the sun in whose presence a million stars of heaven lose their scintillating brilliance."

King Huang and Lady Yang are dead, but Li Po still sings.

My ship is built of spice-wood, and has a rudder of mulan;
Musicians sit at the two ends, with jeweled bamboo flutes and pipes
  of gold.
What a pleasure it is, with a cask of sweet wine,
And singing girls beside me,
To drift on the water hither and thither with the waves!
I am happier than the fairy of the air,
Who rode on his yellow crane,
And, free as the merman who followed the seagulls aimlessly.
Now with the strokes of my inspired pen I shake the Five Mountains.

My poem is done. I laugh, and my delight is vaster than the sea.
O deathless poetry! The songs of (the poet) Ch'u P'ing are ever glorious
  as the sun and moon,
While the palaces and towers of the Chou kings have vanished from
  the hills.

There is so much more to say, but the infernal clock ticks away, so I end with the last paragraph that I wrote about China, about 1932:

No victory of arms, or tyranny of alien finance, can long suppress a nation so rich in resources and vitality. The invader will lose funds or patience before the loins of China will lose vitality; within a century China will have absorbed her conquerors (then the Japanese), and will have learned all the technique of what transiently bears the name of modern industry; roads and communications will give her unity, economy and thrift will give her funds, and a strong government will give her order and peace. Every chaos is a transition. In the end disorder cures and balances itself with dictatorship, old obstacles are roughly cleared away, and fresh growth is free. Revolution, like death and style, is the removal of rubbish, the surgery of the superfluous; it comes when many things are ready to die. China has died many times before, and many times she has been reborn.

Chapter Three

⁕

INDIA—FROM BUDDHA TO INDIRA GANDHI

THE UPANISHADS

Civilization—which we have defined as social order promoting cultural creation—is as old in India as the archeologists care to dig. At Mohenjodaro, on the river Indus, Sir John Marshall and his aides, in 1924, unearthed four or five superimposed cities, with hundreds of solidly built brick houses and shops, ranged along wide streets and narrow lanes, and rising in some cases to several stories. There they found wheeled wagons, household utensils, toilet articles, painted pottery, coins and engraved seals, necklaces, and earrings; all this, we are told, as early as the oldest Egyptian pyramids.

About 1600 B.C. a hardy people called Aryans entered India from the north, settled down as conquerors, became a master class, established or confirmed a caste system, developed a Sanskrit language basically akin to the languages of Europe, and produced a literature of which some fragments have come down to us as four Vedas, or Books of Knowledge. They consist mostly of prayers, hymns, and religious rituals; partly of Upanishads—religiophilosophical conferences between master and pupil. For centuries they were transmitted by word of mouth; then, toward 300 B.C., they were committed to writing, and are now the oldest extant form of Indian philosophy. I am very fond of them, and ask you to share a few of them with me.

Upa means "near," and *shad* means "to sit"; the words suggest one or more pupils seated before a guru, or teacher. The doctrine—which is still taught by gurus today—offers three stages to understanding and salvation. The first is patient, persistent introspection. Ignore sensations, desires, memories, reasoning, thought; put aside all intellectual operations, for these are primarily adapted to dealing with outward things; put aside all actions or thoughts of action; introspect persistently until you see nothing with any shape or substance or individuality, until you feel, behind its operations, the mind itself, and the very consciousness of consciousness. This is the most immediate, most basic of all realities, upon which all phenomena—all perceptions and therefore all things—depend. The gurus called this fundamental reality Atman—which seems to have meant "breath," like our words "spirit" and "inspire."

Secondly, in all things, as in ourselves, there is a breath of this inward, vital, immaterial force, without which matter would be spiritless, motionless, dead, and nothing would live or grow. The sum of all these living forces is Brahma—the one all-pervading immaterial, sexless, impersonal, intangible essence, upon which not only all lives and thoughts, but all forms and forces, depend. This is the one and only god, of whom—or of which—all the gods of the Hindu pantheon are partial aspects and poetic expressions aiding the mortal mind to conceive the varied vitality of omnipresent reality.

Thirdly, Atman and Brahma are one: the nonindividual soul or force within us, or within a tree or a stone, is identical with the impersonal Soul of the World. Hear the most lovable of the Upanishad gurus, Yajnavalkya, explain this to his pupil Shwetaketu:

> "Bring me a fig from there."
> "Here it is, Sir."
> "Divide it."
> "It is divided, Sir."
> "What do you see there?"
> "These rather fine seeds, Sir."
> "Of these please divide one."
> "It is divided, Sir."
> "What do you see there?"
> "Nothing at all, Sir."

"Verily, my dear one, that finest essence which you do not perceive—verily from that finest essence this great tree arises. Believe
me . . . that which is the finest essence—this whole world has as its
soul. That is Reality. That is Atman. Tat tvam asi—that art thou,
Shwetaketu."

"Do you, Sir, cause me to understand even more."

"So be it, my dear one."

The Upanishads teach much more; Yoga as a cleansing of the self,
and rebirth as a punishment for selfishness. But on this matter let us
listen to Buddha, Asia's "Light of the World."

BUDDHA

His story is so shot through with legends that we cannot be sure that
he ever existed. One legend credited him with a virgin birth. He himself, we are told, opened the side of Queen Maya, entered her womb,
stayed there ten months, then came forth, "not stained with impure
matter," but "like a man descending stairs," and "shining like a jewel."
Nevertheless he had a father, the king of Kapilavastu, near the Himalayas. Siddhartha Gautama, as the boy was called, was given every
comfort, was sheltered from pain and grief, chose a wife from five hundred beautiful maidens, became a happy father, and lived in prosperity
and peace.

One day, says a holy tradition, he went forth from his palace into the
streets, and saw an old man. Another day he went forth and saw a sick
man; and on a third day he saw a dead man. "This," he later explained,
"seemed to me not fitting. As I thus reflected, all the elation of youth
disappeared. . . . Thus, O monks, . . . being myself subject to birth, I
sought out the nature of birth; being subject to old age, I sought out the
nature of old age, of sickness, of sorrow, of impurity. Then I thought:
'What if I, being myself subject to birth, were to seek out the nature of
birth; . . . and, having seen the wretchedness of the nature of birth,
were to seek out the unborn, the supreme peace of Nirvana?' " Like one
stricken with "conversion," he resolved to leave his father, wife, and
newborn son, and became an ascetic seeker of fundamental truth.

For six years he lived on seeds and grass. "Then I thought, what if I were to take food only in small amounts, as much as my hollowed palm would hold—juices of beans, vetches, chickpeas, and pulse. . . . My body became extremely lean. The mark of my buttocks was like a camel's footprint through the little food. . . . When I thought I would ease myself I fell prone through the little food."

But one day the thought came to Gautama that self-mortification was not the way. He perceived that no new enlightenment had come to him from these austerities; on the contrary, a certain pride in his self-torture had poisoned any holiness that might have grown from it. He abandoned his asceticism, and went to sit under a shade-giving tree (the "Bodhi tree" still shown to tourists), and resolved never to leave that seat until enlightenment should come. What, he asked himself, was the source of human sorrow, sickness, old age, death? A vision came to him of the infinite succession of births and deaths, each of them darkened with pain and grief. Birth, he concluded, is the origin of all evil.

Why is not birth stopped? Because the law of karma demands new incarnations, in which the soul may atone for evil done in past existences. If, however, one could live a life of perfect justice, of tireless patience and kindness to all; if he could tie his thoughts to eternal things, not binding his heart to those that begin and pass away—then he might be spared rebirth, and for him the fountain of evil would run dry. If one could still all desires for oneself, and seek only to do good to all, then individuality, that fundamental delusion of mankind, might be overcome, and the soul would merge at last with unconscious infinity. What peace there would be in the heart that had cleansed itself of every personal desire!—and what heart that had not so cleansed itself could ever know peace? Happiness is possible neither here, as paganism thinks, nor hereafter, as many believe; only peace is possible, only the cool quietude of craving ended, which is Nirvana. And so, after seven years of meditation, Gautama went forth to preach Nirvana to mankind.

He soon gathered disciples, who followed him as he walked from town to town, teaching as he went. They trusted him, because he seemed to take no thought of himself, and returned good for evil patiently. "Let a man overcome anger by kindness," he counseled them, "evil by good. . . . Never does hatred cease by hatred; hatred ceases only by love." He took no thought of the morrow, but was content to be fed by some local admirer; once he scandalized his followers by eating in the house of a courtesan. They renamed him Buddha; that is, the Enlightened One—but he never claimed that a god was speaking through him. He taught through moral parables, or a pithy pentalog like his "Five Moral Rules":

> *Let no one kill any living being;*
> *Let no one take what is not given to him;*
> *Let no one speak falsely;*
> *Let no one drink intoxicating drinks;*
> *Let no one be unchaste—*

which apparently forbade all sexual actions or desires. Tradition reports a dialogue with Buddha's favorite disciple, Ananda:

> *How are we to conduct ourselves, lord, with regards to women?*
> *As not seeing them, Ananda.*
> *And if we should see them, what are we to do?*
> *No talking, Ananda.*
> *But if they should speak to us, Lord, what are we to do?*
> *Keep wide-awake, Ananda.*

Buddha's conception of religion was purely ethical; he cared everything about conduct, nothing about ritual, worship, or theology. Furthermore, like our latest psychology, he rejected mind if this meant something behind—and performing—the mental operations; mind is an abstract term for those operations taken in their totality. However, Buddha taught, the soul remains, as the living force of a body and a personality; and it is this soul that can be reborn to another earthly life to atone for sins committed in this one.

Sin is selfishness, the seeking of individual advantage or delight; and until the soul is freed from all selfishness, it will be repeatedly reborn. Nirvana is not a heaven after death; it is the quiet content of selfishness overcome. In the end, says Buddha, we perceive the absurdity of moral and psychological individualism. Our fretting selves are not really sep-

arate beings and powers; they are passing ripples on the stream of life,
little knots forming and unraveling in the wind-blown mesh of fate.
When we see ourselves as parts of a whole, when we reform ourselves,
and our desires, in terms of the whole, then our personal disappoint-
ments and defeats, our griefs and pains and inevitable death, no longer
sadden us as bitterly as before; they are lost in the amplitude of infinity.
When we have learned to love not our separate selves but all human
things, then at last we shall find Nirvana—unselfish peace.

TWENTY-FIVE CENTURIES

The soul of India is heat. It seemed so when, in February 1930, the
Durants debarked in Bombay and found the temperature throbbing at
92 degrees Fahrenheit. Could this be the reason why so many Hindus
prayed that they should never be reborn? But then we passed east to
New Delhi and south to Madras, and found many handsome Hindus
eager, active, and creative despite the heat. And in the north the population was kept alert by the cool winds blowing down upon them from
the Himalayas. The English so long maintained their mastery of India
because very few of them stayed there more than five years at a time;
quinquennially they returned to England to get away from the sun.

Buddhism, after its flowering under King Ashoka in the third century B.C., rapidly declined in India and succeeded best in hot Ceylon, at
the cost of a barbarous transformation. I was shocked to find, on the
wall of a Buddhist monastery in Kandy, a spacious painting showing
the gentle founder of Buddhism distributing ferocious punishments in
hell. When I protested against this barbarization of the idealist who
had preached, "Let no man kill any living thing," a monk explained
that unless a religion preached terror as well as virtue and bliss, it could
not control the lawless individualism of mankind. In China, Japan, and
Southeast Asia a theologically reconstructed Buddhism is flourishing,
and the godless Buddha has become a god.

Meanwhile, weakened by heat, by religious, military, and political
divisions, India was invaded by Alexander, then by the Huns, then by
the Arabs, then by the Turks, then by Timor (our Tamerlane), then by
the Portuguese, then by the French, then by the English. In 1686 the
East India Company announced its intention "to establish a large, well-

grounded, sure English dominion in India for all time to come." Most
of the invaders brought some boon to the harassed subcontinent, like
Moslem art and British administration; but each took away some of the
fabled "wealth of the Indies," leaving an impoverished people.

Despite the despotism of Huns, Arabs, Turks, Christians, and the
sun, the patient Hindus found energy enough to develop massive architecture, profuse sculpture, subtle philosophy, and a rich literature in
prose and poetry. Which of you has missed that little gem, in Ra-
bindranath Tagore, where a wise maiden questions her lover's compliments? Let us cool ourselves with it:

> *Tell me if this be true, my lover, tell me if this be true—*
> *When these eyes flash their lightning the dark clouds in your breast*
>   *make stormy answer.*
> *Is it true that my lips are sweet like the opening bud of the first conscious*
>   *love?*
> *Do the memories of vanished months of May linger in my limbs?*
> *Does the earth, like a harp, shiver into songs with the touch of my feet?*
> *Is it true that the dewdrops fall from the eyes of night when I am seen,*
>   *and the morning light is glad when it wraps my body round?*
> *Is it true, is it true that your love traveled alone through ages and*
>   *worlds in search of me?*
> *That when you found me at last your age-long desire found utter peace*
>   *in my gentle speech and my eyes and lips and flowing hair?*
> *Is it then true that the mystery of the infinite is written on this little*
>   *forehead of mine?*
> *Tell me, my love, if all this be true?*

England applauded the poetry, but only the Second World War made
India politically free.

MOHANDAS AND INDIRA GANDHI

Mohandas Gandhi, who had spent three formative years in England,
learned to love the British character and to shrink from the darker side
of British industry. He felt the influence of William Morris, Peter
Kropotkin, John Ruskin, Leo Tolstoi, and the Fabian Socialists. He was

deeply moved by the ethical gospel of Christ and added it to his fervent acceptance of Buddha's major precept—to injure no living thing.

Returning to India, he begged his people to prefer fields to factories. If industrial goods were needed, let the family restore the spinning wheel, and be satisfied with homespun garments and such tools as the village blacksmith could forge. Better the apparent poverty of the rural home than the palaces and tenements of the industrial city; better the friendliness of the village folk than the secret distrust or hostility of the nameless bipeds hurrying through the urban crowd. The vision that drew Gandhi was of a people content with the simplicity of ancient ways.

Like most visions this was not realistic. Whence would iron come to the village smithy except through the industry of workers half-buried in the dungeons of the earth? Whence would come the weapons, the organization, and the martial spirit needed to defend the village against attack? The kindest souls and most peaceful settlements would be at the mercy of the ruthless and the strong. Darwin would again challenge Christ.

After Gandhi's assassination (in 1948) his movement against industrialization was rapidly eroded by the natural acquisitiveness and competitive spirit of men. Town factories lured village youth, and agriculture itself became an industry, wedded to chemistry and costly machines. Even so, population grew faster than the food supply; ancient customs and taboos defeated modern ways and views; and the people canceled their prosperity with their fertility.

Meanwhile studies in science and history, and India's contact with European and American skepticism and permissiveness, had eroded her religious creeds and moral codes, and the new nation found its economic, political, and social life disordered with shoddy work, corrupt administration, and social decay. Suddenly a woman, politically popular, declared a moratorium on democracy, and assumed autocratic control of India's government, economy, and press.

Indira Gandhi took neither her name nor her doctrine from Mohandas Gandhi; the name came from her late husband, Feroz Gandhi, who was no relation to the "Mahatma." Moreover her philosophy of government was almost the opposite of that of her father, Jawaharlal Nehru, the first prime minister of free India, for he had won his people by his gentleness and his power by compromise. Sitting next to her in 1960, when she presided as hostess at a luncheon given to local scribes, I was at first impressed by her beauty—Italian features, flashing eyes—and then more soberly moved by her power as a character and a mind. I was not much surprised, then, when, in 1966, she became prime minister; it seemed almost natural that she should fill the place of her father, who had died two years before.

We need not pretend to sit in judgment on her—we so far away and so imperfectly informed. It may be that the economy, politics, and society of India had fallen into disorder, incompetence, and venality, and called for the stern hand of a central and decisive power. In ancient republican Rome, law allowed—in a crisis—the appointment of a dictator for a year; but when that year had expired, and if the dictator persisted, anyone might depose him, legally or not.

Chapter Four

ﻢﻣﻣ

FROM THE PYRAMIDS TO IKHNATON

THE PHARAOHS

Was the civilization of ancient Egypt the oldest and most lasting in history?

So thought Elie Faure, historian of world art: "It is possible," he wrote, "that Egypt, through the solidarity, the unity, and the disciplined variety of its artistic products, through the enormous duration and sustained power of its effort, offers the spectacle of the greatest civilization that has yet appeared on the earth." (I would rank the civilization of ancient Rome as still greater.)

As to age, the oldest date generally—though still uncertainly—assigned to the Egyptian calendar is 4241 B.C.; if so, Egyptian astronomy and mathematics had reached considerable development by that time. However, a like development had probably been reached in Mesopotamia; and archeologists are inclined to ascribe "the first civilization in known history" to the lands "midway between the rivers" Euphrates and Tigris. If we reckon the specifically Egyptian civilization to have endured from 4241 B.C. to the Greek conquest of Egypt (332 B.C.), we spread Egyptian civilization over 3,809 years. I know of no other culture, not even the Chinese, that maintained itself through so many centuries.

Egypt, as Herodotus said in 430 B.C., was *to doron tou Nilou*, "the gift of the Nile." The most famous of rivers watered the settlements that developed on its banks; it offered a liquid road for communication and commerce; and it annually irrigated the lands of the peasants with its dependable overflow. The Greeks called those settlements *nomes*—i.e., communities accepting laws—and each local ruler became a *nomarch*. When some strong man united several of these *nomes* under his power, the *nomarchs* submitted to a monarch, and the political history of Egypt began.

About 3100 B.C., one such monarch, the half-legendary Menes, issued, for the communities under his rule, a body of laws allegedly given him by the god Thoth. He built his capital on the west bank of the Nile, at a place known to us by its Greek name Memphis; and there he established the First Dynasty of pharaohs.

Some four hundred years later Pharaoh Zozer (c. 2680 B.C.) appointed as his chief minister Imhotep—the first great name in Egyptian history, renowned as both physician and architect. Later generations worshiped him as a god of knowledge, father of their sciences and arts. Tradition ascribed to him the oldest building now extant in Egypt, the step pyramid of Sakkara—a terraced structure of stone near the ruins of Memphis. This is the father of all extant pyramids.

The most famous of these date from the Fourth Dynasty (c. 2613–c. 2494 B.C.). Herodotus celebrated two of its pharaohs as Cheops and Chephren, now more accurately renamed Khufu and Khafre. By their time, Egyptian entrepreneurs had built commercial fleets, and had developed trade with several ports on the Eastern Mediterranean; they had exploited the timber and other resources of Lebanon, and had opened up the mines of Sinai; they had carved out great quarries of stone in the Nubian desert and at Aswan.

The pharaohs became rich and lavished wealth on their palaces and tombs. Herodotus tells how Khufu (r.c. 2590 B.C.) erected the oldest of the many pyramids that adorn the desert near Giza, a suburb of Cairo. So far as we know, this is the largest single structure ever raised by man. It covers thirteen acres, and rises to the height of 448 feet; within its space Rome's St. Peter's, London's Westminster Abbey and St. Paul's, and the cathedrals of Florence and Milan, could all be enclosed.

It is not beautiful, except in the accuracy of its stonecutting and in the symmetry and precision of its geometrical measurements. It impresses us chiefly by its size and history. As a work of engineering it was a miracle of its time: 2,300,000 blocks of stone—each weighing, on the average, two-and-a-half tons—were drawn for miles over the eastern desert and then across the Nile; granite blocks, mostly from Aswan, were carried 555 miles north. Apparently these masses were raised to higher and higher levels of the pyramid by hauling them, on rollers or sledges, along a rising embankment of bricks and earth. According to Herodotus, this rising road took two years to build, and the pyramid itself required the labor of 100,000 men through twenty years. The Greek traveler and historian transmitted an inscription which he claimed to have found on one pyramid, recording the quantity of radishes, garlic, and onions consumed by the workmen in that one enterprise.

Why did the pharaohs and others build pyramids? The Egyptian believed that he had in himself a spiritual counterpart or double which he called his *ka*, and which he hoped would survive indefinitely if his flesh were preserved against hunger, violence, and decay. Hence his corpse was to be embalmed and mummified with expert care; the viscera would be removed by a kind of Caesarian operation; the brains would be drawn out through the nose; the interior would be cleansed with wines and perfumes and aromatic spices; then the body was to be sewn up, steeped in antiseptic chemicals, rubbed with adhesive gum, and wrapped tightly with bandages of waxed cloth; finally it was deposited in a coffin. The ideal tomb should be of stone, of sufficient quantity to make a solid mass impenetrable except for a secret passage to an inner chamber furnished with food, weapons, and a lavatory, and with carved or painted figures which, by a magic formula known only to the priests, would attend to the body, soul, and *ka* forever.

Near the pyramid of Pharaoh Khafre (c. 2550 B.C.) stands the famous monster known to history by its Greek name Sphinx. Apparently, at the ruler's command, a corps of mechanics and sculptors carved out of stone a massive figure with the body of a lion and the head, allegedly, of Khafre himself. The face is dark with a frown, as if to frighten marauders from the royal tomb.

There is something barbarically primitive about the Pyramids—their brute grasp for size, their vain lust for permanence. It may be the memory and imagination of the beholder that, swollen with history, makes these monuments great. Perhaps pictures have too much ennobled them; photography can catch everything except dirt, and enhances man-made objects with noble vistas of land and sky. The sunset at Giza is greater than the pyramids.

THE PEOPLE

Life in ancient Egypt was pleasant for the pharaohs; we see in the pictures and reliefs, and gather from the scrolls, their wealth, luxury, and power.

The clergy cooperated—declared them to be gods, inculcated popular obedience to the royal rule, and received in return a captivating share of the royal revenue. A thousand trained scribes served as a clerical bureaucracy to the pharaohs and clergy, and to the feudal nobles who ruled the provinces as fiefs of the kings. So aided, the government organized a regular postal service, collected taxes, accumulated capital, developed a credit system of finance, distributed funds to agriculture, industry, and commerce, and in some measure achieved a planned economy regulated by the state.

Industry was manned by free labor as well as slaves under the jurisdiction of the provincial governors. The wars brought in thousands of captives, most of whom were sold into bondage; their labor facilitated the exploitation of mines and the triumphs of engineering. Class wars flourished; strikes were frequent. One manuscript preserves the plea of some workers to their overseer: "We have been driven here by hunger and thirst; we have no clothes, no oil, no food. Write to our lord the Pharaoh, and to the governor who is over us, so that they may give us something for our sustenance." However, we hear of no class revolution—unless we describe as such the historic walkout of the Jews.

The industrial arts in ancient Egypt were as advanced and varied as anything in Europe before the Renaissance. Egyptian artisans made weapons and tools of bronze, including drills that bored through the toughest diorite stone and saws that cut the massive slabs of the sarcophagi. They were masters in carving wood: they made merchant vessels a hundred feet long, and coffins so handsome that they almost invited men to die. Egyptian engineering surpassed any before 1800 A.D.; it built canals from the Nile to the Red Sea, and transported over great distances obelisks weighing a thousand tons.

The moral code in Egypt made no objection to incest. We hear of many cases where a man married his sister. Many pharaohs did this, apparently to keep the royal blood pure, or to keep the family property unimpaired—for property was transmitted through the female line. The pharaohs and some nobles kept a harem, but commoners found this impossibly extravagant. Prostitutes abounded, but many pictures celebrate marital love.

Women enjoyed a legal status higher, and a moral and social freedom greater, than in any European state before our time, possibly excepting Imperial Rome. The Greeks, who confined their women narrowly, were astonished to learn that Egyptian women went about their social and business affairs publicly, unattended and unharmed. They used every cosmetic device, even to painting their nails and their eyes; some of them covered breasts, arms, and ankles with jewelry. They spoke of sex with a directness rivaling that of the freest women of today. They could take the initiative in courtship, and could be divorced only for *proved* adultery, or with ample compensation. Some of them, like Nefertiti, earned immortality by their beauty. Some ruled the empire imperiously but well, like Hatshepsut (r. 1503–1482 B.C.), or recklessly like Cleopatra. Motherhood was revered as woman's title to nobility.

Egyptian art is rivaled by the Greek and Roman, but it preceded them by a thousand years, and in a hundred items led the way. I needn't describe—for many of you must have seen them or photographs thereof—the temples, palaces, colonnades, and tombs that rose along the banks of the Nile in the thirty centuries between the age of the pyramids and the time of Cleopatra. At Karnak and Luxor a veritable forest of pillars was raised by Egyptian royalty. The columns seem too plentiful to us, but apparently their obtrusive proximity was intended to break the domineering impact of the sun. Here, long before the Greek flowering, the arch and vault, the column and capital, the architrave and pediment, gave example and challenge to architecture in the Mediterranean world.

• • •

I would not equate Egyptian sculpture with that of classic antiquity, but I know of nothing in Greek statuary finer than the diorite bust of Khafre in the Cairo Museum. It is now forty-two hundred years old, and seems immune to time. It may be idealized, but it probably represents in its essential features the second pharaoh of the Fourth Dynasty. Even more famous is the stone statue of the Scribe, now in the Louvre. Squatting on his haunches, almost totally nude, he holds a pen behind his ear as reserve for the one he holds in his hand. He keeps a record of work done and goods paid for, of prices and costs, of profits and losses, of taxes due or paid. He draws up contracts and wills, and makes out his employer's tax report. His life is monotonous, but he consoles himself by writing essays on the hardships of the manual worker's existence and the princely dignity of those whose food is paper and whose blood is ink.

Beneath and above everything in Egypt was religion. We find it in every stage and form from totemism to theology; we see its influence in literature, government, art—in everything except morality. And its gods were almost as numerous as in India. In the beginning, said the priests, was the sky; and to the end this and the Nile remained the chief divinities. All the heavenly bodies were the external forms of mighty spirits, whose wills ordained their complex and varied movements. The sun was the god Ra or Re or Amon, who had created the world by shining on it; as the god Horus, it was a gigantic falcon flying across the heaven day after day as if supervising its realm. The Nile was the great god Osiris; and—perhaps because the Nile fertilized the adjoining earth—Osiris was also worshiped as the god of male sexual power.

Isis, the sister and wife of Osiris, was the goddess of motherhood; and, as fertilized by Osiris-the-river, the soil of the Delta was one of her forms. Vegetables and animals, too, were worshiped as gods; the palm tree for its shade, the goat and the bull for their reproductive energy, the serpent as a symbol of wisdom and life; at least he knew how to make ends meet. The pharaoh, too, was worshiped as a god, the son of Amon-Re; he was a deity transiently taking the earth as his home. It was through this supposedly divine lineage that he was able to rule so long and with so little use of physical force.

Hence the priests of Egypt were the necessary props of the throne and the secret police of the social order. Through the piety of the people and the politic generosity of the king, they became in time richer and stronger than the feudal aristocracy, or even the royal family itself. They educated the young, accumulated and transmitted learning, and disciplined themselves with rigor and zeal. Herodotus described them almost with awe:

> They are of all men the most excessively attentive to the worship of the gods, and observe the following ceremonies. . . . They wear linen garments, constantly fresh-washed. . . . They are circumcised for the sake of cleanliness, think it better to be clean than handsome. They shave their whole body every third day, that neither lice nor any other impurity may be found upon them. . . . They wash themselves in cold, cold water twice every day and twice every night. (*Histories* 2.37)

Their frailty was a hot devotion to power, and their willingness to recommend, or sell, magic incantations, rites, or charms to the faithful as instruments of earthly welfare or eternal happiness.

According to our great American Egyptologist Professor James Breasted:

> The dangers of the hereafter were now greatly multiplied, and for every critical situation the priest was able to furnish the dead with an effective charm which would infallibly cure him. Besides many charms which enabled the dead to reach the world of the hereafter, there were those which prevented him from losing his mouth, his head, his heart; others which enabled him to remember his name, to breathe, eat, drink, avoid eating his own foulness, to prevent his drinking-water from turning into flame, to turn darkness into light, to ward off all serpents and other hostile monsters, and many others. . . . Thus the earliest moral development which we can trace in the ancient East was suddenly arrested, or at least checked, by the detestable devices of a corrupt priesthood eager for gain.

Such in part was the condition of religion in Egypt when a poet, lover, and heretic came to the throne and announced to a shocked clergy and people that there was only one god.

THE POET

Amenhotep IV was hardly designed to be a king: he cared more for art than for war, wrote the most famous poem in Egyptian literature, and indefatigably loved his wife, Nefertiti. He allowed artists to show him riding in a chariot with the queen, engaged with her in pleasantries with their children.

On ceremonial occasions Nefertiti sat beside him and held his hand, while their daughters frolicked at the foot of the throne. She gave him seven daughters, but no son; he still loved her and took no secondary wife. He spoke of her as "Mistress of my happiness, at hearing whose voice the King rejoices"; and for an oath he used the phrase "As my heart is happy in the Queen and her children."

Next to her he loved the sun. The Egyptians had long worshiped it as the father of all earthly life; but they had also worshiped Amon and a hundred other gods, from the evening star to the onion and the baboon. He was revolted when he saw the high priest of Amon sacrifice a ram to the god; he scorned the traffic of the clergy in magic charms and their use of the pretended oracle of Amon to support their plans.

He abominated the indecent wealth of the temples and the growing hold of a mercenary hierarchy on the nation's life. With a poet's audacity he threw compromise to the winds and announced that these deities and ceremonies were a vulgar idolatry and that there was only one god, Aton—the sun. He threw off his inherited name of Amenhotep, which contained the word Amon, and called himself Ikhnaton, meaning "Aton is satisfied."

Helping himself with some monotheistic poems composed in the preceding reign, he wrote passionate songs to Aton, the god-sun; the longest of these now surviving is the most remarkable remnant of ancient Egyptian poetry:

Thy dawning is beautiful in the horizon of the sky.
O living Aton, Beginning of life.

When thou risest in the eastern horizon,
Thou fillest every land with thy beauty.

Thou art beautiful, great, glittering, high above every land,
Thy rays, they encompass the land, even all that thou hast made.
They are Re, and thou carriest them all away captive;
Thou bindest them by thy love.
Though thou art far away, thy rays are upon earth;
Though thou art on high, thy footprints are the day.

When thou settest in the western horizon of the sky,
The earth is in darkness like the dead;
They sleep in their chambers,
Their heads are wrapped up,
Their nostrils are stopped,
And none seeth the other,
All their things are stolen
Which are under their heads,
And they know it not.
Every lion cometh forth from his den,
All serpents they sting . . .
The world is in silence,
He that made them resteth in his horizon.

Bright is the earth when thou risest in the horizon.
When thou shinest as Aton by day
Thou drivest away the darkness.
When thou sendest forth thy rays,
The Two Lands are in daily festivity,
Awake and standing upon their feet
When thou hast raised them up.
Their limbs bathed, they take their clothing,
Their arms uplifted in adoration to thy dawning.
In all the world they do their work.

All cattle rest upon their pasturage,
The trees and the plants flourish,

The birds flutter in their marshes,
Their wings uplifted in adoration to thee.
All the sheep dance upon their feet,
All winged things fly,
They live when thou hast shone upon them.

The barks sail upstream and downstream.
Every highway is open because thou dawnest.
The fish in the river leap up before thee.
Thy rays are in the midst of the great green sea.
Creator of the germ in woman,
Maker of seed in man,
Giving life to the son in the body of his mother,
Soothing him that he may not weep,
Nurse even in the womb,
Giver of breath to animate every one that he maketh!
When he cometh forth from the body . . . on the day of his birth,
Thou openest his mouth in speech,
Thou suppliest his necessities. . . .
Thy rays nourish every garden;
When thou risest they live,
They grow by thee.

Thou makest the seasons
In order to create all thy work;
Winter to bring them coolness,
And heat that they may taste thee.
Thou didst make the distant sky to rise therein,
In order to behold all that thou hast made,
Thou alone, shining in the form as living Aton.
Dawning, glittering, going afar and returning.
Thou makest millions of forms
Through thyself alone;
Cities, towns and tribes,
Highways and rivers.
All eyes set thee before them,
For thou art Aton of the day over the earth. . . .

Thou art in my heart,
There is no other that knoweth thee
Save thy son Ikhnaton.
Thou hast made him wise
In thy designs and in thy might.
The world is in thy hand,
Even as thou hast made them.
When thou hast risen they live,
When thou settest they die;
For thou art length of life of thyself.
Men live through thee,
While their eyes are upon thy beauty
Until thou settest.
All labor is put away
When thou settest in the West. . . .
Thou didst establish the world,
And raised them up for thy son. . . .
Ikhnaton, whose life is long;
And for the chief royal wife, his beloved,
Mistress of the Two Lands, Nefer-nefru-aton, Nefretiti,
Living and flourishing for ever and ever.

This is not only one of the great poems of history, it is the outstanding expression of monotheism 640 years before Isaiah. Ikhnaton's god is not tribal, like Jehovah; Aton feeds and rules all the nations of the earth. It is a vitalistic conception of deity, as a creative living power animating all things; its heat is the warmth of life and the ardor of love; it nourishes and fertilizes every plant, energizes every animal, and "creates the man-child in woman." It is a god for all nations, for all forms of growth.

Ikhnaton spoiled this by letting egotism cloud his vision: "There is no other that knoweth thee save thy son Ikhnaton. . . . Thou didst establish the worlds, and raised them up for thy son Ikhnaton." Confident of his new religion, he ordered that the names of all gods but Aton should be carved or blotted out from every public place in Egypt. He cut out from his father's name the word Amon, as being a deity now dead; he declared all creeds illegal but his own.

The official hierarchy fumed and plotted; the people, seeing Ikhna-ton's monotheism as a wholesale slaughter of the gods, muttered and rebelled. Even in his palace his ministers hated him, for his scorn of war had weakened the army, and his generals impatiently awaited his death. Subject states refused their customary tribute; one by one they deposed their Egyptian governors and became free; Egypt suddenly fell apart. Ikhnaton found himself almost deserted except for his wife and children. He was hardly thirty years old when he died, mourning his failure as a ruler and the unworthiness of his race.

Two years after his death his son-in-law, Tutenkhamon, a favorite of the priests, ascended the throne. He changed the name Tutenkhaton, which his father-in-law had given him, made his peace with the powers of the Church, and announced to a rejoicing people the restoration of the ancient gods. The words Aton and Ikhnaton were effaced from all the monuments, the priests forbade the name of the heretic king to pass any man's lips, and the people referred to him as "the Great Criminal." The names that Ikhnaton had removed were recarved upon the monuments, and the feast days that he had abolished were renewed. Everything was as before.

Egypt had another great age, under Rameses II, who showed his mettle by reconquering the Egyptian colonies, building immense temples, begetting one hundred sons and fifty daughters on his multiple wives, and leaving behind him a statue of himself as a proud relic of his power. Originally it was fifty-six feet in height; now it is fifty-six feet in length, for the centuries eroded its earthy pediment and let it fall.

Shelley described that statue in a sonnet both beautiful and terrible, entitled by one of Rameses' many names, "Ozymandias":

I met a traveler from an antique land
Who said: Two vast and trunkless legs of stone
Stand in the desert. . . . Near them, on the sand,
Half sunk, a shattered visage lies, whose frown,
And wrinkled lip, and sneer of cold command,
Tell that its sculptor well those passions read
Which yet survive, stamped on these lifeless things,
The hand that mocked them, and the heart that fed;
And on the pedestal these words appear:

"My name is Ozymandias, king of kings:
Look on my works, ye Mighty, and despair!"
Nothing beside remains. Round the decay
Of that colossal wreck, boundless and bare
The lone and level sands stretch far away.

Chapter Five

᭙᭙᭙

PHILOSOPHY AND
POETRY IN THE
OLD TESTAMENT

THE BIRTH OF A NATION

The aim of these chapters is not to compress a history of a civilization into a few pages, but to study and sample the masterpieces of thought and expression left by it. So we shall review here only so much of ancient Jewish history as may help us to understand the philosophy and poetry of the Jews from their appearance in Palestine about 1800 B.C. to their dispersion from their Holy Land in A.D. 135.

The Near, or Middle, East, in pre-Christian times, was a veritable caldron of peoples, hot in temper and pride, restless in their wanderings, impatient in their settlements. They paused long enough to produce extensive civilizations—Sumerian, Babylonian, Assyrian; so the Babylonians advanced science and medicine, and Hammurabi gave them, about 1940 B.C., a remarkably rational code of laws.

One famous wanderer, Abraham, is pictured in our Bible as leaving the town of Ur in Chaldea (now southern Iran) and setting out, toward 1800 B.C., to seek new lands for his growing family and flocks. In a vision, we are told, he saw and heard the god Yahweh, who offered him and his offspring the land of Canaan, on condition that they should worship Yahweh alone and should circumcise their male offspring as a sign of this covenant with their god. Here, as in the case of Moses and the Ten Commandments, we may note the application of religious belief to strengthen the unity, health, morality, and courage of an imperiled people. So Abraham led his followers northwest into Canaan and occupied, some six hundred years before Moses, what they henceforth thought of as their God-given land.

Abraham's eldest son, Jacob, we are told, wrestled with a stranger who turned out to be an angel or a god; and Jacob fought so powerfully that the Lord gave him the new name Israel—"he who has fought with God" (Gen. 32:24–30); this became the name of the tribe and the land. Jacob's favorite son, Joseph, was buried in a pit by his jealous brothers, was rescued, was sold into slavery in Egypt, freed himself by wisely interpreting dreams, became a favorite of the pharaoh, and advised him to store grain in good years in order to feed his people in years of drought. His brothers came down from dearth-stricken Israel to beg food from Egypt; Joseph fed them and invited Jacob and his tribe to come and live in Egypt. They came, and settled in Goshen, about 1650 B.C. (Gen. 46).

Their descendants prospered and multiplied in Egypt through some four hundred years. Then, for reasons unknown, the Egyptians turned against them and laid upon them heavy labor and hateful laws. So, if we may credit the biblical account, a pharaoh who may have been Rameses II (Shelley's Ozymandias) ordered midwives to do away with every male child born to a Jewish mother (Exod. 1:16). Some infants were spared and concealed. It is possible that one of these was Moses. In any case we may accept him as historical and, in its essentials, the story of the years of travail of the Jews in Sinai.

I can readily believe that many of the wanderers, in their suffering, lost belief in the god of their fathers and sacrificed to strange idols in the hope of supernatural aid. I can believe that their leader, by the strength of his character and faith, called them back to order and decency with those Ten Commandments which we wanderers in our moral desert long to hear and obey again. And I can believe that those weary wayfarers, hardened with suffering and battle, fought wildly, even brutally, in the last stages of their trek, to recapture the Canaan from which their forefathers had been driven by hunger and thirst four hundred years before.

For almost two centuries the victors lived in Canaan as a loose association of tribes torn by intermittent strife among themselves and repeatedly harassed by the Philistines, Moabites, Ammonites, and Edomites in peace and war. For a time, law and order were maintained by judges and priests. As the population grew and spread, a demand arose for a central authority with almost absolute command. Samuel, a leading judge, argued against such royal rule. A king, he warned them,

> will take your sons and appoint them . . . to sow his ground and reap his harvest, and make his instruments of war. . . . And he will take your fields, your vineyards, and your olive groves, the best, and give them to his servants; he will take a tenth of your seed and of your vineyards, . . . and your goodliest young men, and your asses, and put them to his work, and ye shall be his servants. And ye shall cry out in that day because of your king which ye shall have chosen; and the Lord will not hear you in that day.

The people rejected Samuel's counsel, saying:

> Nay, but we will have a king over us, that we also shall be like all the nations, and that our king may judge us, and go out before us, and fight our battles.

Saul called the people together, and they chose him to be the first king of the Jews; and all the people shouted, "God save the king" (I Sam. 8:11–20).

Saul failed as a king and died in vain battle against the Philistines. The handsome and melodious David, who had been captain of the royal guard, assumed the throne, about 1000 B.C.; conquered and united all the regions of Israel, and took wives from them to cement his rule; made Jerusalem his capital, reigned for thirty-six years, and left such a memory of prosperity that the Jews, in later misfortunes, longed for a "Messiah"—an "anointed" descendant of David, who would restore the splendor and happiness of David's rule.

Here is one of the earliest and most diverse heroes of history: a victorious warrior, a singer of psalms and player of the harp, a tender lover of Saul's son Jonathan and his own son Absalom (2 Sam. 11); stealing Bathsheba from her husband Uriah, and sending Uriah to die at the front: this is an astonishing but authentic man, of rich and varied elements, bearing within him many vestiges of barbarism, and all the promises of civilization.

His son and successor was called Solomon—from *shalom,* meaning "peace"—and earned the name by preserving peace and prosperity through a reign of thirty-seven years. By maintaining friendly relations with King Hiram of Tyre, he induced Phoenician merchants to direct their caravans through Palestine and developed a profitable exchange of Israel's agricultural products for the manufactured articles of Sidon and Tyre. He built a fleet of mercantile vessels for commerce in the Mediterranean and the Red Sea, and mined the gold and precious stones of "Ophir"—recently discovered in Saudi Arabia. He indulged himself in a harem of "700 wives and 30 concubines"; here we may divide by ten, and count the rest a friendly relationship with other states; besides, the great king may have had a eugenic passion to transmit his superior qualities to a maximum of sons.

He adorned Jerusalem with a great temple whose beauty became the undying pride of the Jews, the apex of their worship, and—as was then the custom—the center of their trade. Before he died, the merchants far outnumbered the priests, dominated the government, and had concentrated the wealth of the nation under their control. A discontented proletariat had been created whose labor found no steady employment or satisfying reward, and whose hardships transformed the warlike cult of Yahweh into the almost socialistic gospel of the Prophets.

THE PROPHETS

They were only incidentally fortune-tellers—inasmuch as they correctly foretold the capture of Jerusalem by a foreign power; but they were denouncers of the present rather than foretellers of the future. Several of them came up to Jerusalem from the countryside; they were shocked by the industrial exploitation and commercial chicanery which they found in the capital, and by the diversion of religion from a call to justice into a ritual of burnt offerings and pious songs.

Amos described himself not as a prophet but as a simple village shepherd who (about 760 B.C.) left his herds to sample the capital. He was dismayed by the unnatural complexity of the life that he saw there, the inequality of fortune, the bitterness of competition, the ruthlessness of exploitation. So he "stood in the gate," and lashed the rich and their luxuries:

> Forasmuch, therefore, as your treading is upon the poor, and ye take from him burdens of wheat, ye have built houses of hewn stone, but ye shall not dwell in them; ye have planted pleasant vineyards, but ye shall not drink wine of them. . . . Woe to them that are at ease in Zion, . . . that lie upon beds of ivory . . . and eat the lambs out of the flock . . . ; that chant to the sound of the viol, and invent . . . instruments of music, like David; that drink wine in bowls, and anoint themselves with the chief ointments. . . . I despise your feast-days (saith the Lord); . . . though ye offer me burnt offerings and meat offerings, I will not accept them. . . . Take thou away from me the noise of thy songs, for I will not hear the melody of thy viols. But let judgment [*justice*] run down as waters, and righteousness as a mighty stream. (Amos 5:6)

A greater prophet, whom scholars call the First Isaiah, advanced this social gospel in some of the noblest prose in the world's literature:

> The Lord will enter into judgment with the ancients of his people and the princes thereof; for ye have eaten up the vineyard, the spoil of the poor is in your homes. What mean ye that ye beat my people to pieces, and grind the faces of the poor? . . . Woe unto them that join house to house, that lay field to field! . . . Woe unto them that decree unrighteous decrees to turn aside the needy from judgment [*justice*], and to take away the right from the poor of my people, that widows may be their prey, and that they may rob the fatherless. And what will ye do in the day of visitation, and in the desolation which shall come from afar? To whom will ye flee for help, and where will ye leave your glory? . . . Wash ye, make ye clean; . . . seek judgment [*justice*], relieve the oppressed, judge [*bring justice to*] the fatherless, plead for the widow. (Isa. 3:14–15; 5:8; 10:1f, 11f)

Isaiah is bitter, but he does not despair; he concludes by formulating the messianic trust of the Jews in a future Redeemer who would bring an era of universal brotherhood and peace:

Behold, a maiden shall conceive and bear a son, and shall call his
name Immanuel. . . . For unto us a child is born, and the government shall be upon his shoulder; and his name shall be . . . the
Prince of Peace . . . With righteousness shall he judge the poor, and
reprove with equity for the meek of the earth; and he shall smite the
earth with the rod of his mouth, and with the breath of his lips shall
slay the wicked. . . . The wolf also shall dwell with the lamb, and the
leopard shall lie down with the kid, and the calf and the young lion
. . . together; and a little child shall lead them. . . . And they shall
beat their swords into ploughshares, and their spears into pruning-
hooks; nation shall not lift up sword against nation, neither shall
they learn war any more. (Isa. 7:14; 9:6; 11:1–6; 2:4)

The evils threatened by the Prophets came, though somewhat de-
layed. In 609 B.C. an Egyptian army defeated the Jews in a bloody battle near the old city of Megiddo; from this, apparently, the apostle John
took the name "Armageddon" for the great conflict that was to decide
the fate of the world (Rev. 16:16). In 597 B.C., Nebuchadnezzar I of
Babylon captured Jerusalem and took 10,000 Jews into captivity.
Against the advice of the grim prophet Jeremiah, King Zedekiah led
the Jews into revolt against Babylon; Nebuchadnezzar returned in
586, ravaged Jerusalem, destroyed Solomon's Temple, and took nearly
all the population of Jerusalem into Babylonian captivity. Then Jeremiah mourned the fulfillment of his prophecies and the desolation of
Jerusalem:

How doth the city sit solitary that was full of people! how is she become as a widow! she that was great among the nations, and princess
among the provinces, how is she become tributary! . . . Is it nothing
to you, all ye that pass by? behold, and see if there be any sorrow like
unto my sorrow . . . Righteous art thou, O Lord, when I plead with
thee: yet let me talk with thee of thy judgments: wherefore doth the
way of the wicked prosper? (Lam. 1:1, 12; 12:1)

Now (about 540 B.C.) a greater prophet than Jeremiah came to the
fore. Scholars call him the Second Isaiah, for he added new chapters to
the First. He preached to the exiled Jews in the name of a god not only

of Israel but of all men, a supreme god "who hath measured the waters in the hollow of his hand, and meted out heaven with the span, . . . and weighed the mountains in a scale, and the hills in a balance. . . . Lift up your eyes on high, and behold who hath made these things."

As for himself, he would no longer curse the people for their sins, but promised that his God would soon lead the Jews out of their bondage in Babylon:

> Prepare ye the way of the lord; make straight in the desert a highway for our God. Every valley shall be exalted, and every mountain and hill shall be made low, and the crooked shall be made straight, and the rough places plain. . . . He shall feed his flocks like a shepherd; he shall gather the lambs with his arm, and carry them in his bosom, and shall gently lead those that are with young. (Isa. 40:3–4, 11) [*Do you hear Handel's music?*]

This prophecy was fulfilled when in 539 B.C. the Persian king Cyrus II captured Babylon, freed the Jews, protected their return to Jerusalem, and pledged his help in restoring the Temple. The Second Temple was completed in 516 and became the center of a religious revival in which the kings relied upon the clergy to maintain social order.

About 444 B.C., Ezra, a learned priest, called the people together, and read to them, several hours daily for seven days, what he called "the Book of the Law of Moses," which the Jews came to call the Torah, or "Guidance," and the Greeks called the Pentateuch, or "Five Rolls"— the first five books of the Bible. In those books are the Ten Commandments and the Mosaic Code, which kept the Jews in order, and in more than average health, through twenty-three centuries of unparalleled tribulation. In that code, in the book called Leviticus is the greatest, boldest, briefest formulation of Christian ethics: "Thou shalt love thy neighbor as thy self" (19:18).

In 332 B.C. the little state, finding itself surrounded by hungry emperors, peacefully accepted Alexander the Great as its protective overlord. After Alexander's youthful death Judea bore the ravages of war among his successors, while its philosophers and poets felt the intoxicating influence of Greek literature and thought.

THE PHILOSOPHERS

Carlyle called the Book of Job "one of the grandest things ever written. . . . There is nothing written, I think, in the Bible or out of it, of equal literary merit." Scholars place it almost anywhere between 500 and 300 B.C. It is a basic book, for it powerfully states the dark question that haunts every theology: How can this world be ruled by a just and loving God, when injustice so often triumphs? Job is represented at the outset as "perfect and upright," yet Yahweh allows a veritable flood of calamities to engulf him. The sufferer listens helplessly to friends who insist that God is just, but finally he turns upon them as blind and insincere. Like pre-Christian Jews in general, he has no belief in an afterlife, and he sees earthly existence as a daily deferment of inevitable death:

> Man that is born of woman is of few days, and full of trouble. He cometh forth like a flower, and is cut down; he fleeth also as a shadow, and continueth not. . . . For there is hope of a tree, if it be cut down, that it will sprout again, and that the tender branch thereof will not cease. . . . But man dieth, and wasteth away; yea, man giveth up the ghost, and where is he? As the waters fall from the sea, and the flood decayeth and drieth up, so man lieth down, and riseth not. . . . If a man die, shall he live again?

Job gives up hope of divine justice, turns upon Yahweh, calls him "Adversary," and plans suicide. Then, in one of the most majestic passages in the world's literature, a voice comes out of the clouds and the "whirlwind," and challenges man:

> Who is this that darkeneth counsel by words without knowledge? Gird up now thy loins like a man, for I will demand of thee, and answer thou me. Where wast thou when I laid the foundations of the earth? . . . Who laid the cornerstone thereof, when the morning stars sang together, and all the sons of God shouted for joy? Or who shut up the sea with doors . . . and said, Hitherto shalt thou come, but no further; and here shall thy proud waves be stayed? . . . Canst thou bind the sweet influence of the Pleiades, or loose the bands of

Orion? . . . Knowest thou the ordinances of heaven? Canst thou set the dominion thereof in the earth? . . . Who hath put wisdom in the inward parts, or who hath given understanding to the heart? . . . Shall he that contendeth with the Almighty instruct him? He that reproveth God, let him answer it. (Job 38:1–40:2)

Job humbles himself in terror before this apparition, saying, "I abhor myself, and repent in dust and ashes." Yahweh relents, forgives Job's challenges, and gives him "twice as much as before;" soon Job has 14,000 sheep, 6,000 camels, 1,000 yoke of oxen, and 1,000 she-asses. He lived thereafter 140 years and saw his sons and his sons' sons even to four generations.

It is a happy ending, but tame and joyless, and yet again the best that we can make. Who are we—mites in a moment's mist—that we should understand the universe? Philosophy is a study of the part in the light of the whole; and its first lesson is that we are very small parts of a very large whole. The harmony of the part with the whole may be the best definition of health, beauty, truth, wisdom, morality, and happiness.

This again is the only answer we can give to Ecclesiastes. The brief book so named is the bitterest message in the Bible. The word *ecclesiastes* is the Greek translation of the Hebrew *koheleth*, which means "preacher." The unknown author calls himself so, and pretends to be Solomon, the wise son of David; but ruthless scholars reduce him to some obscure Hellenized Hebrew about 200 B.C.

I, the Preacher, was King of Israel in Jerusalem. And I gave my heart to seek and search out by wisdom concerning all things that are done under heaven: this sore travail hath God given to the sons of man to be exercised therewith. I have seen all the works that are done under the sun, and behold, all is vanity and vexation of spirit. . . . For in much wisdom is much grief, and he that increaseth knowledge increaseth sorrow. (Eccles. 1:12–18)

He studies history and concludes that this, too, is vanity, for history in the large repeats itself and, like the family Bible, is a record of births and deaths.

One generation passeth away, and another generation cometh, but the earth abideth forever. The sun also ariseth, and the sun goeth down, and hasteth to his place where he arose. . . . All rivers run into the sea, yet the sea is not full; unto the place whence the rivers come, thither they return again. . . . Wherefore I praised the dead which are already dead, more than the living which are yet alive. . . . A good name is better than precious ointment, and the day of death than the day of one's birth. . . . A man hath no pre-eminence over a beast. . . . All go unto one place; . . . all turn to dust again. . . . All is vanity.

THE POETS

Can we find in the poets of the Old Testament any answer to Ecclesiastes and Job? They give two answers: make your peace with God and the universe; and brighten your life with love. One answer is in the Psalms, the other is in the Song of Songs.

Who shall sing a fitting song of praise for those songs of praise called the Psalms? Treasured among my memories of seminary days are the echoes of the Psalms we acolytes sang in the sonorous Latin of St. Jerome's translation; and yet, with all our piety, we could never feel, as deeply as the ancient Jews, the consoling confidence in the divine surveillance of our fate. I cannot forget how, when I attended my wife in the recovery room at Cedars-Sinai Hospital, and Ariel, still in pain, recited the first line of the Twenty-Third Psalm, another patient, just returned from her brush with death, recited the second line, and another patient the third line, of that humble answer to Job:

The lord is my shepherd; I shall not want.
He maketh me to lie down in green pastures; he leadeth me beside the still
    waters. . . .
Yea, though I walk through the valley of the shadow of death, I will
    fear no evil. . . .
Surely goodness and mercy shall follow me all the days of my life.

And was there any sorrow greater than those years of bondage in Babylon?

By the rivers of Babylon we sat down, yea, we wept when we remembered
*   Zion.*
We hanged our harps upon the willows in the midst thereof.
For there they that carried us away captive required of us a song . . .
*   saying, Sing us one of the songs of Zion.*
How shall we sing the Lord's song in a strange land?
If I forget thee, O Jerusalem, let my right hand forget her cunning.
If I do not remember thee, let my tongue cleave to the roof of my mouth; if
*   I prefer not Jerusalem above my chief joy.* (Ps. 137)

I know of no greater glory of language or imagery than in the
Psalms.

The heavens declare the glory of God. . . . In them hath he set a
*   tabernacle for the sun,*
Which is as a bridegroom coming out of his chamber, and rejoiceth as a
*   strong man to run a race.*
His going forth is from the end of the heaven, and his circuit unto the
*   ends of it;*
and there is nothing hid from the heat thereof. (Ps. 19)

Who wrote these psalms? Pious tradition ascribed some seventy of
them to David, and scholars so credit a few; most of them are probably
the voices of many harps through seven centuries from David to Daniel
(900 to 167 B.C.). Many of them were sung in the Temple; we feel in
them the antistrophic rhythm of ancient Oriental poetry, with majestic
choirs in alternate answering.

There is one more poem, in the Old Testament, which we must
honor here. It was formerly called the "Song of Solomon," as being in
part a litany of the young king's charms. The Jews called it *Shir*
Hashirim, which the Catholic Bible translated as *Canticum canticorum*
and which we properly render as the Song of Songs. Seldom has poetry
so frankly and vividly celebrated the joyous surrender of mutual love.

Only God knows how it found its way into the Holy Book. Orthodoxy bravely interprets it as an allegory of the Church's love for Christ.
Scholarship thinks it a relic of some fertility rite, but the ardor of the
poem allows no thought of a field or a child. Its date is unknown; there

are signs of Greco-Egyptian influence, as from Alexandria; the lovers, in Egyptian style, call each other brother and sister.

One famous passage—*Nigra sum sed formosa* in Jerome's translation, "I am black but beautiful"—suggests a lady of African origin and temperature; so my colored brothers and sisters can find biblical warrant for "Black is beautiful." But let the poem speak for itself:

> A *bundle of myrrh is my well-beloved unto me; he shall lie all night betwixt my breasts.*
> *My beloved is unto me a cluster of camphire in the vineyards of Engadi.*
> *Behold, thou art fair, my love; behold, thou art fair; thou hast dove's eyes.* . . .
> *I am the rose of Sharon,* * *and the lily of the valleys.* . . .
> *Stay me with flagons, comfort me with apples, for I am sick of love.* . . .
> *I charge you, O ye daughters of Jerusalem, by the roes, or by the hinds of the field, that ye stir not up, nor awake my love, till he please.* . . .
> *My beloved is mine, and I am his; he feedeth among the lilies. Until the daybreak, and the shadows flee away, turn, my beloved, and be thou like a roe or a young hart upon the mountains of Bether.* . . .
> *Come, my beloved, let us go forth into the field; let us lodge in the villages,*
> *Let us get up early to the vineyards; let us see if the vine flourish, whether the tender grape appear, and the pomegranate bud forth; there I will give thee my loves.*

It is magnificent, and even a tired old man can feel its fever; but one who is an apostle of nonagenarian love may ask for a deeper litany than the splendor of the human form. The joy of the healthy body need not apologize for itself, but how does it answer Job's agony, or the hunger of the soul for a wider significance than physical union or brute survival? De Maupassant suggested a finer devotion when he said that "in true love it is the soul that embraces the body."

The noblest love of all is that which most widens the ego and offers open heart and arms to all living, peaceful things. Happy is the soul that so enlarges its love.

---

* A fertile plain running along the west coast of Palestine.

Chapter Six

ᖰᖰᖰ

THE ROAD TO PERICLES

THE ETHNIC BLEND

Who were the ancient Greeks, and whence did they come? They came from all directions: from western Asia, from the islands of the Aegean Sea, from Crete, Egypt, and the Balkans, some even from "Scythia"—i.e., southern Russia. They pastured flocks, tilled the earth, traded, built villages and towns, fought wars, and submitted to chieftains or kings like Agamemnon of Mycenae and Codrus of Athens.

The Mycenaeans probably derived their civilization from Crete and Egypt, while the settlements of eastern Greece seem to have imported their cultural elements from western Asia and the Aegean isles. The mating of Asiatic and Cretan subtlety and Egyptian refinements with the barbaric vigor of the tribes that had come down into Hellas from the North seems to have set the biological basis of "the glory that was Greece."

THE GEOGRAPHICAL SPREAD

More important than that cross-fertilization was the astonishing spread and development of the Greeks throughout the ancient Mediterranean world, from the Byzantium that became Constantinople to those "Pillars of Hercules" that became Gibraltar. Whether in flight from Dorian or other invasions, or to relieve their own crowding growth, the Greeks, in the six centuries between Agamemnon and Pericles, sent their adventurous surplus from Attica and the Peloponnesus to establish Greek colonies as far north as the Crimea, where Orestes found Iphigenia; as far east as Colchis, at the far end of the Black Sea, where Jason found Medea and the Golden Fleece; along the southern shores of the Black Sea and the eastern shores of the Mediterranean. . . . Let us tarry there a while, for along that famous coastline, or near it, the Greeks, before they made Athens famous, developed a string of twelve cities which came to be called the Dodecapolis of Ionia; these twelve contributed almost as much to Greek history as the cities of Attica. At Teos the poet Anacreon, 570 B.C., sang of inspiring wines and ambidextrous love. At Miletus, 600 B.C., Thales established the first school of Greek philosophy, and powerfully advanced Greek geometry and astronomy.

Heracleitus

At Ephesus, whose temple to Artemis Diana was among the Seven Wonders of the Ancient World, Heracleitus, three hundred years before Plato, expounded, in enigmatic apothegms, a philosophy of evolution that must have delighted Hegel, Darwin, Spencer, and Nietzsche.

Two ideas fascinated him: change is universal, and energy is indestructible and everlasting. Nothing *is,* everything *becomes;* everything is always ceasing to be what it is, and is becoming what it will be; "all things flow" (*panta rei*), and "you can never dip your foot in the same water in a flowing stream"; the universe is one vast, restless, ceaseless "Becoming." Here, in a sentence or two, is half the philosophy that Hegel expounded in 1830 A.D.

But under the flux, Heracleitus saw a never-diminished reality which he called "Fire," by which he seems to have meant "force" or "energy." The individual soul is a passing tongue of the endlessly changing flame of life. Man is a fitful moment in that flame, "kindled and put out like a light in the night." God is the eternal Fire, the omnipresent energy of the fluent world. In the universal flux anything can in time change into its opposite; good can become evil, evil can become good, life becomes death, death becomes life. Opposites are two sides of the same thing; strength is the tension of opposites; "Strife" (competition) "is the father of all and the kin of all; some he has marked out to be gods, and some to be men; some he made slaves and some free." In the end, Heracleitus concluded, "strife is justice"; the competition of individuals, groups, institutions, states, and empires constitutes nature's supreme court, from whose verdict there is no appeal.

Psappha (Sappho)

Just across the water from these Ionian cities lay the island of Lesbos, busy with commerce and sparkling with poetry. In its capital, Mytilene, lived the second most famous of Greek women. Psappha, as she called herself in her soft native dialect, was born about 612 B.C. She was not known for her beauty, but she had the charms of daintiness, refinement, and tenderness. At twenty she married a rich merchant, who soon died.

Eager for an active life, she opened a school for young women, to whom she taught poetry, music, and dancing; it was apparently the first "finishing school" in known history. Manless, she fell in love with one of her pupils, Atthis, and went almost insane when the girl accepted the attentions of a young man. Atthis' parents removed her from the school. Sappho apparently had this in mind when she wrote:

> She [Atthis?] wept full sore to leave me behind, and said: "Alas, how sad our lot! Sappho, I swear, t'is against my will I leave you." And I answered her: "Go your way rejoicing, but remember me, for you know how I doted upon you. And if you remember not, oh, then I will remind you . . . how dear and beautiful was the life we led together. For with many a garland of violets and sweet roses mingled you decked your flowing locks by my side, and with many a woven necklet, made of a hundred blossoms, your dainty throat; and with unguent in plenty, precious and royal, you anointed your fair young skin in my bosom. And no hill was there, nor holy place, nor waterbrook, whither we did not go; nor ever did the teeming noises of the early spring fill the wood with the medley-song of the nightingales but you wandered there with me.

Male posterity avenged itself upon her by handing down, or inventing, the tale of how she died of unrequited love for a man. . . . A passage in Suidas tells how "the courtesan Sappho" leaped to death from a cliff on the island of Leucas because Phaon the sailor would not return her love. In truth we do not know when she died, or how; we only know that she left behind her a vivid memory of passion, poetry, and grace, and that she shone even above Alcaeus as the most melodious singer of her time.

Westward the exuberant Greeks pushed their ships and tents, colonizing the isles of the southern Adriatic, forging forward into Italy, and founding there the once famous cities of Sybaris and Crotona. Sybaris gave its name to lazy luxury; Crotona gave history the vegetarian athlete Milo, winner of both the Olympic and the Pythian games; and Pythagoras, the greatest Greek philosopher before Socrates.

Pythagoras

He was born on the Aegean island of Samos about 580 B.C. and traveled inquisitively in Gaul, Egypt, the Near East, and India. He never recovered from India: he accepted the theory of karma—retributive rebirth; one story tells how he stopped a man from beating a dog, saying that he recognized in its cries the voice of a dead friend. He was over fifty when he settled in Crotona, where his lectures drew enthusiastic students of either sex. He organized the most faithful of his followers into a communistic community pledged to avoid meat, eggs, and beans, to purify their bodies with abstinence and self-control, and to purify their minds with science and music. He gave geometry its classic form two centuries before Euclid; and he himself formulated the theorem that bears his name.

He discovered the numerical relations of musical notes, as on the strings of a harp. Since all bodies moving through space produce some noise, each planet in its orbital motion must make regular sounds; these constitute the "music of the spheres," which we never hear because we hear it all the time. He was the first, says Diogenes Laertius, "to give the name of *kosmos* to the world," because of the order and beauty of the stars. *Kosmos*—i.e., "order"—became a guide word to Pythagoras: virtue is order in our desires and in our relations with the community; and right government is the maintenance of order in the state. This, Pythagoras thought, could be best provided by an educated aristocracy, preferably of Pythagorean graduates. Plato followed

Pythagoras in this and other ways. The Greeks, when they spoke of "the philosopher," meant Pythagoras.

Rounding the toe of Italy, we pass between Italy and Sicily; these "Straits of Messina" are probably the "Scylla and Charybdis" of Homer's *Odyssey*. Soon we reach Velia, the ancient Elea, where Parmenides and one of many Zenos, about 445 B.C., founded a famous school of philosophy and puzzlement. Then north to Pesto, known to its Greek founders as Poseidonia, and to the Romans as Paestum; there, 600 years B.C., the Greeks built temples still bravely beautiful in their ruins. Farther north the Greeks founded Neapolis—"New City"—which we call Naples.

Thence we can fly in an hour to Sicily, where the insatiable Greeks built cities at Syracuse, Messina, Catana, Gela, and Acragas. At Syracuse, Archimedes was born (287 B.C.), greatest of Greek mathematicians, so in love with levers that, he felt, with one of them and a foot of land to stand on, he could move the earth. At Acragas, now Girgenti, on Sicily's southwestern shore, the prosperous colony raised to the goddess Concord a temple that still survives after twenty-three hundred years of war and politics. There Empedocles was born, about the year of Marathon; and perhaps it was there, and not in Etna's crater, that he died; we shall meet him as part of the Golden Age.

Turning north, the Greek merchants built towns at Antipolis (Antibes), Nikaia (Nice), Monoccus (Monaco), and Massilia (Marseilles). Sailing still farther westward, they built castles in Spain, as at Ampurias and Managa (near Malaga). Then, perhaps frightened by winds from the Atlantic, they turned back to their motherlands and enriched them with the proceeds of their conquests and trade.

We need to make this long circuit in order to see and feel the extent, variety, and daring of Greek civilization. Aristotle described the constitutional history of 158 Greek city-states, but there were many more. Each contributed, in commerce, industry, science, philosophy, literature, or art, to what we should mean by "ancient Greece." In the colonies, as well as on the mainland, were born Greek poetry and prose, mathematics and metaphysics. Without those colonial tentacles Greek civilization, the most precious product in our secular heritage, might never have been.

THE HOMELANDS

To mainland Greece—the Peloponnesus, Boeotia, Euboea, Attica—with their vibrant, jealous, competitive city-states—Sparta, Argos, Epidaurus, Corinth, Olympia, Eleusis, Plataea, Athens; to the Greek cities of Ionia—Halicarnassus, Miletus, Sardis, Smyrna, Pergamum; or to those Aegean Isles—Pythagoras' Samos, Sappho's Lesbos, Ariadne's Naxos, Cnidos, Tenedos, St. John's Patmos, Simonides' Keos, Homer's Chios, Samothrace of the Winged Victory—those magic isles where Greek merchants and sailors had been reared almost in smell of the sea: to these, and other places fondly imbedded in Greek memory, returned the avid adventurers when they had tired of trampling the sands of Egypt and the Near East, or plowing through the Mediterranean until it became, in its northern waters, a Greek sea. They brought home with them a thousand facts to arm or prod science, a rich experience to guide philosophy and politics, and an ardent competitiveness to support profound dramas and unsurpassed art.

This ardor for the advancement of knowledge and the adornment of the city seems to have least affected Sparta, which saw itself as guardian of the gates against "barbarian" (i.e., alien) inroads or infiltration from the north, and therefore subjected its citizens and its slaves to a martial discipline that left little room for the humanities and the graces of life. By contrast a dedication to speculation and beauty excited the Athenians, who felt protected by their navy, and so made their theaters the voices of philosophy, and their temples marble hymns to their gods.

We Americans were brought up to think of the Greek gods as creatures of romantic fancy or as metaphors for our poetry; so Zeus was for us an indefatigable adulterer and Aphrodite a dream of beauty; we forgot a thousand passages in classical literature which showed the Greeks as sacrificing toothsome animals to their gods, even as willing, like Agamemnon, to sacrifice a daughter for a breeze. Before the Sophists began, about 450 B.C., to undermine religious belief among the Greeks, religion was dear to the people, and helped them to sustain a moral life. So each household had its gods, whose visible surveillance kept the family together; and every city had its protective deity, as Athens had Athena, in whose worship the citizens could forget, for a while, their often unscrupulous competition and could almost bank-

rupt themselves to build a Parthenon. Their religion, like their patriotism, was mostly of the city and its hinterland, not reaching much beyond Olympia. They had confederacies, but hardly a state; and when a
united Persia challenged them, they came near losing their collective
freedom because they were so fond of their local liberty.

Athens, capital of Attica, particularly interests us because it made
illuminating experiments in government, and reached unsurpassed excellence in things of the mind. It tried monarchy and dictatorship, but,
through most of its famous years, it preferred a limited democracy. Like
our founding fathers, it enjoyed the services of slaves; but these were a
small minority in Athens and were usually war captives who preserved
some memory and hope of freedom.

Again as in the early years of our republic, only property-holders
were accounted citizens, and among these the long-established families
(the eupatrides, or "well-fathered") managed, till 507 B.C., to domi-
nate the Boule, or Court of Judgment, which, from its high seat on the
Acropolis, formulated policies and chose the archons who administered
the state.

Under this semifeudal rule the peasants of Attica approached, in the
7th century B.C., a condition dangerously like that of the French peasantry twenty-five hundred years later. "A few proprietors," wrote Aristotle, "owned all the soil," and the cultivators, with their wives and
children, were liable to be sold into slavery if they failed to pay the interest on their debts. Many peasants struggled on by mortgaging their
land at high interest; if they found themselves unable to pay, they fled
to the towns and surrendered themselves as serfs to the financiers.
Rural poverty in Attica became so great that war seemed to many peasants a secret blessing, since it might win more land for colonization
and leave fewer mouths to be fed.

As the seventh century B.C. approached its close, "the disparity of
fortune between the rich and the poor," says Plutarch, "had reached its
height, so that the city" of Athens "seemed to be in a truly dangerous
condition, and no means of freeing it from disturbances . . . seemed
possible except a despotic government." The poor began to talk of violent revolt, and a complete redistribution of wealth. The rich, unable
any longer to collect the debts legally due them, and angry at the challenge to their property and their savings, invoked ancient laws, sup-

ported the harsh legislation of Draco (620 B.C.), and prepared to defend themselves against an uprising that threatened all property, all established order, even civilization.

SOLON

It seems incredible that at this perilous juncture—so often recurring in history—a man was found who, without any violence of speech or deed, was able to persuade the rich and the poor to a compromise that not only averted social chaos, but established a new and more humane political and economic order for the entire remainder of free Athens' career. Solon's peaceful revolution is one of the encouraging miracles of history.

His father was a eupatrid of purest blood, who, according to Plutarch, "ruined his estates in doing kindnesses to other men." Solon, left to his own resources, consoled himself wisely: the riches of the rich "are no greater than his whose only possessions are stomach, lungs, and feet that bring him joy, not pain; the blooming charms of lad or maid; and an existence ever in harmony with the changing seasons of life." He took to trade, and became a successful merchant with far-flung interests and a rising reputation for intelligence and integrity. He was not yet forty-five when, in 594 B.C., he was chosen archon eponymos (technically, representing a particular locality), and, with the consent of all classes and regions, was entrusted with dictatorial powers to calm the class conflict, draw up a new constitution, and restore stability to the state.

He disappointed the extreme radicals by making no move to redivide the land; such an attempt would have meant civil war, chaos for a generation, and the rapid return of inequality. But by his famous *Seisachtheia* (Removal of Burdens), Solon canceled, says Aristotle, "all existing debts, whether owing to private persons or to the state," and so at one blow cleared Attic lands of all mortgages. All persons enslaved or attached for debt were released; those sold into servitude abroad were reclaimed and freed; and such enslavement was forbidden for the future. The rich protested that this legislation was outright confiscation, but within a decade opinion became almost unanimous that the act had saved Athens from revolution.

More lasting than these reforms were those historic decrees that created the Solonian constitution. Solon prefaced them with an act of
amnesty, freeing or restoring all persons who had been jailed or banished for political offenses short of trying to usurp the government. He
divided the free population of Attica into four groups according to
their wealth, and levied the rough equivalent of an annual income tax
of 12 percent on the first class, 10 percent on the second class, 5 percent
on the third, nothing on the fourth. Feudalism was replaced by a frank
plutocracy, but the new constitution made several moves toward
democracy. It opened the Ecclesia, or National Assembly, to all citizens
regardless of wealth, and gave it the authority to choose the archons
(from the first class) and to hold them subject to scrutiny and censure.
All citizens were eligible to selection by lot (as a means of evading the
power of wealth) to a *heliaea*, a grand jury of 6,000 members, which
served as a supreme court on all matters except murder and treason,
and as a court of appeals from the decision of any magistrate. This
power of public appeal became the wedge and citadel of Athenian
democracy.

Even in the risky realm of morals and manners Solon offered laws.
Persistent idleness was made a crime, and no man who lived a life of
debauchery was permitted to address the Assembly. He legalized and
taxed prostitution, and established public brothels licensed and supervised by the state. He enacted the modest penalty of 100 drachmas
(dollars) for the violation of a free woman, but anyone who caught an
adulterer in the act was allowed to kill him there and then.

He made it a crime to speak evil of the dead, or to speak evil of the
living in temples, courts, or public offices, or at the games; but even he
could not tie the busy tongue of Athens, in which gossip and slander
seemed essential to democracy. He laid it down that those who remained neutral in seditions should lose their citizenship, for he felt
that the indifference of the public is the ruin of the state. He required
that the sons of those who had died defending their country should be
brought up and educated at the expense of the government.

Radicals criticized Solon for failing to establish equality of possessions and power; conservatives denounced him for admitting the commons to the franchise and the courts; and his friend Anacharsis, the
whimsical Scythian sage, laughed at the new constitution, saying that

now the wise would plead and the fools decide. Besides, he added, no lasting justice can be established for men, since the strong or clever will twist to their advantage any laws that are made; the law is a spider's web that catches the little flies and lets the big bugs escape.

Solon accepted all this criticism genially, acknowledging the imperfections of his code; asked if he had given the Athenians the best laws, he answered, "No, but the best that they could receive"—the best that the conflicting groups and interests of Athens could at that time be persuaded to accept. He followed the golden mean and preserved the state; he was a good pupil of Aristotle before Aristotle was born. Tradition ascribed to him the motto written upon the temple of Apollo at Delphi—*Meden agan* (Nothing in excess); and all Greeks agreed in placing him among the Seven Wise Men.

In 572, after serving as archon for twenty-two years, Solon, age sixty-eight, retired from public life and set out to study civilization and government in Egypt and the Near East. "I grow old," he said, "while always learning." Shortly after his return to Athens he was grieved to see Peisistratus establish a dictatorship; but Peisistratus, after consolidating his own position, restored nearly all of Solon's laws.

Meanwhile the spread and profits of Athenian commerce were promoting Athenian industry, and the expanding business class resolved to end the political supremacy of the landed aristocracy. Education spread, and orators found audiences receptive to calls for wider public rule. In 507 B.C., Cleisthenes, himself the grandson of a dictator, established Athenian democracy in the form that it kept till 338 B.C. Supreme authority was placed in the Council of 501, to which every propertied citizen who had reached the age of thirty was appointed by rotation for a year's term. This Council supervised the administrative bureaucracy, determined what matters should be submitted to the Assembly, and served as the final court in law. Every citizen—some 30,000 men—had the right to attend the Assembly; 6,000 sufficed for a quorum. Never before had the world seen so liberal a franchise with so wide a spread of political power.

The Athenians were exhilarated by this leap into sovereignty. From that day they knew the zest of a widening freedom in action, speech, and thought; and from that day they led all Greece in literature, philosophy, and art, even, for a time, in statesmanship and war. When the greatest empire of that age—the Persia that had conquered everything from Afghanistan to Egypt—decided to lay tribute upon the scattered cities of Greece, it forgot that in Attica it would be opposed by men who owned the soil they tilled, and who manned the state that governed them.

It was fortunate for Greece that Cleisthenes completed his work—and Solon's—twelve years before Marathon. There and at Salamis the Athenians led the way to repel the challenge of Persia, and the road was open to Athens' Golden Age.

Chapter Seven

ﬁﬁﬁ

THE GOLDEN AGE
OF ATHENS

PERICLES

"The period which intervened between the birth of Pericles and the death of Aristotle," wrote Shelley about 1820 A.D., "is . . . the most memorable in the history of the world."

Athens dominated that epoch in European civilization because it had led the Greeks to victory over Persia at Marathon (490 B.C.) and Salamis (480), and had emerged from these ordeals with a navy that gave it control of Mediterranean commerce, of its former allies, and of their funds gathered in a temple on the island of Delos. The little city in Attica had become the acknowledged head of an Athenian Empire.

To rule this realm the citizens repeatedly elected Pericles, son of Xanthippus. He had every advantage of breeding and education. His father had fought at Salamis; his mother was a granddaughter of the aristocratic Cleisthenes, who had given Athens an improved form of democracy. The young Pericles, says Plutarch, was "perfectly formed, except that his head was somewhat longish and out of proportion"; his critics were to have much fun with this imperiously dolichocephalic head. He was well tutored in politics, music, and literature, became an ardent pupil of Anaxagoras and Socrates, and the husband of Aspasia— the most liberated woman of her time.

He earned fame by his eloquence, and yet his speech was unimpassioned, and appealed to mature minds. Plutarch described him as "manifestly free from all forms of corruption, and superior to all considerations of money"; this, however, came easily to one who had inherited a comfortable fortune.

Seeing that the landed aristocracy was out of step with the developing commercial economy, he attached himself to the growing party of the *demos*—the free population of Attica. In a long-sustained spirit of admiration and truth, the electorate, thirty times between 467 and 428 B.C., chose Pericles to the ruling body of *strategoi* (state leaders); these usually chose him to be *strategos autokrator,* or commander-in-chief. He increased his hold on the commonalty by arranging payment for jury service or attendance at the Dionysiac drama or the official games. The archonship, hitherto confined to the rich, was opened to all classes. He gave work to the unemployed by inaugurating great public enterprises, like building the "Long Walls," which enclosed Athens and its ports—Phalerum and the Piraeus—in a closed area accessible to enemies only by the sea, which was firmly controlled by the imperial fleet.

Hoping to make his capital the cultural crown of all Hellas, and to rebuild on a grander scale the ancient shrines which the Persians had destroyed as a prelude to the battle of Salamis, he engaged the artists of Athens, and the remaining unemployed, in a bold program for the architectural adornment of the Acropolis. To finance this massive enterprise he persuaded the hesitant Assembly to transfer to Athens the treasury accumulated by the Delian Confederacy from Delos, where it lay idle and insecure; and to use some of the fund for the beautification of a vibrant capital.

While these works proceeded, and Pericles' special protection and support were given to Pheidias, Ictinus, and the other artists who labored to realize his dreams, he lent his patronage also to literature and philosophy; and whereas in other Greek cities in this period the strife of parties consumed much of the energy of the citizens, and literature languished, in Athens the stimulus of growing wealth and democratic freedom was combined with enlightened leadership to produce the Golden Age. When Pericles, Aspasia, Anaxagoras, and Socrates together attended a play by Euripedes in the Theater of Dionysus, Athens could see in the flesh the zenith and unity of Greek life—statesmanship, art, science, philosophy, literature, religion, and morals living no separate careers as in the pages of books, but woven into one many-colored fabric of a nation's history.

THE PEOPLE

There are some aspects of this Golden Age that may alarm and offend us, but we must give them a passing mention if only to avoid a romantic idealization of a human-all-too-human scene.

First, of the 315,000 inhabitants of the little peninsula called Attica, only 43,000 were enfranchised citizens, and there were 115,000 slaves. These were recruited from unransomed prisoners of war, from slave raids upon non-Greek states, and from criminals and impressed wastrels. Greek traders bought slaves as they bought merchandise, and sold them in Athens, Corinth, or wherever they found purchasers. At Athens there were (as in the United States till A.D. 1863) markets where naked slaves were inspected and bought. Even the poorest citizen had a slave; Aeschines, to prove his poverty, complained that his family had only seven. All miners, including the superintendents and engineers, were slaves, and all Attic mines and miners were owned by the state.

The Athenian economy was still chiefly agricultural. Industry was carried on mostly in the house, but Athens had several factories; Pericles owned one. The esurient Greeks took rather to commerce than to industry; to buy cheap in one place and sell dear in another became half the life of Greece. The five-mile road between Athens and its chief port, the Piraeus, was usually alive, in daytime, with commercial traffic. Merchant vessels, powered both by sails and slave rowers (sometimes two hundred in one ship), pushed their prows through the sea at eight miles an hour to a hundred trading centers on the Mediterranean's eastern and northern shores.

Given naval supremacy and commercial prosperity, luxury grew and morals declined. Prostitutes were plentiful, and their patrons suffered hardly any reproof from public opinion. Athens officially recognized and legalized the business, and taxed its professionals. Some of these were trained in music, dance, and other forms of entertainment. The highest class among them—the *hetairai*, or companions, sought education, and amused cultured patrons by discussing literature, art, or philosophy; one of them pleased Sophocles, and another—Aspasia—married Pericles.

Their problem was not the law but the boys. Merchants imported handsome lads to be sold to the highest bidder, who would use them first as concubines and then as slaves. Athenian law forbade unisexual relations, but public opinion tolerated them. When Plato, in the *Phaedrus*, talks of human love, he means homosexual love; and the disputants in his *Symposium* exalt it above love between man and woman.

Aristotle attributed the custom to fear of overpopulation; perhaps it was part of Europe's Oriental heritage, and owed much to the seclusion of women. The life of the agora, gymnasium, and palaestra in Athens showed the youth only the male form; even art did not announce the physical beauty of women until Praxiteles, a century after Pericles. In married life the men seldom found mental companionship at home; the rarity of education among women created a gulf between the sexes, and men sought elsewhere the charms that they had not permitted their women to acquire. To the Athenian his home was not a castle but a dormitory; from morning to evening, in most cases, he lived in the city, and rarely had social contacts there with respectable women. Greek society was unisexual, and missed the excitement, grace, and stimulation that the spirit and charms of women were to give to Renaissance Italy and Enlightenment France.

Consequently the average Athenian male was lacking in the softer elements of character. Except in his first six years he lived with other males; and his adult personality was formed by the marketplace, by the competitions of commerce, by the problems of politics, philosophy, and war, by the sharp interplay of realistic minds shorn of a religion-based morality. The Greeks might admit that honesty is the best policy, but they tried everything else first.

Thrasymachus, the Sophist, identified might with right, and Thucydides, greatest of Greek historians, agreed with him on every other page. Most Greeks were kind to animals and cruel to men; they regularly used torture in eliciting information from unaccused slaves, and slept heartily after slaughtering a cityful of noncombatants; however, the oppressed and hunted of other states found sympathetic refuge in

Athens. War of some kind was a normal condition in Hellas. Greek met Greek in a thousand battles; and, a century after Marathon, the most brilliant civilization in ancient history consumed itself in a twenty-seven-years war that was almost a national suicide.

The Athenians were too brilliant to be good, and they scorned simplicity more than they abominated vice. No people ever had a readier fancy, or a livelier tongue. Clear thought, and its child, clear expression, seemed divine things to the Athenian; he had no patience with learned obfuscation, and looked upon informed and intelligent conversation as the highest sport of civilization. He agreed with Protagoras that man is the measure of all things. The desire to know and understand was his noblest passion, as immoderate as the rest. Later he would discover the limits of reason, and would fall into a pessimism strangely discordant with the natural buoyancy of his spirit. Even in his Periclean exuberance the thought of his profoundest men—who were not his philosophers but his dramatists—would be clouded over with the brevity of beauty and the patient pertinacity of death.

PERICLEAN ART

The Greek pursuit of wealth was limited only by an intense love of beauty. "I swear by all the gods," says a character in Xenophon's *Banquet*, "that I would not choose the power of the Persian king in preference to beauty." And a character in Xenophon's *Economics* adds: "It is beautiful too, despite the jeers of the witless, . . . to see cooking-pots arranged with sense and symmetry. All things without exception, because of symmetry will appear beautiful when placed in order."

This feeling for order and proportion, for form and rhythm, for precision and clarity, is the central fact in Greek culture. It enters into the shape and ornament of every bowl and vase, of every statue and painting, of every temple and tomb, of every poem and drama, of all Greek work in science and philosophy; it is wanting only in Greek conduct, religion, and statesmanship. Greek art is reason made manifest: Greek painting is the logic of line, Greek sculpture is a worship of symmetry, Greek architecture is marble geometry. There is no extravagance of emotion in Periclean art, no *bizarrerie* of form (as in Dionysian ritual), no striving for novelty through the abnormal or unusual; "we love beauty without extravagance," says Thuycides' Pericles. The purpose is not to represent indiscriminately the myriad details of the real, but to catch and hold the essence of things, and portray ideal possibilities of form and life.

Whatever the romanticists of less virile ages may have fancied of him, the Greek was no effeminate esthete murmuring mysteries of art for art's sake. He thought of art as subordinate to life, and of living as the greatest art of all; he had a healthy utilitarian bias against any beauty that could not be used; the useful, the beautiful, and the good were almost as closely bound together in his thought as in Plato's philosophy. Having a vivid sense of the state, he identified himself with the power and glory of his city, and employed a thousand artists to embellish its public places, celebrate its festivals, and commemorate its history.

Above all, he wished to honor and propitiate the gods, to express his gratitude for life, escape, or victory; he offered votive images, spent lavishly on temples, and engaged statuaries to give his gods or his dead an enduring similitude in stone. Hence, Greek art belonged not to a museum, where men might contemplate it in borrowed awe, but to the actual interests and enterprises of the people. The artist here was not an insolvent recluse in a studio, working in a language alien to the common citizen; he was an artisan toiling with laborers of all degrees in public and intelligible tasks. Athens brought together, from all the Greek world, a greater concourse of artists, as well as of poets and philosophers, than any other city of ancient Europe; and these men, competing in fervent rivalry, and cooperating under enlightened statesmanship, realized in heroic measure the visions of Pericles.

I will say nothing of Greek pottery except to remind you how much Keats saw on a painted Grecian urn, that "still unravished bride of quietness"; there is so much in anything if we perceive it in "silence and slow time." But how can we feel today the genius of Periclean painters like Polygnotus or Zeuxis, who left us hardly a line that careless, burdened history has not erased? I can only tell you a story of Zeuxis, who, when another painter boasted of his rapid execution, said quietly, "I take a long time."

The sculptures fared better than the paintings. I will speak of only two masterpieces from that age. *The Birth of Aphrodite* is a marble relief found in the ruins of the Roman Villa Ludovisi in 1887: the goddess of beauty, whose name means "foam-born," rises dripping from the sea, emerging victorious from a massive wave. Or you may prefer the *Discobulos,* or *Discus-Thrower,* cast in bronze by Myron about 470 B.C.; this athlete is no frenzy of strained muscles, but a man calm in the confidence of ability, a man of refinement and sensitivity, who could write books if he would so condescend.

Pheidias, who remained unrivaled in sculpture till Michelangelo, was dear to Pericles as a reckless consumer of gold and as leader of the corps of sculptors who worked on the Parthenon. He designed the groups and figures that were to fill the metopes, friezes, and pediments, and left it to his pupils to execute the plan. He himself molded for the Acropolis three statues of the city's guardian goddess, Athene. The most renowned of them, *Athene Parthenos,* rose thirty-eight feet high in the Parthenon as the virgin deity of wisdom and chastity.

The Parthenon—temple "of the virgins"—was only one of the architectural masterpieces that sprouted in Athens and its affiliated cities during the administration of Pericles. The ravaging of the capital by the Persians in 480 had burned to the ground almost every building of any value or prominence. The returning victors were at first dispirited by the ruins; but the agricultural hinterland sent them food, their victorious fleet brought them sustenance from a score of towns, the Treasury of Delos provided funds, the profits of trade brought more; the eloquence of Pericles stirred the chords of courage and pride; in the last eighteen years of his life (447–29) the city voted $60,000,000 for architecture, sculpture, and painting. The savings of the rich were spread among the artists, artisans, and slaves, and Athens became for a century a wonder of the world.

THE PHILOSOPHERS

Amid the new wealth, science and philosophy began to make themselves heard. Many Greek cities—above all, Sparta—forbade the public consideration of philosophical theories, "on account," says Athenaeus, "of the jealousy and strife and profitless discussions to which they give rise." But in Periclean Athens the "dear delight" of philosophy (as Plato was to call it) captured the imagination of the educated classes; rich men opened their homes in the manner of the French Enlightenment; philosophers were lionized, and clever arguments were applauded like sturdy blows at the Olympic games.

To Athens, in this period, came the Sicilian physician, vegetarian, poet, and mystic Empedocles, who expounded a theory of the evolution of man and all other species through the struggle for existence, the survival and selection of the fittest, and the elimination of forms and species through the internal forms of decay. From Abdera, in the supposedly barbarous north, came Democritus, and informed the Athenians that nothing existed except material particles, and that ideas were merely especially fine and smooth particles. But Zeno of Elea had already come to Athens and amused the philosophers with intellectual puzzles designed to prove his master Parmenides' psychological idealism—that since matter is known only through mind, materialism is logically illogical. Philosophy became a fever in Athens, and conservative statesmen began to fear the dissolution of morals and the state.

About 440 B.C., Anaxagoras, a friend of Pericles, issued the treatise *On Nature.* It pictured the universe as a conglomeration of particles animated by a tenuously physical *nous,* or mind, akin to the source of life and motion in ourselves. All organisms were generated originally out of earth, moisture, and heat, and thereafter from one another. All phenomena should be explained by natural causes. When no other way could be found to weaken Pericles, his demagogic rival, Cleon the Tanner, brought a formal indictment of impiety against Anaxagoras on the charge that he had described the sun (still to the people a god) as a mass of stone on fire, and pursued the case so relentlessly that the philosopher, despite Pericles' defense of him, was convicted (c. 434 B.C.). Anaxagoras fled to Lampsacus on the Hellespont, where he died a few years later, at the age of seventy-three.

Obviously the fear of the gods had faded in the intellectual minority in Athens. Two processes had led to this: the growth of the widely traveled middle class, and the spread of secondary education through itinerant scholars who lectured on rhetoric, literature, science, philosophy, and politics. Some of them, like Protagoras, called themselves *sophistai,* "teachers of wisdom"; some of them charged high fees. Since many of their students lost their religious faith, their teachers were accused of the venal sophistry which still clings to their name. Protagoras startled his time by declaring that "man is the measure of all things," and in the home of Euripides he preached a frank agnosticism: "With regards to the gods, I know not whether they exist or not." The Athenian Assembly ordered him to leave Athens; it commandeered all copies of his books and burned them in the marketplace.

It is in the perspective of this conflict that we must see the career and fate of Socrates. He is probably the most famous of Periclean Greeks; half of the Western world knows his bald head, broad face, thick nose, and spreading beard; his neglected wife; his irritating way of questioning others while rarely committing himself; but we hear little, in histories of philosophy, of his pupils' inclination to abandon their religious faith. One of these skeptical youths was the son of Anytus, who was a leader of the democratic party in Athens. Anytus did not like Socrates' criticism of democracy. He waited watchfully for a chance to destroy him—but first let us ascend to the peak with Greek drama.

THE GREEK DRAMA

Normally the philosophy of one age is the literature of the next: the ideas and issues that in one generation are fought out on the field of speculation or research provide in the succeeding generation the background of drama, fiction, and poetry. But in Greece, the literature did not lag behind the philosophy; the poets themselves were philosophers, did their own thinking, and were in the intellectual vanguard of their time. That same conflict between conservatism and radicalism which agitated Greek religion, science, and philosophy found expression also in poetry and drama, even in the writing of history; Thucydides invented speeches for his historical characters in order to play philosopher. Since excellence of artistic form was added, in Greek letters, to depth of speculative thought, the literature of the Golden Age reached heights never touched again until Shakespeare and Montaigne.

About 500 B.C., the wooden benches of a major Athenian theater collapsed, causing such alarm that the government built, on a slope of the Acropolis, a majestic amphitheater largely of stone, which they dedicated to the god Dionysus. In that roofless edifice, rising in fantastic semicircles of tiers toward the Parthenon, and facing Mount

Hymettus and the sea, the tragedies and comedies of the Greeks were played, in tribute to the gods, and before the high priests and officials of the state; and in those dramas was fought out one living phase of that war—between the old faith and the new philosophy—which binds into one vast process of thought and changed the inner history of classical Greece.

As early as 460 B.C., when Pericles was thirty-five, Aeschylus produced his first great drama, *Prometheus Bound.* He told the story of a man who had challenged the gods by teaching men the arts of fire and civilization, and was punished, at Zeus's command, by being chained to a rock in the Caucasus, and having his heart eaten out by a vulture and repeatedly restored and eaten again. In the lost conclusion of a trilogy, Aeschylus showed Prometheus making his peace with Zeus; but the theme of man's revolt against a cruel deity survived through twenty-two centuries to find wild utterance in Shelley's *Prometheus Unbound.*

In another trilogy, the *Oresteia* (438 B.C.), Aeschylus took up both sides of the argument, and pictured man's crimes as both shared and punished by the gods. Agamemnon, his fleet becalmed on the way to Troy, slays his daughter Iphigenia in a ritual sacrifice to obtain from heaven a cooperative breeze. While he besieges Troy his wife, Clytemnestra, having lost all love for her husband, gives herself to Aegisthus. On his return from Troy, Agamemnon is murdered by his fearful wife and her paramour. Her son, Orestes, growing up amid these horrors, and urged on by his sister, Electra, kills his mother and Aegisthus, and then is pursued in body and mind by the relentless fury of the avenging gods. How had so much evil come into the ritual of worship, and into the soul of man? This bloody trilogy is no mere murder story. It is a powerful indictment both of men and of the gods whom they had conceived. After the *Iliad* and the *Odyssey*, this *Oresteia* is the highest achievement in Greek literature, and perhaps Shakespeare himself never equaled it.

In 468 B.C., Aeschylus, then fifty-seven, lost the prize for drama to a youth of twenty-seven, who bore the challenging name of Sophocles—that is, "Wise and Acclaimed." He was both, for he won prize after prize, both in the Theater of Dionysus and on the stage of life. His father made swords, and grew rich, for the Greeks had a passion for war. The son had not only good fortune but good looks and genius; he was a skilled ballplayer, harpist, and dancer. He became a friend of Pericles and held high office under him; in 443 he was imperial treasurer; in 440 he was a leading general. He was very pious, and loved pleasure; in his maturity he had a fancy for boys, but in his old age he preferred courtesans. He enjoyed every favor of life, counted that man most blessed who had never been born, and lived to be ninety-one.

His plays were known only to scholars until our century, when Freud and his acolytes informed us that a girl like Electra will usually fall in love with her father and be jealous of her mother, while a full-blooded son like Oedipus, will, however unwittingly, kill his father and marry his mother. Sophocles must not be blamed for these inflations of occasional neuroses; he was merely telling a story familiar to his listeners. What he added was the subtle structure of his plays, and the melodious flow of his solemn verse. His is the typically "classic" form of utterance: polished, placid, and serene; vigorous but restrained; every line relevant; every incident moving toward the climax, and revealing significance.

Nevertheless, admiring the classical, loving the romantic, I prefer Euripides. He was unabashedly romantic: soaking his reason in feeling, hating injustice madly, dreaming of saner worlds. Only eighteen of his seventy-five plays survive, but nearly all were enlisted in his campaign against superstition, oppression, and war. He told the Athenians that the gods they were asked to worship were childish fancies, more cruel than beneficent. He presented Medea in all her barbaric violence and hatred, but he told the proud males—who ruled Athens—that:

Of all things upon earth that bleed and grow,
A herb most bruised is woman. We must (in a dowry) pay
Our store of gold, hoarded for that one day,
To buy us some man's love; and lo, they bring
A master of our flesh! . . . And then the jeopardy,
For good or ill, what shall that master be. . . .
Home never taught her that—how best to guide
Toward peace that thing that sleepeth at her side;
And she who, laboring long, shall find some way

Whereby her lord may bear with her, nor fray
His yoke too fiercely, blessed is the breath
That woman draws! Else let her pray for death.

Bravest of all was his play *The Trojan Women*, produced in 415 B.C.
amid the long, ferocious Peloponnesian War between Athens and
Sparta; daring to show the feelings of the defeated enemy; picturing
the desolation of Troy after the victors had burned down the city, and
while they were taking its widowed women into concubinage or slavery. King Priam is dead; his son and heir, Hector, has died in battle
with Achilles; his old widow Hecuba begs Hector's young widow An-
dromache to yield herself silently to concubinage in hope that her cap-
tors may spare her royal infant, Astyanax. But the Greeks fear that the
child may later claim vengeance and the throne of Troy; they fling it to
death over the city's wall. The corpse is brought to Hecuba for proper
burial; she speaks to it in the climax of Euripidean feeling and courage,
challenging and shaming the victorious Greeks:

(She takes the body.)

HECUBA: *Ah, what a death has found thee, little one! . . .*
Ye tender arms, the same dear mold have ye
As his. . . . And dear proud lips, so full of hope,
And closed forever! What false words ye said
At daybreak, when ye crept into my bed,
Called me kind names, and promised, "Grandmother,
When thou art dead, I will cut close my hair
And lead out all the captains to ride by
Thy tomb." Why didst thou cheat me so? 'Tis I,
Old, homeless, childless, that for thee must shed
Cold tears, so young, so miserably dead.
Dear God! the pattering welcomes of thy feet,
The nursing in my lap; and oh, the sweet
Falling asleep together! All is gone.
How should a poet carve the funeral stone
To tell thy story true? "There lieth here
A babe whom the Greeks feared, and in their fear

Slew him." Aye, Greece will bless the tale it tells! . . .
Oh, vain is man,
Who glorieth in his joy and hath no fears,
While to and fro the chances of the years
Dance like an idiot in the wind! . . .

(She wraps the child in the burial garments.)

Glory of Phrygian raiment, which my thought
Kept for thy bridal day with some far-sought
Queen of the East, folds thee for evermore.

The wave of public resentment that met *The Trojan Women* led Euripides to feel that, aside from Socrates, he had hardly a friend left in Athens; Pericles was long since dead. In 408, age seventy-two, he accepted the invitation of King Archelaus to be his guest in Pella, the Macedonian capital. There, for eighteen months, he found comfort and peace, and there, in 406, he died, attacked and dismembered, said pious Greeks, by the royal hounds.

He achieved postmortem popularity even in Athens. The ideas for which he had fought became the dominant conceptions of the following centuries, and the Hellenistic age looked back to him and Sophocles as the greatest intellectual stimuli that Greece had ever known. The plays of his predecessors slipped into comparative oblivion, while his were repeated in every year, wherever the Greek world had a stage. When, in the collapse of the Athenian expedition to Syracuse (415), the captive Athenians faced a living death as chained slaves in the quarries of Italy, those were given their freedom (Plutarch tells us) who could recite passages from the plays of Euripides. The revival of liberalism and humanitarianism in the eighteenth and nineteenth centuries made Euripedes almost a contemporary figure. All in all, only Shakespeare has equaled him; and Goethe did not think so. "Have all the nations of the world," asked Goethe, "produced one dramatist worthy to hand him his slippers?" Not more than one.

DISASTER

The remainder of the story of Periclean Athens is *decrescendo doloros*. From the peaks of drama we pass to the comedies of Aristophanes— brilliant, coarse, merciless; ridiculing Pericles, Euripides, and Socrates; attacking democracy, skepticism, and moral laxity; calling for a return to an almost forgotten morality, and crying for an end to war.

In 431 B.C., Sparta and Athens had begun the Peloponnesian War, which was to continue for twenty-seven years, spreading poverty and cruelty and darkening the spirit of Greece. Thucydides took part in the conflict, and recorded it blow by blow, in one of the classics of the world's literature. Sparta, fearing encirclement by Athens' growing empire and fleet, gathered allies, declared war, invaded Attica, and laid it to waste. Athens, which had neglected its army in too great reliance on its navy, could not defend her hinterland, and was forced to call its population to come and live within the city walls. There the crowded families bore an entire generation of siege, hunger, plague, and political turmoil. Pericles himself died (429), after two years of the war, and the Athenians, tired of his aristocratic democracy, submitted to an oligarchy of demagogues who led them from one calamity to another.

At last (404) the war ended, leaving Athens disordered and spiritless. Taking advantage of the political chaos, a group of aristocrats, led by Critias, established the Council of Thirty to rule Athens (404). It confiscated the property and alienated the support of many rich merchants; it plundered the temples, and sold for three talents the wharves of the Piraeus which had cost a thousand; it exiled 5,000 democrats, and put 1,500 others to death; it ended all freedom of assembly and speech; and Critias forbade Socrates to continue his public discourses.

All the blunders of the democracy were forgotten as the crises of the oligarchs multiplied. The number of men, even of substantial means, who began to seek an end to the tyranny grew from day to day. When a thousand armed democrats under Thrasybulus approached the Piraeus, Critias led a small band against them, was defeated and killed. Thrasybulus entered Athens and restored democratic government.

Among the victorious democrats was the same Anytus who, years before, had promised to revenge himself upon Socrates for some dialectical wounds and the "corruption" of his son. He could not forget that when he had been exiled by the Thirty his son had stayed in Athens with Socrates, and had become a drunkard. It seemed to Anytus that Socrates, more than any Sophist, was an evil influence on religion and morality, and had undermined the belief of educated Athenians in democracy. The tyrant Critias had been one of Socrates' pupils; the immoral and treasonable Alcibiades had been Socrates' brazen lover; Charmides, his early favorite, had just died in battle against democracy. It seemed fitting to Anytus that the philosopher should leave Athens—or die.

The indictment was brought forward by Anytus, Meletus, and Lycon in 399 B.C. "Socrates is a public offender in that he does not recognize the gods that the state recognizes . . . he has also offended by corrupting the youth." The trial was held before a popular court of some five hundred citizens, mostly of the less educated class. Socrates replied that he believed in the state gods, even in the divinity of the sun and the moon. He refused to promise silence: "I shall never cease from the practice and teaching of philosophy. . . . Whatever you do, know that I shall never alter my ways, not even if I have to die many times." He was pronounced guilty by a majority of sixty.

He had the privilege of proposing an alternative penalty instead of death; on the urging of Plato and other friends, who underwrote his pledge, he offered to pay a fine of thirty minas ($5,000?). The second polling of the jury condemned him by eighty more votes than the first. His friends offered to bribe his way to escape; he refused, saying that he relinquished only the most senile and burdensome part of life.

The Golden Age ended with the death of Socrates. Athens was exhausted in body and soul and felt the degradation of character that had gone on through a generation of ruthless conflict. Two things sustained her: the restoration of democracy, and the consciousness that during the last sixty years, even during the war, she had produced such art and literature as surpassed the product of any other so brief period in the memory of man.

Anaxagoras had been exiled, and Socrates had been put to death, but the stimulus given to philosophy sufficed to make Athens generate, in the next sixty years, systems of thought that would flourish in Europe through centuries to come. Soon the wandering Sophists would be replaced, in higher education, by universities that would make Athens "the school of Hellas." Through the bloodshed and turmoil of conflict the traditions of art had not quite decayed; Apelles and Praxiteles were soon to come; and through many more centuries the painters, sculptors, and architects of Greece were to draw, carve, and build for the Mediterranean world.

Out of the despair of her defeat Athens raised herself with startling virility to new wealth, culture, and power; and the autumn of her life was bountiful.

Chapter Eight

〽️

FROM PLATO
TO ALEXANDER

AFTER THE WAR

We begin at 399 B.C., the year in which Socrates died and Plato was twenty-eight. Athens was rising out of defeat. Sparta was relaxing in victory.

Athens had a reviving commerce and industry; Sparta had a stagnant agriculture listlessly manned by slaves. "Some Spartans," wrote Aristotle, "owned domains of vast extent, the others have nearly nothing: all the land is in the hands of a few." When Sparta sought to dictate to Thebes, a Theban army led by Epaminondas (and 300 "Greek lovers" bound in homosexual attachment) defeated the Spartans at Leuctra (371 B.C.), and ended Sparta's domination of Greece.

Freed from fear of Sparta, Athens rebuilt her mercantile fleet, her martial navy, and her Mediterranean empire. The mines of Laurium were reopened with slaves, and silver was mined in such quantity that money grew faster than goods, prices rose faster than wages, and the poor bore the burden of the change. Fortunes were made by buying domestic products cheaply and selling them for a profit at home or abroad. The clever flourished; the simple or disadvantaged looked in growing resentment at the rapid concentration of wealth. Banks multiplied their number and services, their investments and loans; a credit system developed. The change from landed to movable wealth produced a struggle for money, and led to new words like *chrematistike*, the feverish pursuit of riches; *pleonexia,* the appetite for more and more; *neoplutoi,* the newly rich.

In the midst of wealth, poverty increased, for the same variety and freedom of exchange that enabled the clever to make money enabled the simple to lose it faster and more diversely than before. Athens, said Plato, had become "two cities, one of the poor, the other of the rich, the one at war with the other." The poor schemed to despoil the rich by legislation or revolution; the rich organized for protection against the poor. The intellectuals generally took the side of the poor, and even the rich among them, like Plato, flirted with communistic ideas.

Finally the poorer citizens captured the Assembly, and began to vote the property of the rich into the coffers of the state, for redistribution among the lower classes. Legislators strained their ingenuity to discover new sources of public revenue. The result of these imposts was a wholesale hiding of wealth and income. Evasion became universal, and as ingenious as taxation. Houses were entered, goods were seized, men were jailed to enforce payments. Isocrates, old and rich, complained in 353 B.C.: "When I was a boy wealth was regarded as a thing so secure and admirable that almost everyone affected to own more property than he possessed; . . . now a man has to be ready to defend himself against being rich as if it were the worst of crimes." The middle classes, as well as the rich, began to distrust democracy as empowered envy, and the poor began to distrust it as a sham equality of votes stultified by a gaping inequality of wealth. The increasing bitterness of the class war left Greece internally divided when Philip of Macedon pounced down upon it, and many rich Greeks welcomed his coming as the alternative to revolution.

Moral laxity accompanied the growth of luxury and the liberation of the intellect. The masses cherished their superstitions and clung to their consoling myths; the gods of Olympus were dying, but new ones were being born, and exotic divinities were imported from Egypt and Asia. The rising and half-alien bourgeoisie of Athens had little awe for the traditional faith. "Now that a certain portion of mankind," wrote Plato, "do not believe at all in the existence of the gods, . . . a rational legislation ought to do away with the oaths of the parties on either side."

Philosophy struggled to find in civic loyalty and educated intelli-

gence some natural substitute for divine commandments and surveil-
lant deities, but sexual, social, and political morality continued to decline. Bachelors and courtesans increased in fashionable cooperation,
and free unions gained ground on legal marriage. "Is not a concubine
more desirable than a wife?" asks a character in a fourth-century B.C.
comedy. "The one has on her side the law that compels you to retain
her, no matter how displeasing she may be; the other knows that she
must hold a man by behaving well, or else look for another." Limitation
of the family was customary, whether by contraception, abortion, or infanticide.

Political morality continued to be low. Bribery prospered at every
level of government. Persia had no difficulty in bribing Greek politicians to foment war among Greek states. Greek mercenaries sold themselves impartially to Greek or "barbarian" (i.e., non-Greek) generals;
the Persian armies that Alexander faced were full of Greeks. Meanwhile
the rising class of rhetors, or orators, had taken on more and more the
work and character of lawyers and political managers; they planned and
directed campaigns and raised funds by promising favors. Politics became more intense than ever, but patriotism waned and corruption
grew. Individualism flourished, the state decayed.

Meanwhile, in mountainous and half-barbarous Macedonia, a lusty
monarch pondered the conquest of Greece.

PHILIP AND DEMOSTHENES

Philip was prepared for his role in history by a mixture of primitive
vigor and martial training with a touch of education and subtlety.

He was strong in body and will, athletic and handsome, a magnificent animal trying to be civilized. Like his son, here was a man of violent temper and abounding generosity, loving battle much, and drink
more. Unlike Alexander, he was a jovial laugher. He liked boys, but
women better, and married many of them. For a time he tried
monogamy with Olympias, the wild and beautiful Molossian princess
who gave him Alexander; but then his fancy roamed, and Olympias
brooded over ways of revenge.

Most of all he liked stalwart men who would risk their lives all day and carouse with him half the night. He was, before Alexander, the bravest of the brave, and left a part of himself on every battlefield. "What a man!" exclaimed his greatest enemy, Demosthenes. "For the sake of power and dominion he had an eye struck out, a shoulder broken, an arm and a leg paralyzed." In diplomacy he was affable but treacherous; he broke a promise with a light heart but was always ready to make another; he recognized no morals for governments, and looked upon bribes and lies as humane substitutes for slaughter. But he was lenient in victory, and gave the defeated Greeks better terms than they gave one another. All who met him—except Demosthenes—liked him, and ranked him as the ablest and most interesting character of his time.

He found and drilled an army of cavalry trained to confuse the enemy by repeated attacks diversely aimed; of infantry arranged in successive phalanxes and wielding lances twenty-one feet long; of archers sending their arrows over their phalanxes to their foes; and of a siege force with catapults and battering rams. With these weapons he proposed to drive the Persians again out of the Greek cities of Asia; but first, he felt, he must unify all European Greeks under his hegemony.

He began by seizing some cities, allied with Athens, on the coasts of Macedonia and Thrace. These towns not only blocked the way to Asia; they also controlled gold mines and taxable trade. While the Athenians were absorbed in another war, he took Pydna and Potidea (356 B.C.), and answered Athenian protests with compliments on Athenian literature and art. But when he proposed to bring the Athenians themselves under his rule, they were aroused to resistance by the passionate eloquence of the most famous orator in history.

Demosthenes

The Vatican statue of Demosthenes shows a deeply careworn face, as if every advance of Philip had cut a new furrow in the brow. The body is thin and wearied. The aspect is that of a man who has made his final appeal for a desperate cause.

His father left him a moderate fortune, but the executors consumed it. He made his own fortune as a rhetor, writing speeches for litigants;

sometimes, according to Plutarch, he prepared pleas for both parties to a dispute. He could compose better than he could speak, for he was weak in body and defective in articulation. To overcome these handicaps he addressed the noisy sea with his mouth half filled with pebbles, or he declaimed while running uphill. After years of effort he became one of the richest lawyers in Athens, flexible in his morals, but fearless in his views.

He told the Athenians that they were degenerate slackers who had lost the martial will necessary to national survival. He denounced Philip's call for the unification of Greece as a device for its subjugation to Macedonia. He begged his countrymen to resist Philip to their last man. His rival, Aeschines, defended Philip. Both were accused of receiving bribes—Aeschines from Philip, Demosthenes from the Persian king.

Finally Philip's southward drive so reinforced Demosthenes' eloquence that the Athenians turned the dole for the poor into preparation for war. In 338 they marched north to face Philip's phalanxes at Chaeronea. Sparta refused to help, but Thebes sent its "Sacred Band" to fight beside the Athenians. Every one of its 300 members died on that battlefield. The Athenians, too, fought bravely, but they were not organized or equipped to resist the sea of lances that fell upon them as if from the sky; they fled, and Demosthenes fled with them.

Philip punished the Thebans severely but he freed the 2,000 Athenians who had been taken prisoner and sent his charming son Alexander to offer peace on condition that Athens should accept Philip as the general of all Greece against the common Persian foe. Athens agreed. Philip convened at Corinth an assembly of the Greek states, and outlined his plans for the liberation of Hellenic Asia from Persian domination. He was unanimously chosen commander in this enterprise. He left to the constituent states a large measure of freedom, and prepared for a holy war.

He had won over all his foes except his wife Olympias, who resented his amours. Two years after Chaeronea, one of Philip's officers, Pausanias, brooding over an offense and teased by Olympias, killed the king. Alexander, idealized by the army, took the throne, and prepared, at age twenty, to conquer the world.

ART

After the eruption of dramatic genius in the fifth century B.C., Greek literature subsided into minor figures like Xenophon, the general who marshaled modern youth through Greek with his *Anabasis,* and Isocrates, the teacher and pamphleteer who invented the essay.

Art continued to flourish. "Apelles of Cos," wrote Pliny the Elder, "surpassed all other painters who either preceded or followed him." He must have been supreme, since he could afford the rare extravagance of praising his rivals. Learning that the greatest of these, Protogenes, was living in poverty, Apelles sailed for Rhodes to visit him. Unwarned, Protogenes was not in his studio when Apelles came. An old woman attendant asked Apelles whom she should name as visitor when her master returned. Apelles replied only by taking a brush and tracing upon a panel with one stroke an outline of exceeding fineness. When Protogenes came back, the old woman could not name the vanished visitor, but Protogenes, seeing the outline, exclaimed, "Only Apelles could have drawn that line." Then he drew a still finer line within that of Apelles, and bade the woman show it if the stranger should return. Apelles came, marveled at his absent rival's skill, but drew between the two lines a third of such slenderness and delicacy that when Protogenes saw it he confessed himself surpassed, and rushed to the harbor to overtake and welcome the master.

The panel was transmitted as a masterpiece from generation to generation, was bought by Julius Caesar, and perished in the fire that destroyed his palace on the Palatine Hill. A picture by Apelles, Pliny adds, sold for a sum equal to the treasuries of whole cities. Nothing remains of these masterpieces.

Sculpture took more time, and time preserved it. In many respects this arduous art now reached its apogee. It lacked the stimulus of religion, and fell short of the Parthenon pediment and frieze, but it took new inspiration from feminine grace, and it achieved a loveliness never surpassed.

The fifth century had modeled nude men and draped women; it had idealized its types, and had cast or chiseled the buffeted life of man into emotionless repose; the fourth century tried to realize in stone something of human individuality, feeling, and pain. In male statuary the head and face took on more importance, the body less; the study of character replaced the idolatry of form; portraits in stone became the fashion. The body abandoned its stiff, straight pose, and leaned at ease upon a stick or tree; and the surface was modeled to let in the living play of light and shade. Anxious for realism, Lysistratus of Sicyon, apparently first among the Greeks, fitted a plaster mold upon the subject's face, and made a guiding cast.

The representation of sensual beauty came near perfection in Praxiteles. All the world knows that he courted Phryne, and gave life beyond death to her loveliness, but no one knows when he was born or when he died. He was both the son and father of sculptors, so that we picture him as the climax of a family tradition of patient artistry. He worked in bronze as well as marble, and won such repute that a dozen cities competed for his services.

About 360, Cos commissioned him to carve an *Aphrodite;* with Phryne's help he did, but the Coans were scandalized to find the goddess quite nude. Praxiteles mollified them by making an *Aphrodite* clothed, while Cnidus bought the first. King Nicomedes of Bithynia offered to pay the city's heavy public debt in return for the statue, but Cnidus preferred immortality. Tourists came from every nook of the Mediterranean to see the work; critics pronounced it the finest statue ever made in Greece; gossip said that men had been stirred to amorous frenzy by viewing it.

The geographer Pausanius remarks, with irritating brevity, that among the statues in the Heraeum at Olympia was "a stone *Hermes* carrying Dionysus as a babe, by Praxiteles." German excavators digging on the site in 1877 crowned their labors by finding this figure, buried under centuries of rubbish and clay, as if time had been stone blind. Descriptions, photographs, and casts miss the quality of the work; one must stand before it in the little museum at Olympia, and clandestinely pass the fingers over its surface, to realize the smooth and living texture of this marble flesh. The head is a special delight, with its aristocratic shapeliness, its chiseled refinement of calm features and curly hair; the right foot is perfect—where perfection in statuary is rare. Antiquity considered this a minor work; judge from this the artistic wealth of the age.

We miss, in the scant remains of Praxiteles, the strength and sublimity of Pheidias; the gods have made way for Phryne, and the great issues of national life have been put aside for private love. But no sculptor has ever surpassed the sureness of Praxiteles' technique, the almost miraculous power to pour into stone ease and grace and tender sentiment, woodland joy and sensual delight.

Hovering between sculpture and architecture is the Mausoleum of Halicarnassus, an Ionian city-state whose ruler Mausolus was so loved by his wife Artemisia that when he died, in 353 B.C., she brought together Scopas and other artists to build and adorn his tomb. The vivid frieze, now in the British Museum, is among the triumphs of Greek sculpture. The monument gave a word to a score of languages, and was numbered by the ancients among the Seven Wonders of the World.

In the same list antiquity included the third temple, built at Ephesus in 356 B.C. to the goddess Artemis. Rising through the labor of fifty years, this became the largest temple in the Greek world. There the virgin goddess was worshiped first by the Greeks as Artemis, then by the Romans as Diana, then by the Christians as Mary the Mother of God. In history, as in newspapers, only the names and dates change; the events are always the same.

PLATO

In our mental youth we discover Plato, and think of a handsome young man fondling philosophy as a "dear delight," and imagining a utopia guided by virtuous philosophers; in old age we discover him proposing a government by dictators controlling or banishing artists and poets, and enforcing a state religion on penalty of death. How did he manage this transformation?

Let us recall, from our sophomore studies, that Plato was born in 427 B.C., of good family and fortune; that for many years he was an ardent follower of Socrates, and readily seconded his master's dislike of democracy; that the execution of Socrates by a democratic government fused dislike into scorn. He saw democratic politicians catering to the whims of the common herd until, in his view, liberty had become anarchy; and old standards of conduct and taste, which had protected civilization in manners, morals, and arts, were debased by a spreading and triumphant vulgarity. And he made his imaginary Socrates go on, as if describing today:

SOCRATES: In such a state the anarchy grows and finds a way into private homes. . . . The father gets accustomed to descend to the level of his sons, and the son to be on a level with his father, having no fear of his parents, and no shame. . . . The teacher fears and flatters his pupils, and the pupils despise their teachers. . . .

ADEIMANTUS: But what is the next step? . . .

SOCRATES: The excessive increase of anything often causes a reaction in the opposite direction. . . . The excess of liberty, in states or individuals, seems only to pass into slavery . . . and the most aggravated form of tyranny arises out of the most extreme forms of liberty.

In the second book of the *Republic,* Plato considered a communistic utopia, but explained that it was impractical because men are by nature individualistic, acquisitive, and, occasionally, murderous. He went on to portray a "second-best" state, organized around a system of education open to all, and ruled by "guardians" emerging alive, aged fifty, from the severest tests of the educational mill. These guardians, Plato argued, should have no property, no money, no wives, but should be dedicated to plain living and high philosophy; they should be a communistic isle ruling a surrounding sea of free enterprise. They would supervise, on eugenic principles, all mating and all marriages; "the best of either sex should be united with the best as often as possible, and the inferior with the inferior; they are to rear the offspring of one sort of union, but not of the other; for this is the only way of keeping the flock in prime condition."

All children are to be brought up by the state, and given equal educational opportunity; classes are not to be hereditary. Girls shall have an equal chance with boys; and no position shall be closed to women because they are women. It may seem impracticable, but Plato concluded: "Until philosophers are kings, or the kings and princes of this world have the spirit and power of philosophy, . . . cities will never cease from ill, nor the human race."

In old age he had not lost the ardor for utopias, but he reacted against the continuing laxity of Athenian democracy with the dictatorship of his last major work, the *Laws*. His new ideal is a rural community, situated sufficiently inland to be free from disturbance by foreign ideas. The voters shall be 5,040, for that is a conveniently divisible number. They shall elect 360 guardians, who will administer the economy and the laws, and will elect a Nocturnal Council of 26, who will legislate on all vital matters, economic or cultural. Everyone is to be encouraged to be an active farmer; all complex financial operations should be avoided; economic bequests are to be strictly limited. Women are to have equal opportunity—educational, economic, and political. Drinking and public amusements are to be regulated by religion and the state to protect the morals of the people. Authority is to replace freedom in the family and the school. Since obedience to parents, teachers, and the laws can be secured only through supernatural beliefs, the state shall determine what gods shall be worshiped, and how. Literature, science, and art are to be censored to prevent the spread of ideas hostile to religion or the state. Anyone who questions the state religion shall be imprisoned, and if he persists, put to death.

When Athens' most famous philosopher could find so little to say for freedom, philosophy was ripe for a new religion, and Greece was ripe for a new king.

ARISTOTLE

We play with Plato, but we must *work* with Aristotle.

It is one of the pranks of history that Plato's popular *Dialogues* survive and often enchant us, while his technical treatises were swamped in the flotsam of time, whereas Aristotle's popular works have perished, and only his technical treatises remain, demanding laborious attention as the price of their concentrated lore.

Son of a physician in Thracian Stageirus, he inherited a wide interest in science. Coming to Athens, he registered in Plato's Academy, whose main portal warned, "Let no one without geometry enter here." After Plato's death Aristotle went to the court of Hermeias, who had studied with him at the Academy, and had raised himself from slavery to be dictator of Atarneus and Assos in Asia Minor.

Aristotle married Hermeias' daughter Pythias, and was about to settle in Assos when Hermeias was assassinated by a Persian. Aristotle fled with Pythias to Lesbos, where she died after giving him a daughter. Later he married—or lived with—the hetaira Herpillis, but he maintained to the end a tender devotion to Pythias, and at his death he asked that his bones be laid beside hers. He was not the emotionless bookworm that seems to emerge from his surviving works.

In 343, Philip invited him to come to Pella to undertake the education of Prince Alexander, then a wild lad of thirteen. Aristotle labored at this task for four years. In 334 he returned to Athens—perhaps aided by funds from the now King Alexander—and opened a school of rhetoric (literature and philosophy). He chose as its home the most elegant of Athens' gymnasiums—a group of buildings dedicated to Apollo Lyceus (God of Shepherds) and surrounded with shady gardens and covered walks.

The school came to be called the Lyceum, and the group and its philosophy were named Peripatetic from the walks (*peripator*) along which Aristotle liked to move with his pupils as he discoursed. He set them to gathering and arranging knowledge in almost every field: the customs of foreign peoples, the constitutions of the Greek city-states, the chronology of Greek victors in the Pythian games and the Athenian Dionysia, the organs and habits of animals, the character and distribution of plants, the history of science and philosophy. These researches became a treasury of data upon which he drew—sometimes too confidently—for his diverse and numerous treatises. If we sample them, we must expect no Platonic duel of lively converse, but only a rich argosy of knowledge and thought, and such conservative wisdom as befitted the friend and pensioner of kings.

In science he covered the field with observations, reports, and experiments, and was the first man known to have organized a group for scientific research. He made a hundred brilliant perceptions, and a hundred glaring mistakes—like his reassuring discovery that women have fewer teeth than men. But his *History of Animals* came near to a theory of evolution and his *Treatise on the Soul* defined the soul, or psyche, as the vital "powers of an organism for nourishment, growth, and decay." His conception of God as the Prime Mover, or basic and omnipresent energy, accords with the modern conception of the world as energy in action.

The goal of conduct is happiness, but the secret of happiness is virtue, and the best virtue is intelligence—a careful consideration of the reality, the goal, and the means; usually "virtue" is a golden mean between extremes. Politics is the art of compromise between the classes that constitute a society. All men are created unequal, and the upper classes will as readily revolt if an unnatural equality is enforced, as the lower classes will rebel when inequality is unnaturally extreme. So Aristotle favored a "timocracy" (rule by honor)—a combination of aristocracy and democracy, in which the suffrage would be restricted to property owners, and a numerous middle class would be the pivot and balance wheel of power.

All in all, Dante was justified in calling Aristotle *il maestro di color chi sanno*—"the master of those who know"—and Europe was justified in calling him, through almost fifteen hundred years, *ille philosophus*— "the philosopher."

ALEXANDER

His famous pupil, Alexander, pleased his teacher for some years after becoming king of Macedonia and commander-in-chief of all Greek forces against Persia. "For my part," Alexander wrote to Aristotle, "I had rather surpass others in the knowledge of what is excellent than in the extension of my power and dominion." "He had," says Plutarch, "a violent thirst and passion for learning, and this increased as time went on." But the philosopher's instructions were only a small part of the influences forming the young monarch's character and policies.

He heartily accepted his father's plan for liberating Greek Asia from Persia, but he expanded that plan with every victory. His mother claimed descent from Achilles, and met Philip's infidelities by intimating that the real father of her son was the god Ammon; Alexander never quite rejected this heroic and divine genealogy. He read and reread the *Iliad* until he knew a hundred passages by heart, and he envied Achilles for having had a Homer to sing his story. He grudged the time he gave to sleep, saying that Sleep and the act of generation made him sensible that he was mortal.

Physically he was next to godliness. He excelled in every sport, and hunted lions for play; once, after a duel with a lion, he was pleased to hear it said that he had fought as though it had been to decide which of the two should be king. All the world knows how he tamed the giant horse Bucephalus when all other riders had failed. Thereupon, Philip exclaimed: "My son, Macedonia is too small for you; seek out a larger empire, worthier of you." Add to this that Alexander was handsome beyond all precedents for a king.

It was impossible for a youth so saddled with perfections and power to develop mature judgment or an educated mind. A crown burdened him at twenty, war and government absorbed him till he died; death cut him down in his thirty-third year before he could reach the clear intelligence of Caesar or the instant understanding of Napoleon. He could talk brilliantly, but fell into a hundred errors when he wandered from politics and war. He rose above dogma, but was to the end a slave of superstition; his court was crowded with astrologers. He could govern millions, but not his temper. He allowed his judgment to be blurred by daily adulation. He lived in a frenzy of excitement and glory, and so loved war that he rarely knew an hour of mental peace.

In morals, too, he never achieved consistency or maturity. Sexually he was almost virtuous, not so much on principle as from preoccupation. He took several wives, but as tools of statesmanship. He was gallant to ladies, but preferred generals and boys; he loved young Hephaestion to madness, and gave to friendship the tenderness and solicitude that other men might give to love. He endeared himself to his soldiers by his consideration for them; he risked their lives, but not heedlessly, and he seemed to feel all their wounds. He repeatedly forgave offenses, and made friends of captive generals. His reputation for generosity became international. Many enemy troops allowed themselves to be taken prisoner, confident of easy terms; and cities, unresisting, opened their gates at his coming. Yet he was his mother's son;

he had a tigress in his blood, and could be unmanned by paroxysms of cruelty.

You know the story of his conquests. With his 30,000 soldiers he met (we are told) 600,000 Persians at the river Issus (333 B.C.), and so confused them with incalculable cavalry dashes that they gave up and fled with Darius III, who left his purse and princess behind him. Alexander went on to take Damascus, Sidon, and Tyre, received courteously the surrender of Jerusalem, marched across the Sinai desert into Egypt, expelled the Persians (who had ruled there since 525 B.C.), founded Alexandria, marched back into Asia, met the vast polyglot army of Darius III near Arbela, and was at first so dismayed by their number that his soldiers reassured him: "Be of good cheer, Sire; . . . they will not be able to stand the smell of goat that clings to us." Their bravery, cavalry, phalanxes, and orderly acceptance of wise generalship won the day; Darius fled again and was killed by his retinue. Alexander took Babylon, marched on to Susa, found the government's hoarded treasure, and divided some of it among his men.

Drunk with victory and gold, he led his reluctant troops over the Himalayas into India. He crossed the Indus, defeated King Porus, and announced his intention to press on to the Ganges. But his soldiers were exhausted in body and spirit; they knew they were leaving their families and Greek civilization ever farther behind them; victory itself had become a bore. Sadly he yielded to them, and followed them back to Persia in a retreat almost as long and disastrous as Napoleon's from Moscow. When they reached Susa, 10,000 of them had died from heat or thirst.

Now, among the Persians, Alexander perceived that his warriors had conquered a people more civilized than themselves. He conceived the idea of intermarriage between conquered and conquerors; he married two Persian princesses, and proposed to his officers and soldiers that they should take Persian brides. Thousands of them did. He opened lands in Persia and Mesopotamia to Greek colonization. This interplay of diverse cultures furthered the Hellenization of the Near East, and then, by a reverse movement, facilitated the eastward flow of Oriental religions; so Judaism—and later Christianity—spread across the Aegean, and a faith born in Jerusalem became the creed of Europe.

Alexander still dreamed of victories and continents, but his soldiers threatened mutiny. Finally he gave them permission to go home, but he added a reproof: "Go back and report that you deserted your king and left him to the protection of conquered foreigners." Then, says a perhaps apocryphal story, he retired to his room and refused to see anyone. Stricken with remorse, the leaders of the revolt came and lay down before his door, saying that they would not leave till he had forgiven them and reaccepted them into his army. When at last he reappeared, they broke down and insisted on kissing him; and after being reconciled with him they went back to their camp shouting a song of thanksgiving. *Si non è vero è ben trovato.*

While he was in Ecbatana with his army, his beloved young friend Hephaestion died. Feeling that half of his own flesh and blood had been torn away, Alexander broke down in almost uncontrolled grief. Back in Babylon, he abandoned himself to drink. One night, reveling with his officers, he proposed a drinking match. Promachus quaffed twelve quarts of wine and won the prize, a talent ($12,000); three days later he died. Shortly afterward, at another banquet, Alexander drained six quarts. On the next night he drank heavily again; cold weather suddenly set in; he caught a fever and took to his bed. He lingered for eleven days, and then died, 323 B.C., age thirty-two. When his generals asked him to whom he left his empire, he answered, "To the strongest."

It was just as well that he died at his zenith; added years would almost surely have brought him disillusionment. Perhaps if he had lived, he might have been deepened by defeat and suffering, and might have learned—as he was beginning—to love statesmanship more than war. But he had undertaken too much; the strain of holding his swollen realm together, and watching all its parts, was probably disordering his brilliant mind. Energy is only half of genius; the other half is harness; and Alexander was all energy.

We miss in him—though we have no right to expect—the calm maturity of Caesar, or the subtle wisdom of Augustus. We admire him (as we admire Napoleon), because he stood alone against half the world, and because he encourages us with the thought of the incredible power that lies potential in the individual soul.

And we feel a natural sympathy for him, despite his superstitions and his cruelties, because we know that he was at least a generous and affectionate youth, as well as incomparably able and brave; that he fought against a maddening heritage of barbarism in his blood; and that through all battles and all bloodshed he kept before his eyes the dream of bringing the light of Athens to a larger world.

THE ROMAN REPUBLIC

We shall, in these introductory pages, undertake not a history of republican Rome, but a brief analysis of how family, religion, and discipline produced the Roman character; how the conflicts of classes and generations produced the Roman government; and how the cooperation of character and accident enabled Rome to master the Mediterranean world.

First, then, the people.

THE PEOPLE

Who were they? They had been the indigenous tribes—Umbrians, Sabines, Latins . . . plowing and fighting in and around Rome. They had been hardy immigrants from Central Europe, surmounting the Alps and spreading over the lake region—Maggiore, Como, Garda—into the fertile valley of the Po. Some may have been adventurers from Asia Minor who came to mingle with natives to become the obscure Etruscans of ancient Tuscany. And a dozen varieties of Greeks had developed lively settlements in the foot of that Magic Boot which is called Italy.

"Those who are the best judges in that country," says Aristotle, "report that when Italus became King of Oenotria, the people there changed their names to Italians." Oenotria was the toe of the Italian boot, so teeming with grapes that the word meant "land of wine." Italus, according to Thucydides, was a king of the Sicels, who conquered Sicily. Just as the Romans called all Hellenes *Graeci*, Greeks, from a few Graii who had emigrated from north Attica to Naples, so the Greeks gradually extended the name Italia to all the peninsula south of the Po.

Most of the population lived by agriculture; a minor part constituted the precarious population of the towns. Competition by slaves depressed the wages of free workers, and reduced many of them to life in slums. Strikes were few among the free, who had to compete for jobs; but slave uprisings were frequent. The "First Servile War" (139 B.C.) was not the first, and Spartacus was not the last slave to die in revolt (71 B.C.).

Criminals were added to slaves in building the great roads that stimulated trade, quickened the movement of armies and ideas, and finally made Italy one. In 312 B.C., Appius Claudius directed the construction of the Appian Way from Rome to Capua; year after year it was extended until it reached the Adriatic at the modern Brindisi. In 241, Aurelius Cotta began the Via Aurelia that made Nice an outpost of Rome.

Social order, which is the fount and prop of civilization, was maintained by the family, the clergy, the school, the law, and the varied arms of the state. Order in the family, in the early Republic, was based on the almost absolute power of the father; he alone had any right before the law; even his wife's dowry belonged to him. If his wife was accused of a crime, she was committed to him for judgment and punishment; he could condemn her to death for infidelity, or for stealing the keys to his wine. Over his children he had the power of life and death, or sale into slavery; over his slaves his power was limitless.

These rights of the paterfamilias were gradually checked by public opinion, custom, the clan council, and the growth of security and law; otherwise they lasted till his death. Presumably they reflected the frequency of war, and the need of habituation to strict discipline. They were harsher in the letter than in practice, and did not bar a deep and natural *pietas*, or reverential affection, between parents and children. The tomb statuary of the Romans is as tender as those of Greece and our own.

Over the family as protectors, lawgivers, and moral forces, hovered a multitude of gods, conceived not as having human form, but as spirits wielding supernatural power over all things and all phases and periods of life. So the goddess Venus symbolized the life and continuity of the family by the fire on the hearth; that fire was never allowed to die, and must receive a bit of every meal. Over the hearth were little icons representing the gods of the family: the Lares that guarded its buildings and fields, and the Penates, or gods of the interior, protecting the accumulations of the family in its cupboards, storerooms, and barns.

Hovering, invisible but potent, over the threshold, was the god Janus, two-faced not as deceitful but as watching all entry and exit at every door. The child was taught that its mother bore in her a Juno, as the spirit of her capacity to bear new life, and that its father enclosed a *genius* as the spirit of his power to beget. The child too had its *genius* or Juno, as both its guardian angel and its soul—a godly kernel in a mortal husk. Everywhere about it were the *Di Manes,* or Kindly Shades— death masks hanging on the walls, warning the child not to stray from the ways of its ancestors, and reminding it—as Burke reminded the revolutionary French—that the family is composed not only of those few individuals who were now alive, but also of those that had once been, or would some day be, members of it in the flesh, and who therefore formed part of it in its spiritual multitude and timeless unity. In Rome the family ruled the state.

When the child stepped out of the house, it found itself again and everywhere in the presence of gods. The earth itself was a deity, sometimes Tellus, or Terra Mater—"Mother Earth"; sometimes Bona Dea, the "Good Goddess" who gave rich wombs to women and fields. On the farm there was a helping god for every task or spot: Pomona for orchards, Saturn for sowing, Ceres for crops, Vulcan for making the fire. Other religions may have looked to the sky, and the Roman admitted that there, too, were gods, but his deepest piety and sincerest propitiations turned to the earth as the mother of his life, the home of his dead, and the magic force in the sprouting seed.

The very air and soil of Italy were alive with divinities: spirits of the season like Maia, water gods like Neptune, woodland sprites like Silvanus, or gods that dwelt in trees. There were spirits of procreation: Tutumus was tutelary deity over conception, Lucina over menstruation and delivery. Priapus was a Greek god readily domiciled in Italy; maidens and matrons sat on the male member of his statue as a means of ensuring pregnancy; figures of him, without scandal, adorned many a garden; images of him were worn to bring fertility or good luck.

Over all gods and men reigned Jupiter, or Jove, the god of the sky or the sun, as a bolt of thunder, Jupiter Tonans; or Jupiter Pluvius, of rain. Quite as old in popular regard was Mars, god of war; every tribe in Italy named a month after him. These major gods were identified with deities seeping in from Greece: so Athena became Minerva, Hera became Juno, Aphrodite became Venus, Vulcan became Mars, Artemis became Diana. Never before had a religion had so many gods; Petronius complained that in some towns of Italy there were more gods than men.

Did this religion help Roman morals? In some ways it seems to us immoral: its ritual suggested that the gods rewarded not goodness but gifts and formulas; and its prayers were nearly always for material goods or martial victory. Nevertheless the religion made for order and strength in the individual, the family, or the state. Before the child could learn to doubt, faith molded its character into discipline, duty, and decency. Religion gave divine sanctions and support to the family; it instilled in parents and children a mutual respect and piety never surpassed. It invested every phase of public life with religious solemnity, and fused the state into such intimacy with the gods that piety and patriotism became one, and love of country rose to a passion stronger than in any other society known to history. Religion shared with the family the credit for forming the iron character that for five hundred years enabled Rome to govern the classic world.

THE GOVERNMENT

In her long and wide experience Rome tried and illuminated many forms of government. The family conflicts and sexual diversions of its possibly legendary kings surfeited the Romans with monarchy. The terminal king, Tarquinius Superbus, or the "Proud," had a reckless son who raped the virtuous Lucretia—Livy and Shakespeare have told that story. Lucretia proclaimed her misfortune, and killed herself. The patrician class to which she belonged rose to revenge her; it deposed Tarquinius, established a republic, and chose two consuls to govern under a supreme senate composed of fathers claiming descent from the founding fathers of the state.

Like our own founding fathers, or *patres,* the Roman patricians did not intend the new republic to be a democracy. The right to vote was limited to holders of property; the term *res publica* meant the "common wealth." The heads of old clans or families formed a senate of some three hundred members, replenished by the automatic admission of consuls and tribunes who had honorably completed their terms. These early senators were not such lords of comfort and luxury as some of their descendants; often they put their own hands to the ax or plow; they lived vigorously on simple fare, and wore clothing spun in their own homes. The plebs admired them even when it fought them, and applied to almost anything pertaining to them the term *classicus*—"classical," of the highest class.

Close to them in wealth, far below them in political power, were the equites—literally the "horsey set," actually the business class. The word *populus,* "people," included only these two upper classes. Below them were the slaves and the plebs. When Rome began her career of conquest, war captives were sold in rising number to the aristocracy, businessmen, even to prosperous plebeians.

The plebeians were the residue of Romans, aside from the patricians, the businessmen, and the slaves. They consisted of farmers, workingmen, traders, professional men, artists, teachers, bankers, and others. Some were rich, some were powerful, most were poor; all felt that Roman law was unfair to them; and most of Roman history before Caesar is the story of the plebeians' struggle for a share in power. They fought the harsh law that allowed a creditor to imprison a persistently defaulting debtor in a private dungeon, to sell him into slavery, even to kill him. They demanded that lands won in war should be distributed among the poor instead of being given, or sold at nominal prices, to the rich; that plebeians should be eligible for the magistracy and the priesthood, and have a representative of their class among the highest officials of the government. The Senate sought to frustrate the agitation by fomenting wars, but it was shocked to find its calls to the colors ignored.

In 494 B.C., large masses of the plebs "seceded" to a "Sacred Mount" on the river Anio, three miles from Rome, and declared that they would neither fight nor work for Rome until their demands were met. Fearing that external attack might coincide with revolt within, the Senate agreed to a cancellation or reduction of debts, and the establishment of two tribunes as the elected defenders of the plebs. This was the opening battle in a class war that ended only with the republic that it destroyed.

The next step in the climb of the plebs was a demand for definite, written laws, free from ecclesiastical interpretation and control. After a long resistance the Senate (454) sent a commission of three patricians to Greece to study, and report on, the legislation of Solon and other lawmakers. When they returned, the Assembly of the Centuries—i.e., of the army—chose ten men to formulate a new code. This commission transformed the old custom-based law of Rome into the famous Twelve Tables, and displayed them in the Forum for all to read. This was the first written form of that body of laws which was to be one of Rome's most signal contributions to civilization.

The power of the Senate remained supreme despite these advances toward democracy. The cost of winning and holding office—which was unpaid—disqualified the poor. The richer plebeians now cooperated with the patricians in checking radical movements. Businessmen fell in with patrician policy because it gave them contracts for public works, openings for colonial and provincial exploitation, and commissions to collect taxes. The Senate took the lead in legislation, and custom sanctioned its authority far beyond the letter of the law.

As foreign affairs became more important, the Senate's firm and skillful administration of them raised its prestige and power. When, in 264 B.C., Rome entered upon a century of war with Carthage for control of the Mediterranean, it was the Senate that led the nation through every trial to victory; and an imperiled people yielded with little protest to its leadership and domination.

CONQUEST

Rome became a military power because she found herself hemmed in between the sea and a dozen Italian states fiercely independent and half in love with war. With arms and diplomacy, she fought or bought them off, and absorbed most of them under her rule. Two problems remained: Italy north of the Po was still under control by Gauls, and even the Romans called it Gallia Cisalpina—Gaul this side of the Alps; and south of Rome were Naples, Paestum, Crotona, Sybaris, Tarentum—all proudly fond of their Greek origin and culture, and their commercial wealth.

Fearing a Rome made powerful by her victories, they appealed to Pyrrhus, the brilliant young king of Epirus, to come to their aid. Hoping to divide Italy for his own security, Pyrrhus crossed the Adriatic and defeated the Romans at Heraclea (280 B.C.) and Asculum (279); there, however, his losses were so discouraging that he reckoned, "One more such victory and we are undone"—so giving us an adjective. Nevertheless, hearing that Carthaginian invaders were besieging Syracuse, he led his depleted army into Sicily and drove the Carthaginians from nearly all their posts on the island. But his imperious rule offended the Sicilian Greeks, who thought they could have freedom without order; Pyrrhus returned to Italy, saying, "What a prize I leave to be fought for by Carthage and Rome!" He met the reinforced Romans at Beneventum (275), and suffered so decisive a defeat that he withdrew to Epirus. Three years later he was killed in battle at Argos, age forty-six.

Rome was now lord of all Italy, but across the narrowing sea was a power older and richer than Rome. Phoenician merchants, plying between the Near East and Spain, had established intermediate trading posts on the north coast of Africa. Legend, as in Virgil's *Aeneid,* told how Dido, daughter of the king of Tyre, had founded, near Utica, a Semitic settlement called Kart-hadasht, or Newtown, which the Romans modified into Carthago. The settlers hired or enslaved African natives, developed large-scale agriculture, built a merchant navy, and carried goods to and between Tyre and Sidon, Spain and Britain. By the third century B.C., Carthage had become the richest city in the Mediterranean world, with a population of 250,000, with revenues twenty times greater than those of Athens at her peak; and with palaces and temples splendid enough to inspire, across two thousand years, the gilded prose of Flaubert's *Salammbo.* Government was by a popular Assembly, and a merchant-dominated Senate. The secret pride of the city-state was its navy of five hundred quinqueremes, which controlled all the southwestern Mediterranean. When that navy transported an army to Sicily, the Roman Senate decided that Carthage must be destroyed.

We need not repeat what our schooldays told us—that Rome and Carthage debated, from 264 to 146 B.C., which of the two should hold Sicily, Corsica, and Spain, and call the Mediterranean *Mare nostrum,* "Our Sea." Many heroes were projected into history in those three Punic (i.e., Phoenician) Wars: Regulus, Hamilcar, Hannibal, Hasdrubal, Scipio Africanus. Before leaving Carthage on a final campaign, Hamilcar led his nine-year-old son Hannibal to the altar of the god Baal-Hamen, and bade him swear that some day he would avenge his country against Rome. Hannibal swore.

His famous exploits were made possible by Rome's intermittent conflict with the Gauls for control of Italy north of the Po. To secure herself in the West she signed a treaty by which the Carthaginians in Spain agreed to stay south of the Ebro. In 225 B.C., a Gallic army of 50,000 foot and 20,000 horse swept down from Cisalpine Gaul in an attempt to destroy Rome. The inhabitants of the capital were so terrified that the Senate returned to the primitive custom of human sacrifice and burned two captive Gauls alive. The Roman legions met the invaders near Telamon, killed (they said) 40,000 of them, and went on to subjugate Cisalpine Gaul. Now master of Italy, Rome resumed her duel with Carthage.

In 221 the Carthaginian army in Spain chose Hannibal to be its commander. He was twenty-six years old, in the prime of body and mind. He had received some education in the history, languages, and literatures of Phoenicia and Greece, and had absorbed a soldier's training in camp and war. He had disciplined his body to hardship, his appetite to need, his thought to fact, his tongue to silence. He was "the first to enter the battle," said the hostile Livy, "and the last to leave the field." Veterans loved him because in his commanding presence they saw their old leader Hamilcar returning to them in fresh youth; the recruits liked him because he never rested till he had provided for his army's needs, and shared with them all sufferings and gains. The Romans could not forgive him for winning battles with his brains rather than with the lives of his men.

He saw his opportunity now that the Gauls rivaled him in hatred of Rome. He could not invade Italy by sea, for the Roman navy was too

powerful; but if he might march through Gaul and over the Alps . . .
He crossed them by almost the same route that Napoleon would take
two thousand years later. The Cisalpine Gauls welcomed him; some
joined him, but the 50,000 men he had led from Spain were now reduced to 26,000. He met Roman armies near the river Ticino (218) and
again by Lake Transimene (217), and overwhelmed them with African
elephants and wild Numidian cavalry. Hannibal led his exhausted
forces over the Apennines and down the Adriatic coast. The Senate
made Quintus Fabius Maximus dictator, and bade him pursue and en-
gage Hannibal's army. Fabius thought it wiser to pursue than to en-
gage; like Pyrrhus, he gave the European language an adjective. The
Senate replaced this Fabian with two commanders, one of whom, Caius
Varro, insisted on battle.

The two forces clashed at Cannae, in Apulia (216). The Romans had
80,000 infantry, 6,000 cavalry; Hannibal had 19,000 veterans, 16,000
unreliable Gauls, and 10,000 horse; and he lured Varro to fight in a
plain ideal for cavalry. He placed his Gauls at the center, expecting
them to give way. They did; and when the Romans pursued them into
the pocket, Hannibal, himself in the thick of the fray, ordered his veterans to close in on the Roman flanks, and bade his cavalry break
through the opposed horsemen and attack the legions from behind.
The Roman army, surrounded, lost all chance of maneuvering, and was
almost annihilated; 44,000 Romans died there, including 80 senators.
Hannibal lost 6,000 men, two-thirds of them Gauls. It was a supreme
example of generalship, rarely bettered in history. It ended Rome's reliance upon infantry, and set the lines of military tactics for two thousand years.

It was a battle immediately decisive and ultimately futile. For a time
the Mediterranean world thought Rome's power shattered. A dozen
Italian states allied themselves with Hannibal; Syracuse declared for
Carthage; Philip V of Macedon, fearing Roman expansion into Greece,
opened war on Rome. But amid these triumphs Hannibal found his depleted army surfeited with battle and needing time to heal its wounds.
He appealed to the Carthaginian Senate to send him reinforcements; it
responded minimally; meanwhile Rome was assembling and equip-
ping a new army of 200,000 men.

In 208 B.C., Hannibal's younger brother Hasdrubal led a Carthaginian army from Sparta through Gaul and over the Alps; he died in defeat at the river Metaurus (207); his severed head was thrown into Hannibal's camp by order of a Roman general. Publius Cornelius Scipio, soon to be Africanus, now brought all Spain under Roman control, and then led an army into Africa. Carthage, disordered and besieged, begged Hannibal to come to its aid. He came, formed a new army, and engaged Scipio's forces at Zama, fifty miles from the capital. He was defeated, and the helpless submission of Carthage ended the Second Punic War (202).

No Mediterranean state could now stop the expansion of Rome. She proceeded almost at once to discipline Philip V of Macedon. In 200 B.C., a Roman force under Titus Quinctius Flamininus crossed the Adriatic, and, after years of maneuvering, overwhelmed Philip at Cynoscepalae (197). All Greece now expected to become another spoke in the wheel of Rome. But Flamininus had grown up in the liberal Hellenizing circle of the Scipios; his awe before the accumulated heritage of Greek history, literature, philosophy, and art matched the awe of Greek cities quieted in their quarrels and humbled to peace. In an epochal convocation at Corinth he announced to the Greeks that Rome would not be their master but their protector; they were to be free from tribute, even from garrisons, and left to rule themselves, on the sole condition that they should end internal and interstate strife. So great a cheer rose from the multitude, says Plutarch, that crows passing over the stadium fell dead in their flight. Flamininus withdrew his troops to Italy.

The Greeks sang odes to liberty, but they were too intensely divided to bear with peace; war and class strife were resumed. In 146, while Rome was fighting the Third Punic War, the Achaean League of Greek states opened a war of liberation from Rome. A Roman army under Mummius captured Corinth, slew nearly all its men, sold its women and children into slavery, and transported its movable art and wealth to Rome. Athens and Sparta were allowed to remain under their own laws, but the other Greek states were molded into a province under a Roman governor.

Roads were opened for the transport of men, goods, and ideas between the old civilization and the new. Thousands of Greeks crossed into Italy, bringing shreds of their heritage with them. The Greek cultural conquest of Rome slowly followed the Roman military conquest of Greece.

A united classical heritage grew, and passed over Roman roads and Alps to northern Europe, and, in the leisure of time, to you and me.

LUCRETIUS

Parts of the rich heritage that slowly crossed to Rome in the wake of the returning conquerors were the literature and art, philosophy and science, religious creeds and doubts, that had accumulated through half a millennium in the scattered cities of mainland and colonial Greece.

Among these treasures were the manuscripts and oral traditions transmitting the materialism of Democritus and the ethics of Epicurus. A Roman poet, Titus Lucretius Carus, on fire with these survivors of carnage and slow time, set himself the pleasant, exhilarating task of expressing in Latin poetry, for a nation still intellectually young, the problems of philosophy and the earthly sources of sane delight.

He called his philosophical epic *De rerum natura* (*On the Nature of Things*), and wrote it in Homeric hexameters succinct, rich, and powerful, as if Achilles had composed verse. He began with a fervent apostrophe to Venus as the goddess of fertility and the conqueror of the god of war:

> Mother of Aeneas' race, delight of men and gods, O nurturing Venus: . . . through thee every kind of life is conceived and born, and looks upon the sun; before thee and thy coming the winds flee, and the clouds of the sky depart: to thee the miraculous earth lifts up sweet flowers; for thee the waves of the sea laugh, and the peaceful heavens shine with overspreading light. For as soon as the spring-time face of day appears, and the fertilizing south wind makes all things fresh and green, then first the birds of the air proclaim thee and thy advent, O divine one, pierced to the heart by thy power; then the wild herds leap over the glad pastures, and cross the swift streams; so, held captive by thy charm, each one follows thee wherever thou goest to lead. Then through seas and mountains and rush-

ing rivers, and the leafy dwellings of the birds, and the verdant
fields, thou strikest soft love into the breasts of all creatures, and
makest them, to propagate their generation after their kinds. Since,
therefore, thou alone rulest the nature of things; since without thee
nothing rises to the shining shores of light, nothing joyful or lovely
is born; I long for thee as partner in the writing of these verses. . . .
Grant to my words, O goddess, an undying beauty. Cause, meanwhile, the savage works of war to sleep and be still. . . . As Mars re-
clines upon thy sacred form, bend thou around him from above,
pour sweet coaxings from thy mouth, and beg for thy Romans the
gift of peace.

Venus is the only god Lucretius worships. For the rest of the Roman
gods he has no use; they may exist, but they have no influence on
human affairs. He denounces the pagan rituals of animal or human sacrifice; he tells the story of Iphigenia sacrificed for a breeze.

O miserable race of men, to impute to the gods such acts as these,
and such bitter wrath! . . . For piety lies not in being often seen
turning a veiled head to stones, . . . nor in lying prostrate . . . before
the temples, . . . nor in sprinkling altars with the blood of
beasts, . . . but rather in being able *to look upon all things with a mind
at peace.*   The terror and gloom of the mind must be dispelled not
by the sun's rays, . . . but by the aspect and law of nature.

And so, "touching with the honey of the Muses" the rough materialism of Democritus, Lucretius proclaims as his basic theorem that
"nothing exists but atoms and the void"—i.e., matter and space. All
was once formless but the gradual assortment of the moving atoms by
their size and shape produced—without design—air, fire, water, and
earth; and, out of these came sun and moon, planets and stars. In the infinity of space new worlds are ever being born, and old worlds are wast-
ing away. A portion of the primeval mist broke off from the mass, and
cooled to form the earth. Earthquakes are not the growling of deities
but the expansion of subterranean gases and streams. Thunder and
lightning are not the voice or breath of a god, but natural results of

condensed and clashing clouds. Rain is not the fitful gift of *Jove,* but the return to earth of moisture evaporated from it by the sun.

Lucretius was a thorough evolutionist.

> Nothing arises in the body in order that we may use it, but what arises brings forth its own use. . . . It was no design of the atoms that led them to arrange themselves in order with keen intelligence, . . . but because many atoms in infinite time have moved and met in all manner of ways, trying all combinations. . . . Hence arose the beginnings of great things, . . . and the generations of living creatures. . . . Many were the monsters that the earth tried to make: . . . some without feet, and others without hands or mouth or face, or with limbs bound to their frames. . . . It was in vain; nature denied them growth, nor could they find food, or join in the way of love. . . . Many kinds of animals must have perished then, unable to forge the chain of procreation. . . . For those to which nature gave no (protective) qualities lay at the mercy of others, and were soon destroyed.

The soul (*anima*) is a "vital breath" which is spread as a very fine matter throughout the body and animates every part. It grows and ages with the body, and its atoms are apparently dispersed when the body dies. Life is given us not in freehold but on loan, and for good so long as we can make good use of it. When we have exhausted our powers, we should leave the table of life as graciously as a grateful guest rising from a feast.

Death itself is not terrible; only our fears of the hereafter make it so. But there is no hereafter. Hell is here in the suffering that comes from ignorance, passion, pugnacity, and greed; and heaven is here in the *sapientum tempela serena*—"the serene temples of the wise."

Virtue lies not in the fear of the gods, nor in the timid shunning of pleasure; it lies in the harmonious operation of senses and faculties guided by reason: "the real wealth of a man is to live simply with a mind at peace." Marriage is good, but passionate love is a madness that strips the mind of clarity and reason. No marriage, no society, no civilization can find a sound basis in such erotic befuddlement.

How civilization developed, Lucretius tells in a pretty summary of ancient anthropology. Social organization gave man the power to survive animals far stronger than himself. He discovered fire from the friction of leaves and boughs, developed language from gestures, and learned song from the birds; he tamed animals for his use, and himself with marriage and law; he observed the heavens, measured time, and learned navigation. History is a procession of states and civilizations rising, prospering, decaying, dying; but each in turn can transmit the civilizing heritage of customs, morals, laws, and arts; "like runners in a race they hand on the lamps of life" (*et quasi cursores vitai lampada tradunt*).

Looking back over this "most marvelous performance in all antique literature," we may first recognize its shortcomings: the chaos of its contents, left unrevised by the poet's early death; the conception of sun, moon, and stars as no larger than we see them; the difficulty of explaining how dead atoms become life, consciousness, and foresight; a certain insensitiveness to the insights, consolations, and inspirations of faith, and the moral and social functions of religion.

But how light these faults are in the scale against the brave attempt at a rational interpretation of the universe, of religion, of disease ("There are many seeds of things that support our life; and on the other hand there must be many flying about that make for disease and death"); the picture of nature as world of law, in which matter and motion are never increased or decreased; the sustained power of imagination that feels everywhere "the majesty of things" and lifts the visions of Empedocles, the science of Democritus, and the ethics of Epicurus into some of the loftiest poetry that any age has known.

In the endless struggle between East and West, between "tender-minded" and consoling faiths versus a "tough-minded" and materialistic science, Lucretius waged almost alone the most far-reaching conflict of his time. He is, of course, the greatest of philosophical poets.

In him—as soon thereafter in Catullus, Cicero, and Virgil—Latin literature came of age, and leadership in letters passed from Greece to Rome.

Chapter Ten

꩜

THE ROMAN REVOLUTION

Now let us consider the chief causes, persons, and crises of the Revolution that agitated Rome in the period between the liberal legislation of Tiberius Gracchus in 133 B.C. and the defeat of Antony and Cleopatra at Actium in 31 B.C.

If you are the alert and subtle minds that I feel you to be, you will see in the narrative many analogues of our country's history in the last hundred years. As Horace put it, "*De te fabula narratur*"—"Of you the story is told."

OMENS

Some factors underlay the Revolution. The import of cheap slave-grown grains from the provinces ruined the freeman farmers of Italy by forcing them to sell their crops below the cost of production. The replacement of family farms by latifundia—i.e., broad estates operated by slaves and owned by senators or businessmen—drove the free peasant to join the turbulent proletariat of the city. There he watched without cost the games of the amphitheater, received a dole of corn from the government, sold his vote to the highest bidder, and lost himself in the impoverished and indiscriminate mass. The city worker himself was so harassed by the competition of slaves that he found it almost as profitable to be idle as to toil.

Slaves abounded throughout the Empire, but mostly in Italy. To the war prisoners brought in after a victorious campaign were added the victims of pirates—who made a business of human bondage—or Rome's colonial officials whose organized manhunts impressed into slavery any person caught on the loose and without a protective friend. Every week slave dealers brought their human prey to be auctioned off in public markets; at Delos 10,000 were sold in a single day. In 177 B.C., 40,000 Sardinians, in 167 B.C. 150,000 Epirotes, were captured by Roman armies and sold at approximately a dollar a head. In the cities the lot of the slave was mitigated by humanizing contacts with his master, but on the latifundia he rarely saw his owner, and the rewards of the overseer depended upon how much profit he could make for his master from the labor of his men; and these had no incentives to work except fear of the lash or the *ergastulum*—the underground prison that was a regular feature of the massive farms. Now and then there were slave revolts—most notably in the First Servile War in 139 B.C., and in 73–71 B.C. under Spartacus. When that famous rebellion failed, 6,000 captives were crucified along the Appian Way—from Rome to Capua. Their rotting bodies were left to hang for months, so that all masters might take comfort, and all slaves take heed.

Meanwhile, in Rome and its empire, as in every civilization and in almost every generation, the natural inequality of economic ability, and the popular institution of inheritance, had produced an increasing concentration of wealth, which, through imperial conquest and exploitation, had grown to a degree hardly rivaled in history. Periodically such concentration is challenged by social unrest, sometimes by revolution. We have seen one case, at Athens, peaceably resolved in the archonship of Solon (594 B.C.). Now, in 133 B.C., a like crisis rose in Rome, but here statesmanship failed and was replaced by a hundred years of class war, bringing the Roman Republic to an ignominious close.

CORNELIA'S JEWELS

Tiberius Sempronius Gracchus (162?–133 B.C.) was almost fated to greatness: he was the son of a man twice consul, and of a mother, Cornelia, daughter of the Scipio Africanus Maior who had defeated Hannibal at Zama. Her husband died after begetting her twelve children; nine of these died in adolescence, leaving a daughter and two sons, Tiberius and Caius, her consolation and pride. When a visitor asked if she wore jewels, she showed him her boys; "these," she said, "are my jewels."

Brought up in the atmosphere of literature, statesmanship, and philosophy, Tiberius and Caius Gracchus knew the speculations of Greek thought and the problems of Roman government. Traveling in Italy, Tiberius noted the paucity of freemen on the soil; what sort of army would Rome have if the sturdy peasants who once manned it were displaced by captured slaves hating Rome? How could Rome have any political stability with a city proletariat festering in poverty, instead of a proud yeomanry owning and tilling the land? A distribution of state terrain among the poorer citizens seemed the obvious and necessary solution.

Elected a tribune in 133, Tiberius prepared for the Tribunal Assembly three proposals: (1) that no citizen should have more than 333—or if he had two sons, 667—acres of land bought or rented from the state; (2) that all other public lands that had been sold or leased to private individuals should be returned to the state for the purchase or rental price, plus an allowance for improvements made; (3) that the returned lands should be divided into twenty-acre lots among poor citizens, on condition that they agree never to sell their allotment and to pay an annual tax on it to the Treasury. Tiberius, before an assembly of indigent plebeians, defended his proposals in an appeal to class interests:

> The beasts of the field and the birds of the air have their holes and hiding places, but the men who fight and die for Italy enjoy only the light and the air. Our generals urge their soldiers to fight for the graves and shrines of their ancestors. The appeal is idle and false. You cannot point to a paternal altar. You have no ancestral tomb. You fight and die to give wealth and luxury to others. You are called the masters of the world, but there is not a foot of ground that you can call your own.

The Senate denounced the proposals as confiscatory, charged Tiberius with seeking a dictatorship, and persuaded Octavius, another tribune, to prevent by his veto the submission of the bills to the Assembly. Tiberius thereupon moved that any tribune who acted contrary to the wishes of his constituents should be immediately deposed. The Assembly passed the measure, and Octavius was forcibly removed from the tribune's bench by the lictors of Tiberius. The original proposals were then voted into law, and the Assembly, fearing for Tiberius' safety, escorted him home.

His illegal overruling of a tribunician veto, which the Assembly itself had long ago made absolute, gave his opponents a handle with which to frustrate him. They declared their purpose to impeach him at the end of his one-year term, as having violated the constitution further by seeking reelection to the tribunate for 132. When election day came, Tiberius appeared in the Forum with armed guards and in mourning costume, implying that his defeat would mean his impeachment and death. As the voting proceeded, violence broke out on both sides. Scipio Nasica, crying that Tiberius wished to make himself king, led the senators, armed with clubs, into the Forum. The supporters of Tiberius, awed by patrician robes, gave way; he was killed by a blow on the head, and several hundred of his followers perished with him. When his younger brother Caius asked permission to bury him, he was refused, and the bodies of the dead rebels were thrown into the Tiber.

Cornelia was desolate. She had no consolation except in her surviving son, Caius Sempronius Gracchus. He had served with courage and intelligence in Spain, and had won the admiration of all groups by the integrity of his conduct and the simplicity of his life. In the fall of 124 he was elected tribune by the Assembly. His proposals to it aimed to win diverse classes to his support: the peasantry by renewing his brother's program for redistribution of state lands; the middle classes by establishing new colonies in Narbo, Capua, Tarentum, and Carthage, and developing these as thriving centers of trade; and the urban masses by his *lex frumentaria,* or corn law, which committed the government to distribute grain at half the market price to all who asked for it. It was a measure shocking to old Roman ideas of self-reliance and was destined to play a vital role in Roman history. It enriched contractors and reduced unemployment by a program of road-building in every part of Italy. It was one of the most radical measures offered to Rome before Caesar.

Armed with such varied support, Caius was able to override custom and win election (123 B.C.) to a second and successive tribunate. But when he proposed to extend a full franchise to all the freemen of Latium (the little state of which Rome was the capital), and a partial franchise to all the freeman of Italy, the Assembly, jealous of its privileges, demurred; and when, a year later, he flouted a tradition by seeking election for a third year, he was defeated. Some of his followers charged that many ballots had been falsified. He counseled against violence and retired to private life.

The Senate, which Caius had reduced to apparent impotence, now regained some of its power. In the year 121 it proposed the abandonment of the colony at Carthage; all sides interpreted the measure, openly or privately, as the first move in a campaign to repeal the Gracchan laws. Some of Caius' adherents attended the Assembly armed, and one of them cut down a conservative who threatened to lay hands upon Caius. On the morrow the senators appeared in full battle array, each with two armed slaves, and attacked the popular party entrenched on the Aventine. Caius did his best to quiet the tumult and avert further violence. Failing, he fled across the Tiber; overtaken, he ordered his servant to kill him; the slave obeyed and then killed himself. A friend cut off Caius' head, filled it with molten lead, and brought it to the Senate, which had offered a reward of its weight in gold. Of Caius' supporters 250 fell in the fight, 300 more were put to death by senatorial decree. The city mob that he had befriended made no protest when his corpse, and those of his followers, were flung into the river; it was busy plundering his house. The Senate forbade Cornelia to wear mourning for her son.

SULLA THE HAPPY

The *populares* slowly reorganized and began a "Civil War" under the brilliant leadership of Caius Marius, who periodically abandoned war to enjoy his spoils. Against him the Senate raised, as the military defender of the *optimates* ("the new people"), Lucius Cornelius Sulla, one of the most indescribable characters in history.

Sulla, who lived from 138 to 178 B.C., was unprepossessing, and he took his revenge upon life for having made him at once patrician and penniless; when he conquered money, he made it serve his appetites without qualm or restraint. He had glaring blue eyes in a white face mixed with rough blotches of fiery red, "like a mulberry sprinkled over with flour." His education belied his looks. He was well versed in Greek as well as Roman literature, was a discriminating collector of art (usually by military means), had the works of Aristotle brought from Athens to Rome as part of his richest spoils, and found time, between war and revolution, to write his *Memoirs* for the misguidance of posterity. He was a jolly companion and a generous friend, devoted to wine, women, battle, and song. "He lived extravagantly," says Sallust, "yet pleasure never interfered with his duties, except that his conduct as a husband might have been more honorable." He made his way rapidly, above all in the army, his happiest medium; he treated his soldiers as comrades, shared their work, their marches, and their dangers; "his only effort was not to allow anyone to surpass him in wisdom or bravery." He believed in no gods, but many superstitions. Otherwise he was the most realistic as well as the most ruthless of the Romans; his imagination and his feelings were always under the control of his intellect. It was said of him that he was half lion and half fox, and that the fox in him was more dangerous than the lion. Living half the time on battlefields, spending the last decade of his life in civil war, he nevertheless preserved his good humor to the end, graced his brutalities with epigrams, filled Rome with his laughter, made a hundred thousand enemies, achieved all his purposes, and died in bed.

Such a man seemed chemically compounded of the qualities needed for surpressing revolution at home and rebellion abroad. His 35,000 trained troops quickly overcame the peasant or proletarian regiments that Marius had improvised. But after Sulla had led his forces out of Italy—to bring Mithridates VI back to Roman allegiance—Marius assembled another army, proclaimed freedom to slaves, and captured Rome. Drunk with battle, and hot with the hatred of many years, the victors slaughtered thousands and paraded with noble heads held up on pikes as a model for future eruptions. All captured friends of Sulla were slain, his property was confiscated, he was declared a public enemy, and Valerius Flaccus, with 12,000 men, was sent east to depose him from his command. Lucius Cinna, elected consul for four successive years (87–84 B.C.) transformed the Republic into a dictatorship.

Meanwhile, Athens joined Mithridates in revolt against Rome. Sulla reconquered the once illustrious city, allowed some slaughter, then stopped it, saying that he would "forgive the living for the dead." He ferried his army across the Hellespont, seeking Mithridates, but he found that Valerius Flaccus and his legions had also reached Asia, bringing him dismissal and outlawry. He persuaded Flaccus to give him time to discipline Mithridates. One Fimbria killed Flaccus and advanced against Sulla; Sulla made peace with Mithridates and advanced against Fimbria; Fimbria's troops went over to Sulla; Fimbria killed himself; Sulla led 40,000 men across the Aegean, Greece, the Adriatic, and Italy to the gates of Rome.

The revolutionary government slaughtered all the patricians they could find, and then evacuated the capital. Sulla entered it unhindered, but he soon had to lead his 50,000 veterans out to meet a rebel mass of 100,000 men at the Colline Gate, in one of the goriest battles of ancient times. Sulla won, and the humbled Assembly appointed him dictator. Massacre, banishment, and confiscation of property spread from Rome, and fell upon rebels and followers of Marius everywhere. Sulla issued a series of edicts designed to establish a permanently aristocratic constitution, for he was certain that only a monarch or an aristocracy could administer an empire. After two years of absolute rule he resigned all his powers and retired to private life.

He was safe, for he had killed nearly all who could be suspected of planning his assassination. He dismissed his guards, walked unharmed in the Forum, and offered to give an account of his official actions to any citizen who would dare to ask for it. Then he went to spend his last years in his villa at Cumae. Tired of war, power, glory—tired perhaps of men—he surrounded himself with singers, dancers, actors, and actresses. He wrote his *Commentaries,* hunted and fished, ate and drank his fill. His men called him Sulla Felix, because he had won every battle, known every pleasure, reached every power, and now lived without fear or regret.

He married five women, divorced four, and made up for their inadequacies with mistresses. At fifty-eight he developed an ulcer of the colon so severe that "the corrupted flesh," says Plutarch, "broke out into lice. Many men were employed day and night in destroying them, but they so multiplied that not only his clothes, baths, and basins, but his food were polluted by them." He died of intestinal hemorrhage, after hardly a year of retirement. He had not neglected to dictate his epitaph: "No friend ever served me, and no enemy ever wronged me, whom I have not repaid in full."

THE MORAL COLLAPSE

Within a decade after Sulla's death his policy for restoring economic and political order had come to ruin. He had dealt with the phenomena, not the causes, of Rome's decay. The causes were the multiple spawn of an economic revolution: the passage from village tillage to urban industry; from the family as the unit of economic production, moral discipline, and social order to town and city individuals competing in labor, trade, and finance, and shedding morals in the mechanism of industry and the protective anonymity of the crowd. The rising business class had no taste for the ornate ritual of the official religion, whose chief ministrants were skeptical senators; Caesar smiled while officiating as *pontifex maximus*. The growth and concentration of wealth made for an epicurean secularism in the upper classes. Art passed from religious to political subjects and forms. Literature dared to preach a materialistic atheism, as in Lucretius' philosophic epic *De rerum natura* (59 B.C.); or it combined a hilarious obscenity with exquisite poetry, as in Catullus (60 B.C.), who said that he had to salt his verses with dirt to hold his audience. In the agricultural regime, poverty had been familial or individual, and had found solace in religion; in the city, poverty became a class and corporate condition, and led the way increasingly to social revolt.

So the class war became bitterer, finally shedding all moral restraint. The *optimates* cherished government by the well-born and the Senate; the *populares* demanded government by the popular assemblies, with free land for the poor; and both parties practiced intimidation and venality without conscience, concealment, or restraint. Cicero described candidates going about, purse in hand, ready to buy any vote at a reasonable price. Pompey had his mediocre friend Afranius elected consul by inviting the leaders of the tribes to his gardens, and there paying them for the wholesale ballots of their groups. So much money was lent and borrowed to finance candidacies that the campaigns raised the interest rate to 8 percent per month—96 percent per year.

The courts, though now preempted by senators, rivaled the polls in corruption. Oaths had lost all worth as testimony, and almost any verdict could be bought. Lentulus Sura, having been acquitted by two votes, mourned the extra expense he had gone to in bribing one more judge than he had needed. Protected by such courts, the senatorial proconsuls, the generals, the tax-gatherers, the moneylenders, and the business agents milked the provinces at a rate that ultimately poisoned Rome with unearned wealth. Lucullus financed his famous meals with his gleanings from the East; Pompey brought back $11,000,000 for the Treasury, $21,000,000 for himself. Cicero thought himself a painfully honest man, having made only $110,000 in his one year as governor of Cilicia. Antiquity had never known so powerful—and so corrupt—a government.

The business classes accepted aristocracy and democracy almost with indifference, apparently confident that they had transformed both of them into plutocracy. The millionaire Atticus contributed to both parties, knowing that neither would venture far from his purse.

Patrician senators and business magnates competed in luxurious display, while revolt brewed in the provinces and men starved in the slums. Senators lounged in bed till noon. Some of their sons dressed and walked like courtesans, decked themselves with jewelry, sprinkled themselves with perfume, and emulated the bisexual impartiality of the Greeks. All men of any pretension had at least one palace, plus a villa at some resort like Baiae, where they took to the baths and declared a moratorium on monogamy. In their palaces a horde of specialized slaves served them—valets, messengers, lamplighters, secretaries, musicians, doctors, philosophers, cooks. Eating was now the chief occupation of upper-class Romans; "everything good," said Metrodorus, "had reference to the belly."

Sex came a close second. Despite increasing competition from women and men, prostitutes were plentiful. Adultery was common, and women divorced their husbands as readily as men their wives. There were still many loyal unions, but marriage was increasingly political; so Caesar gave his daughter Julia to Pompey as an item in their triumviral alliance.

There was much love of children—but a dearth of them—among the educated Romans, who had long since learned contraceptive arts. Caesar worried lest the native stocks should be swamped by the immigrant households that were growing in number and size in the cities. In his legislative days he promised the ladies state rewards for large families, but he found that children were a luxury which only the poor could afford. Meanwhile a rising proportion of women sought expression in cultural pursuits—learned Greek, studied philosophy, wrote poetry, lectured, and opened literary salons.

Beneath the layer of luxury the poverty of the masses continued, and broke out now in the slave revolt led by the heroic Spartacus in 71 B.C., and, in 65, in an uprising of the plebs under Lucius Catiline. According to Sallust, writing in the next generation, Catiline addressed his followers in terms of open class war:

> Ever since the state fell under the sway of a few powerful men . . . all influence, rank, and wealth have been in their hands. To us they have left danger, defeat, prosecutions, poverty. . . . What have we left save only the breath of life? . . . Is it not better to die valiantly than to lose our wretched and dishonored lives after being the sport of other men's insolences?

The program on which he proposed to unite the heterogeneous elements of revolution was simple: *novae tabulae*—"new records"—i.e., a clean sweep and abolition of all debts. Cicero—the outstanding orator and essayist of the time—attacked Catiline in those furious "philippics" that some of us studied in college as models of Latin prose. In the year 64 B.C., Catiline opposed Cicero as candidate for the consulate, and waged so violent a campaign that many upper-class citizens took fright and prepared to leave Italy. Cicero won; Catiline took to war and organized an army of 3,000 men; all of them fell in battle, Catiline fighting till he was dead. Many years afterward his followers still strewed flowers upon his grave. Caesar was accused of having secretly supported him and narrowly escaped assassination. A year later he formed a triumvirate with Crassus and Pompey and began his own revolution.

CAESAR

Caius Julius Caesar traced his genealogy through Aeneas to Venus, daughter of Jupiter, and lived up to his pedigree in war and love. The Julian gens, or clan, though impoverished, was not without repute or power; it had given Rome consuls in 489, 482, 473, and 157 B.C. Caesar was born in 100 B.C., allegedly by the operation that later took his name.

"Now was this Caesar," says Suetonius, "wondrous docible and apt to learn." He developed a perilous facility in oratory and juvenile authorship. He was saved by being made a military aide to Marcus Thermus in Asia. Nicomedes, ruler of Bithynia, took such a fancy to him that Cicero later taunted him with having "lost his virginity to a king." Returning to Rome in 84 B.C., he married Cossutia to please his father; when his father died, he divorced her and married Cornelia, daughter of the Cinna who had taken over the revolution from Marius. When Sulla came to power, he ordered Caesar to divorce Cornelia; when Caesar refused, Sulla confiscated his patrimony and Cornelia's dowry, and listed him for death. Caesar fled, was captured by pirates, escaped, and went to Rhodes to study rhetoric and philosophy.

Back in Rome, he divided his energies between politics and philandering. He was handsome, but worried about his thinning hair. When Cornelia died, he married Pompeia, granddaughter of Sulla. As this was a purely political marriage, he did not scruple to carry on liaisons in the fashion of his time, in such number and with such ambigendrous diversity that Curio called him *omnium mulierum vir et omnium virorum mulier*—"the husband of every woman and the wife of every man." The aristocracy hated him doubly—for undermining their privileges and seducing their wives. We must think of Caesar as at first an unscrupulous politician and a reckless rake, slowly transformed by responsibility into one of history's most conscientious statesmen. We must not forget, as we rejoice at his faults, that he was a great man notwithstanding. We cannot equate ourselves with Caesar by proving that he seduced women, bribed ward leaders, and wrote books.

In 68 B.C., at age thirty-two, he was chosen quaestor to serve in Spain. He led military expeditions against rebel tribes and collected enough plunder to pay off some of his debts. In 65, as commissioner of public works, he spent his money—or the money of his rich friend Crassus—in adorning the Forum with new buildings and courting the populace with games. Sulla had removed from the Capitol the trophies of Marius—pictures and spoils representing the features and victories of the old radical; Caesar had these restored, and by that act announced his developing *populares* policy.

The conservatives protested, and marked him out as a man to be broken. In 64 B.C., as president of a commission appointed to try cases of murder, he summoned to his tribunal the surviving agents of Sulla's proscriptions and sentenced several of them to exile or death; a year later, in the Senate, he voted against the execution of some captured leaders of Catiline's revolt. When he decided to run for the consulate, the senators, almost to a man, opposed him. He foiled them by winning Pompey, idol of the business class, to an alliance with him and Crassus in the First Triumvirate (60 B.C.), in which each member pledged himself to oppose any legislation displeasing to any one of them. With Pompey's support and Crassus' money Caesar was elected consul for the year 59.

His term was almost consumed in a battle to reenact the Gracchan legislation. He proposed to allot government lands to 20,000 returning soldiers and to poor citizens who had three children. To bring the contest to public scrutiny he hired clerks to record senatorial and other political activities by inscriptions on prominent walls of Forum buildings as Acta Diurna, or Daily Actions; these graffiti were carried by journalistic messengers to various parts of Rome and other cities, and constituted, in a sense, the first newspaper in known history, the beginning of the vital role of "the press" in influencing legislation.

After consuming most of his year's consulate in carrying these and other popular measures, Caesar, with an eye to his personal safety, had himself appointed governor of Cisalpine and Narbonnese Gaul for five years with command of the only army that would be legally stationed in Italy. Before leaving for his post he divorced his third wife, Pompeia, on suspicion of adultery with Publius Clodius Pulcher; nevertheless he lent his decisive aid to the election of Clodius as tribune for the year 58.

He refused to bring any moral charge against Clodius; when he was asked why, then, he had divorced Pompeia, he replied, "Because my wife must be above suspicion." He secured the election of Gavinius Piso as consul, took Piso's daughter Calpurnia as his fourth wife, and went off to conquer Gaul.

Probably he had at first no such intent. The Gauls appealed to him to help them against Germans invading Gaul at several points along the Rhine. He consented; repulsed, near Autun, a vast horde that had come through Switzerland; marched north, defeated a German multitude under Ariovistus, and drove them back across the Rhine. The Gauls thanked him and asked him to suggest a reward. He proposed that all Gaul should accept inclusion, and therefore protection, in the Roman Empire. They refused, and fought his legions bravely—but in vain; he lived to tell the tale in *De bello Gallico.* Though a German Frank some five hundred years later gave the land a German name, Gallia became, through Caesar, a Latin land with a Latin language absurd but beautiful; the rough Latin of Roman soldiers was transformed into the music of Racine and Anatole France; *corruptio pessimi optima.*

While Caesar was unwittingly preparing Gaul to inherit and transmit classic civilization, the Roman Republic was dying in a pool of corruption and brutality. In 53 B.C. the first voting division in the Assembly was paid 10,000,000 sesterces for its vote. When money failed, murder was available; or a man's past was raked over and blackmail brought him to terms. Crime flourished in the city, brigandage on the road; no palace force existed to control it. Rich men hired bands of gladiators to protect them, or to support them in the comitia. Any man who would vote as paid was admitted to the rolls, whether citizen or not; sometimes only a minority of those who cast ballots were entitled to vote; and those who voted the wrong way were beaten to within an inch of their lives, after which their houses were set on fire. Following one such fracas, Cicero wrote: "The Tiber was full of the corpses of citizens; the public sewers were stuffed with them; and slaves had to mop up with sponges the blood that streamed from the Forum." Clodius the Handsome and Titus Milo were Rome's most distinguished experts in this brand of democracy. They organized rival bands of ruffians for political purposes, and hardly a day passed without some trial of their strength. One day Clodius assaulted Cicero in the street; another day his warriors burned down Milo's house; at last Clodius was caught by Milo's gang and killed. The proletariat, not privy to all his plots, honored Clodius as a martyr, gave him a mighty funeral, carried his body to the Senate house, and burned the building over him as his funeral pyre. Pompey brought in his soldiers and dispersed the mob. As reward he asked from the Senate, and received appointment, as "consul without colleague," a phrase which Cato the Younger recommended as nicer than dictator. All the elements of wealth and order in the capital resigned themselves to the dictatorship of Pompey, while the poorer classes hopefully awaited the coming of Caesar.

A century of revolution had broken down a narrow and selfish aristocracy but had put no other government in its place. Unemployment, bribery, and bread and circuses had corrupted the Assembly into an ill-formed and passion-ridden mob clearly incapable of governing itself, much less an empire. Democracy had succumbed to Plato's formula: liberty had become license, and chaos begged an end to liberty.

Caesar agreed with Pompey that the Republic was dead and that dictatorship was unavoidable. But he had hoped to establish a leadership that would be progressive, that would not freeze the status quo, but would lessen the abuses, inequities, and destitution which had degraded democracy. He was now fifty-four, surely weakened by ten years of campaigns in Gaul. He made every effort at conciliation. He proposed to the Senate that both he and Pompey should lay down their commissions; Pompey refused. After long negotiations the Senate gave Pompey orders and powers to "see that no harm should come to the state"—the Roman phrase for dictatorship and martial law. Caesar hesitated beyond his wont.

Finally he summoned his favorite Thirteenth Legion and laid the situation before them. His first word won them: *"Commilitones!"*— "Fellow soldiers!" He reminded them that an idle and corrupt aristocracy would not give Rome order, justice, and prosperity. Would they follow him? Not one refused. When he told them that he had no money with which to pay them, they emptied their savings into his treasury. On January 10, 49 B.C., he led one legion across the Rubicon, a small stream that marked the southern boundary of Cisalpine Gaul. Now, he is reported to have said, *"Iacta est alea"*—"The die is cast." One by one the cities on his route opened their gates to him; some turned out en masse to welcome him; "the towns," wrote Cicero, "salute him as a god." Pompey, though his forces far outnumbered Caesar's, fled from Rome, from Italy. Caesar pursued him, and at Pharsalus, in Thessaly, though outnumbered two to one, he won one of the bloodiest battles in Roman history—August 9, 48 B.C. Caesar asked his men to spare the young senator Marcus Junius Brutus. Pompey escaped, and found his way to Egypt, where an agent of Ptolemy XII stabbed him to death. When Caesar arrived there, the killers offered him the severed head. He turned away in horror, and wept at this new proof that by diverse ways men come to the same end.

He found many things charming in Egypt: its treasury was full, apparently his for the asking, and Ptolemy's sister, Cleopatra, was beautiful and eager. He stayed long enough to assist at her delivery of his son, whom they named Caesarion. In October, 47 B.C., he reached Rome, bringing with him Cleopatra, her husband-brother, and Caesarion. Apparently Caesar's wife, Calpurnia, took all this as in the normal routine of Roman politics. Some surviving aristocrats whispered that he was planning to make himself king and remove the capital of the empire to Alexandria. Nevertheless, awed by his legions, the Senate heaped lands and dignities upon him and in 44 B.C. made him "dictator for life," which, in this case, meant five months.

In those months he labored to revive Rome as a city and a state. He reduced the Senate's powers by increasing its membership from 600 to 900; its number invited debate, discouraged decision, and freed Caesar to rule. The Assemblies elected him tribune, which made his person legally inviolable. He controlled all important appointments and initiated the most significant legislation.

Continuing the work of the Gracchi, he distributed lands to his veterans and the poor. He relieved the pressure of a growing population by sending 80,000 citizens to colonize Carthage, Corinth, and other centers thinned by war. To provide work for the unemployed, he allotted substantial sums to building programs in many cities in Italy, Spain, Gaul, and Greece. To reduce the leakage of funds in administering welfare to the poor, he required a means test for eligibility to the state dole of grain; soon the number of applicants fell from 320,000 to 150,000. He scaled down debts, enacted several laws against excessive rates of interest, and relieved extreme cases of insolvency by establishing the laws of bankruptcy—essentially as they stand today.

Noting that the calendar of the priests had lost all connection with the seasons, he commissioned the Alexandrian astronomer Sosigenes to devise an Egyptian model, the "Julian" calendar, which allotted 365 days to the year, with an added day in every fourth February. Cicero complained that Caesar, not content with ruling the earth, was now regulating the stars, but the Senate welcomed the reform, and gave the dictator's family name, Julius, to the month Quinctilis, which had been fifth when March opened the year.

But this great statesman was not above vanity. He continued to wear daily, in order to hide his baldness, the laurel crown that had been placed upon his head in a triumph. He ordered his statue to be erected in the Capitol next to those of Rome's ancient kings, and he deposed from office the tribunes who removed from his statue the royal diadem placed upon it by his friends. At the feast of the Lupercalia, February 18, 44 B.C., the consul Antony, drunk, tried thrice to place a royal crown upon Caesar's head; three times Caesar refused it, but was it because the crowd had murmured disapproval?

The aristocrats who had been deprived of their wonted powers could not be mollified by his pardoning their past resistance; it is difficult to forgive forgiveness. Shortly after the Lupercalia, Caius Cassius, described by Plutarch as a sickly man, "pale and thin," suggested to Marcus Brutus the assassination of Caesar. He had already won several men to the project; they agreed that if Brutus would join them, his reputation for virtue would glorify their cause.

Brutus believed himself descended from the Lucius Junius Brutus who had expelled the kings from Rome 464 years before. The historian Appian remarks that Caesar was a lover of Brutus' mother Servilia; and Plutarch reports that Caesar believed Brutus to be his son. Brutus pondered moodily over these matters, and is alleged to have written to a friend, "Our ancestors thought that we should not endure a tyrant even if he were our own father." Brutus yielded, and the conspirators drew up a plan. In a moment of unforeseeing sentiment, Brutus insisted that Antony should be spared.

On the evening of March 14, to a gathering at his home, Caesar proposed, as a topic of conversation, "What is the best death?" and gave his own answer: *"Subito"*—i.e., a sudden one. The next morning his wife begged him not to go to the Senate, saying that she had dreamt of seeing him covered with blood. On his way to Pompey's Theater, where the Senate was to convene, he met a soothsayer who had once whispered to him, "Beware the Ides of March"; he remarked that the Ides had come, and all was well; to which Spurinna answered, "But they have not passed." When Caesar entered the theater and took his seat, the "Liberators" flung themselves upon him without delay. "Some have written," reports Suetonius, "that when Marcus Brutus rushed at him, Caesar said in Greek, *"Kai su teknon?"*—("You too, my child?") Feeling Brutus' weapon, Caesar, says Appian, ended all resistance. One wish had been granted to the most complete man that antiquity produced.

Technically, the Roman Republic came convulsively back to life: Antony's appeal to the commonalty seemed to offer it another chance to rule. Actually all that remained was the struggle of Antony against Brutus for the privilege of ruling the ruins, and then the struggle of Antony against Caesar's adopted son and heir, Gaius Octavianus, for the reins of power. After his defeat of Antony and Cleopatra at Actium in 31 B.C., and their dual suicide in Egypt, Octavian, later renamed Augustus, established (27 B.C.) and maintained a monarchical rule which he called a "principate." So Plato's wheel of political history completed its circle from dictatorship to monarchy to aristocracy to democracy to dictatorship to monarchy . . .

Rome, for two centuries more, would remain, *diminuendo,* the Western center and summit of the glory and cruelty of history.

Chapter Eleven

ııııı

THE ROMAN EMPIRE
(27 B.C.–A.D. 180)

AUGUSTAN STATESMANSHIP

Gaius Octavianus, grandnephew and adopted son and heir of Julius Caesar, returned to Rome in 29 B.C., after defeating Antony and Cleopatra at Actium (31 B.C.), establishing Roman control over Egypt, dipping into its treasury, and restoring order and taxes in the Eastern dependencies of a Roman Empire that had almost been dismembered by war, revolution, and anarchy.

The capital welcomed him as an opulent savior and gave him a triumph that lasted three days. He responded by awarding to each of his soldiers a substantial sum of money, and to each honorably discharged veteran an allotment of arable land. He forgave property owners all tax arrears and publicly burned all records of their debt to the state. Out of his inherited and accumulated funds he paid for the corn dole, undertook public works to reduce unemployment and beautify Rome, made up deficits in the national treasury, and sent large sums for the relief of provinces suffering from "acts of God."

Armed with this irresistible beneficence, and with a genius for easing change with gradations and courtesy, he readily persuaded the restored Senate to name him *princeps senatus,* a title which had meant "first on the roll call of the Senate," but which soon took on the dignity of "prince." In the year 27 B.C., Octavian asked to be relieved of all his offices and powers, and to be allowed to retire to private life. The Sen-

ate begged him to continue to rule; he consented, and it confirmed his
princely title for life. Soon it bestowed upon him the religious title *Augustus*—the "Divine Augmentor" or "Provider"; and this term became
his name for history.

The people of Rome, and of Italy, accepted this disguised monarchy
with the humility of experience. They were no longer enamored of freedom, but wearily wished for security, order, and peace; any man might
rule them who guaranteed them games and bread. Vaguely they understood that their clumsy comitia, clogged with corruption and racked
with violence, could not govern an empire. Now the whole Mediterranean world lay in disorder at Octavian's feet, waiting for statesmanship.

He eased the death of the Republic by keeping republican terms and
forms. He professed to be merely chairman of the Senate, but no measure was proposed to it except by his instigation or consent. He allowed
the assemblies to meet; he ran for the consulate thirteen times, and can-
vassed—even paid—for votes like the rest; it was a concession to custom. Consuls and tribunes continued to be elected till the fifth century,
but their functions became administrative rather than executive, and
they yielded their powers to the prince. Political corruption continued,
but was lessened by requiring every candidate to deposit a financial
guarantee that he would abstain from bribery. However, Augustus violated a vital precedent. He kept under his control three cohorts of soldiers in the city, and six near it, to ensure public order and *his* rule.
These nine cohorts became the Praetorian Guard, which in A.D. 41
raised Claudius to power and began its fatal subjection of the government.

Armed with so much authority, and aided by administrators whom
he found in the rising business class, Augustus brought a productive
order back to the economy and the state. He spread landownership
among the poor, lent money without interest to responsible farmers,
opened new mines, roads, and routes, controlled brigandage and
piracy, protected and enlarged the great aqueducts that brought water
to Rome; mollified the poor with cheap wheat, exciting lotteries, and
spectacular games; protected all classes with well-administered laws,
and, for the rest, left to hunger, greed, competition, and free enterprise
the stimulation of production, distribution, and finance. With public

and private money, and helped by the genius of Marcus Agrippa, he carried out a massive program of public building which relieved unemployment and justified his later boasts that he had found Rome a city of brick and left it a city of marble.

He found it easier to restore prosperity than to reform morals. The decline of the ancient faith among the educated classes had dissolved the supernatural supports of marriage, fidelity, and parentage; the passage from farm to city had made a child less of an asset, more of a liability and expensive toy; women wished to be sexually desirable rather than maternally revered; many native Romans avoided wedlock, or limited their families by contraception, abortion, or infanticide. Augustus saw in these phenomena the decay of parental authority, social order, and the Roman character. By his powers as censor and tribune he induced the Assembly to pass laws that brought marriage under state control, and punished adultery in the woman with banishment and the confiscation of a third of her fortune and half her dowry; the wife, however, could not accuse her husband of adultery, and he might with impunity patronize registered prostitutes.

Another law made marriage obligatory, imposed economic penalties upon celibates, and offered social and economic rewards for begetting and rearing children. Historians, from Tacitus onward, reported these laws as failures; men and women found ways of evading them. Sexual immorality continued, even openly; in Ovid's *Amores* it has become a fine art, taught by experts to apprentices. The native Romans began to lose number and vigor, while the immigrants, closer to the family and religion, multiplied in number and power.

Augustus was more successful in giving the Empire a structure of law and stability, one that held for two hundred years. He began, like any Roman general, by seeking to expand the Empire by conquests; he sent abortive expeditions to absorb Ethiopia and Arabia, and bade his stepsons Drusus and Tiberius to punish new German invasions of Gaul by conquering Germany to the Elbe. But in the ninth year of the Christian era the Germans lured three Roman legions into a trap, surrounded them, and killed every man of them. Augustus ordered Tiberius to exact some revenge, but ordered him to withdraw the Roman frontier to the Rhine.

Having expanded the Empire to its greatest extent—from Britain and Spain to the Black Sea and the Euphrates—he called a halt to further conquest and resolved to replace war with legislation. He expressed his surprise "that Alexander did not regard it as a greater task to set in order the empire that he had won than to win it." The Pax Romana had begun.

THE POET'S HOUR

Under this Roman peace every part of the realm could export goods and ideas, import the latest fads and creeds. Now the Hellenistic world—Greece, the Near East, and Egypt—creators and inheritors of rich and diverse cultures—could pour their poetry and prose, their old faiths and new doubts, their sciences and philosophies and arts, into a Rome still intellectually eager, ready to receive new religions, poetical ecstasies, and architectural forms.

A timid youth from Mantua—so modest that some wits turned his name "Virgil" into "Virgin"—was inspired by the Greek pastorals of Syracusan Theocritus to write *Eclogues* (*Selections*) of pastoral life, in delightfully melodious hexameters. The millionaire philanthropist Maecenas persuaded him to tune his lyre to some more substantial celebration of rural tasks and joys. When Octavian returned from his arduous victories over Antony and Cleopatra, Maecenas lured him in to listen, during four days, to the 2,000 lines of Virgil's *Georgics*—lyrics of the land. They harmonized delightfully with the young conqueror's hope to lure Romans back to the soil. He rewarded the poet imperially, and Virgil, grateful, retired to secret lairs where, for the next ten years, he composed his epic *Aeneid,* designed to do for Aeneas and Rome what Homer's *Iliad* had done for Achilles and Troy. The meticulous author died, aged fifty-one (19 B.C.), before completing his masterpiece.

The Aeneid lacks logical structure, but logic rarely chimes with poetry; it lacks the vigorous flow of the *Iliad,* the masculine thought of the *Odyssey,* but it is a veritable archipelago of melodious episodes, *rari nantes in gurgite vasto*—"swimming here and there in a vast sea." Here, for example, is a passage anticipating and rivaling Keats's finest ode:

The nightingale mourning, beneath the poplar's shadow, the loss of her young ones, whom some hard plowman has seen and torn unfledged from their nest; all night long she cries, and perched on a spray, renews her pitiful song, filling the woods with her sad lament.

And of course there is a story of Dido, Queen of Carthage; her passionate surrender to Aeneas' strong arms; his leaving her to follow his assumed destiny to establish Rome; her despondent plunge alive into a funeral pyre. Horace equated the *Aeneid* with the *Iliad;* the Middle Ages revered Virgil as (like Plato in Pater's phrase) *anima naturaliter Christiana*—"a soul by nature Christian" before Christ; Dante chose him as his guide through hell, purgatory, and heaven; Purcell put Dido to music; and Voltaire capped all by ranking the *Aeneid* as the finest literary monument left by antiquity.

One of the pleasantest pictures in the world of letters—where jealousy is only less rife than in love—is of Virgil introducing Horace to Maecenas. The man of the world enjoyed in Horace's subtly crafted poems a sophistication complementing the simplicity of Virgil's character and verse. In 34 B.C. he gave Horace a spacious house and an income-producing farm in the Sabine Valley some forty-five miles north of Rome. So freed to speak his mind, Horace satirized, in almost colloquial hexameters, the typical figures that he had found in Rome: the caustic slave, the vain author, the gabbing bore, the place-hunting philosopher, the crafty Oriental, the businessman, the streetwalker, the philanderer who, tired of his wife, itches for another woman, who herself has become prose to another man: this, we feel, is the living Rome.

Comfortable in his twenty-four rooms with three bathing pools, Horace idealized the farmer who, "far from business cares . . . tills with his own oxen his patrimonial fields." To fill out his dreams he composed odes to or about his real or imagined mistresses, of whom he named thirteen. Conscious of his own skill, he composed a letter later entitled *The Art of Poetry,* telling young scribblers the rules for good writing: clarity, directness, mingling the useful with the pleasant. Art assumes feeling as well in the artist as in the recipient: "If you wish me to weep, you must first grieve yourself." But art is not feeling alone; it is feeling conveyed in disciplined form—"emotion remembered in tranquility"; here is the challenge of the classic to the romantic style.

To achieve form, study the Greeks day and night. Avoid words that are new, obsolete, or sesquipedalian—"foot-and-a-half words." If your product survives all this, hide it away for eight years. If then it still pleases you, publish it, but remember that it may shame your maturity. If you write dramas, obey the three unities—of action, time, and place. Study life and philosophy, for without study and understanding, a perfect style is an empty vessel, too fragile for our use.

Horace did not doubt his own art, and its survival. *Exegi monumentum aere perennius*—"I have raised a monument more lasting than bronze, loftier than the royal peak of the pyramids. . . . I shall not wholly die"—*non omnis moriar.* In the year 8 B.C., having bequeathed his property to Augustus, he surrendered his body to the earth and was laid to rest near Maecenas' tomb.

A third poet graced the Augustan Age, or—in this case, Augustus thought—disgraced it criminally. Publius Ovidius Naso made himself the model and laureate of those epicurean Romans who resented the prince's legislation against sexual freedom, and laughed at warriors who foraged for death on alien soil when they might have been exploring the charms of Rome's liberated women. His rich middle-class father sent him to the capital to study law and was shocked to learn that the youth proposed to be a poet. Ovid managed to rise to the quite uncongenial post of judge, but *en route* he wrote a book of poems in praise of promiscuity.

After studious experience in the amorous chase he issued a manual of seduction entitled *Ars amatoria* (2 B.C.), but judiciously bade its readers to apply its precepts only to courtesans and slaves. These and later volumes sold so well that Ovid reached dizzy heights of fame and hubris: "So long as I am celebrated all the world over, it matters not what one or two pettifoggers say about me." He did not know that one of those pettifoggers was Augustus, who was pondering ways of putting teeth into the Julian Laws that he had passed in 13 B.C.

Ovid prospered, married three times, found a new happiness with Fabia, cooled his fires, and in A.D. 7 published his most enduring work, *Metamorphoses,* which recounted in lively and fluent hexameters some famous cases of transformation in objects, animals, men, and gods; from this treasury, almost till our time, a thousand poems, paintings, and statues took their themes. At the end, the confident author announced his immortality: *Per saecula omnia vivam*—"I shall live through all ages." He had hardly issued this prophecy when, in the eighth year of our era and the fifty-first of his age, he received imperial notice of banishment to Tomi (now Constanta), a cold and misty town on the Romanian shores of the Black Sea.

Often the poet sent, to his wife or friends, poems later gathered as *Tristia.* When, in that somber port, he thought of Italy's warm women and cheerful skies, his heart broke, and his verses, still beautiful in form and phrase, took on a depth of feeling that they had seldom shown before. He humbly appealed for pardon, but no answer came, and he died in exile, A.D. 17. There must have been something dearly lovable in him, for his third wife, who had stayed behind at his bidding, remained loyal to him to the end.

THE MORTAL PRINCE

The man whose word had become law from York to Baalbek to Cádiz lived all the while a life of unassuming simplicity, shunning the luxuries of wealth and the emoluments of office, wearing the simple garments woven by the women in his home, and sleeping in a small room of what had been the palace of the orator Hortensius.

Augustus was so unpretentious that a Gaul who came to kill him thought this could not be the Imperial ruler that he sought. Through nearly all his life he suffered from some chastening ailment—ringworm, arthritis, typhus, catarrh, stones in the bladder, sleeplessness; in some campaigns, too weak to ride a horse, he had to be carried in a litter to the battlefield. After trying many physicians he doctored himself with sulfur baths and a diet of coarse bread, cheese, fish, and fruit. Old at thirty-five, he lived to be seventy-six.

His character contained contrary elements which could be brought out alternately by the whim of circumstance. In his youth—fortunate in family and loved by Caesar—he shared in the sexual laxity of the time. Then, shaken by Caesar's assassination, he joined Antony against Brutus; but Antony's reckless ambition, his heartless treatment of his wife, Octavia—Octavius' sister—turned Octavius into a merciless enemy. When at thirty-three he became master of Rome, his virtues flowered in prosperity. Power humbled rather than corrupted him. He accepted too many powers, but he put on no airs. He smiled at the lampoons that wits and poets composed about him. As the supreme court in the land he judged with wisdom and mercy. In his final years a series of misfortunes embittered and hardened him. We must consider the frailty of his body and the sorrows of his old age before our hearts can go out to him as to the murdered Caesar and the beaten Antony.

His failures and tragedies were almost all within his family. His daughter Julia seemed destined, by her beauty and vivacity, to brighten his declining years, but her warm passions and volatile temperament gave no welcome to her father's legislation on marriage, parentage, and morals. Wedded at fourteen and widowed at sixteen, she enjoyed her freedom with such abandon that her father hastened to marry her to his favorite aide, Marcus Agrippa, who was forty. Julia gave Agrippa five children; but when he died (12 B.C.), she entered upon a succession of amours which became the scandal and delight of a Rome fretting under the "Julian laws." Forced to marry her father's adopted son Tiberius, she continued her amours; Tiberius fled to Rhodes to study philosophy and astrology. His friends reminded Augustus that, according to his laws, an adulteress must be denounced to the courts by her husband, or, if the husband refused, by her father. In the year 2 B.C., Augustus issued a decree banishing his daughter to the island of Pandateria, a barren rock off the Campanian coast. Many, including Tiberius, begged Augustus to pardon Julia; he refused, and Julia died after six years of imprisonment. Meanwhile her daughter, also named Julia, imitated her mother's morals until Augustus exiled her to an island in the Adriatic (A.D. 8). The broken old ruler longed for death.

It came to him quietly in his seventy-sixth year. To friends at his bedside the greatest of Roman statesmen uttered the words often used to conclude a Roman comedy: "Since well I've played my part, clap now your hands, and with applause dismiss me from the stage." He embraced his wife, saying, "Remember our long union, Livia; farewell"; and with this simple parting he passed away.

Some days later his corpse was borne through Rome on the shoulders of senators to the Field of Mars, and there cremated while children of high degree chanted the lament for the dead.

Chapter Twelve

᠆᠊᠊᠊

NERO AND AURELIUS

NERO

From the death of Augustus in A.D. 14 to the accession of Odoacer in 476 as the first "barbarian" ruler of Rome, the Roman Empire survived every trial of external challenge and internal decay.

Tiberius, who succeeded, as his adopted son, to the power of Augustus, governed well till family troubles soured him and absolute power clouded his mind. Caligula began his reign with popular benefactions, but soon fell into cruelties that led to his assassination. Claudius astonished Rome by governing well despite having written books of philosophy and history and an autobiography; but, says Suetonius, he "was immoderate in his passion for women."

We are unreliably told that his fourth wife, Messalina, brought him concubines as a reward for his toleration of her adulteries. After some soldiers killed her, Claudius married Agrippina, who was already the mother of Nero; she persuaded Claudius to adopt Nero as his son; finally she fed the emperor poisonous mushrooms; Claudius died, and Nero, age seventeen (A.D. 54), mounted the throne.

Nero became the most famous of Rome's emperors because he was falsely believed to have ordered the burning of Rome, and because he arranged theatrical displays of his artistic skills. Nevertheless the great Trajan, accounted the first five years of Nero's rule the best period in the history of the Imperial government. Acknowledging his youth, he surrendered to the Senate nearly all royal powers except command of the army.

He accepted Seneca as his guide, and promised to illustrate throughout his reign that virtue of mercy which the philosopher was inculcating in the treatise *De clementia;* however, when he learned that his mother was intriguing to replace him on the throne with her other son, Britannicus, he arranged (we are told) to have him poisoned. In any case, the Empire prospered in his first quinquennium: corruption was checked, the administrative bureaucracy was improved, the Black Sea was cleared of pirates, and Parthia signed a peace that endured for fifty years.

Seneca was probably the guiding spirit in that quinquennium. To divert Nero from state affairs he allowed him a loose rein in morals. The youth developed a fancy for expensive banquets, gay youths, and prostitutes. He dismissed his gentle wife Octavia and married Poppaea Sabina, who spent half the day polishing her person, and the other half in stimulating desire. When Nero's mother opposed her, Poppaea prodded the youth into ordering Agrippina's death. Viewing the naked corpse, he remarked, "I did not know I had so beautiful a mother."

It is hard to believe these stories of a youth of twenty-two years with an acknowledged passion for poetry, drama, music, art, and athletic games. He practiced all of these laboriously, and neared excellence in some of them. He gathered artists and poets around him, and compared his work with theirs. In A.D. 64, in Naples, he gave a public concert as a harpist, and, a year later, as harpist and singer in Pompey's Theater in Rome. He appeared on the boards as an actor, and thrilled to public applause. Learning that Alexandria and Antioch had been rebuilt according to scientific designs, he mourned that Rome had grown so haphazardly, mingling palaces with slums; he dreamed of rebuilding it and renaming it Neropolis.

On July 18, 64, a fire broke out in the Circus Maximus, spread rapidly, burned for nine days, and razed two-thirds of Rome. Nero was at Antium (now Anzio), thirty-three miles away, when news of the conflagration reached him. He hurried up to the capital, did what he could to control and localize the flames, and energetically organized relief. He raised a city of tents on the Field of Mars and brought in food from the surrounding country to feed the homeless. He was wrongly accused of having started the fire, and of having watched it from a tower while singing lines from his epic on the burning of Troy. He himself, according to Tacitus, accused the little group of Christians that the apostles Peter and Paul had found there some three years before. Nero, says the strongly anti-imperial historian, had a number of them "put to death with exquisite cruelty." Meanwhile he began the restoration of the city according to his dream.

A year later he learned of a conspiracy to depose him; some prisoners implicated Seneca and the poet Lucan; Nero ordered them to kill themselves; they obeyed. He seemed now at the height of his power. In 66 he thought himself so secure that he left Italy to compete in the national games of Greece. At Olympia he drove a four-horse chariot. He was thrown, was severely injured, remounted his quadriga, resumed the race, gave up exhausted before the finish, but was awarded the crown of victory—whereupon he freed Greece from all further tribute to Rome. He went on to compete in the Pythian, Nemean, and Esthonian games as singer, harpist, actor, and athlete. He was regularly given the prize, and consoled his vanquished competitors with Roman citizenship.

Amid his conquests he received news that Judea was in revolt and that nearly all the West was rising against him. In 68, Vindex, governor of Lyons, and Galba, commander of the Roman army in Spain, joined in rebellion. Nero looked to the Praetorian Guard to defend him; it declared for Galba, and the Senate proclaimed Galba emperor. Nero appealed to favored friends; none came to his help. He fled along the road to Ostia, hoping to find a vessel with a loyal crew, but the soldiers of the Senate overtook and surrounded him. He tried to drive a poniard into his throat; his hand faltered; his freedman helped him press the blade home. "*Qualis artifax pereo!*" he mourned—"What an artist dies in me!"

DECADENCE

The death of Nero marked the apex of Epicurean Rome, as the death of Cato the Censor, in 149 B.C., had marked the zenith of Stoic Rome.

Soon after Cato's death the Roman conquest of Greece (146 B.C.) and of the Hellenistic East lengthened westward that economic and cultural road which Alexander's conquests had opened two centuries before the taxes, peoples, customs, philosophies, and religions of the East poured into Rome and began to transform its stoic vigor into epicurean ease. The first conquest of Rome was not by barbarian tribes from the north but by literate peoples from the East: Greeks, Syrians, Jews, Egyptians, Parthians, Ethiopians . . . ; Juvenal complained that the Orontes (Syria's river) was flowing into the Tiber, and Tacitus, proud senator, called Rome "the cesspool of the world."

There were many virtues in the newcomers; the family life of the Jews was a pillar of strength to them, and the little Christian enclaves were astonishing the Romans by their piety and decency. But many of the newcomers were demoralized by removal from their native surroundings and disciplines, and frequent mingling with alien codes eroded their own. This diversity of codes, this submission of racial unity and vigor in a maelstrom of diverse stocks, faiths, purposes, and ways, may have shared with Rome's imported wealth in relaxing her moral life into the reckless hedonism of Ovid, Horace, and Martial, the diversions and crimes of Nero, and the infidelities of Roman queens. All the more astonishing is the sudden appearance, in the second century of our era, of the most stoic and dedicated rulers in the history of post-Augustan Rome.

THE PHILOSOPHER KINGS

Hear Gibbon's judgment: "If a man were to be called upon to fix the period, in the history of the world, during which the condition of the human race was most happy and prosperous, he would without hesitation name that which elapsed from the accession of Nerva (A.D. 96) to the death of Aurelius (180). Their united reigns are possibly the only period in history in which the happiness of a great people was the sole object of government."

Ernest Renan agreed: the principle of royal adoption gave Rome "the finest succession of good and great sovereigns the world has ever had." That principle had been established by Augustus; it had been set aside after Nero's death; it was restored by Nerva (A.D. 98) when he adopted Trajan as his successor. The Senate had accepted the principle on the assumption that the adoption would be of a man already known for administrative and military ability. The principle worked well because Nerva, Trajan, Hadrian, and Antonius Pius had no son, and had time to study and train their choice.

Marcus Cocceius Nerva was sixty-six when the Senate appointed him *princeps*. He distributed land among the poor, annulled many taxes, freed the Jews from the tribute laid upon them, and strengthened the finances of the state by economy in his household and his administration. Three months before his death (98) he appointed, as his successor, Marcus Ulpius Trajanus.

Trajan loved the Empire so well that he wanted more and more of it, and spent most of his mature life in protecting and expanding it. He conquered and absorbed Dacia (now Romania) as necessary to control the Danube as the best barrier to the multiplying "barbarians." He gave Dacia a Latin language and took her gold mines in return. Enriched, he distributed 650 denarii ($260?) to all Roman citizens who applied; he built the still-flourishing amphitheater in Verona, and the vast Forum Traianum in Rome; there the triumphal arch, and the column with spiral carvings, commemorating his victories, stand to inspire Napoleon's.

In 113 he set out again with his legions, hoping to conquer Parthia and open a commercial road to India. He made new provinces of Armenia, Assyria, Mesopotamia, and Parthia, and triumphantly reached the Red Sea. Then he suffered a paralytic stroke and died at Salinus in 117, after transmitting his imperial powers to his nephew, Publius Aelius Hadrianus.

Hadrian, like Trajan, was born in Spain, but differed from him in almost everything else. He disliked war, loved dogs, horses, hunting, literature, philosophy, and half a dozen arts. He restored independence to Armenia, Assyria, Mesopotamia, and Parthia. Returning to Rome, he reorganized the government, kept watch over every branch of it, and (like Napoleon, who learned much from Rome) astonished each administrative head by detailed knowledge of each field.

Over all departments he put an *advocatus fisci*, or "defender of the treasury," to detect corruption or deceit. As the Empire's supreme court he earned the reputation of a fair and learned judge, usually favoring the poor against the rich, the weak against the strong. Under his care the Empire was better governed than ever before or afterward.

Restless, and abounding with ideas, Hadrian set out to share with the provinces some of the wealth they had yielded to Rome. In Gaul he brought relief to localities stricken by inadvertent "acts of God." At the German border he reinforced the line of defense against the ever-pressing "barbarians"—by which the Romans meant anyone outside of the Empire. Sailing down the Rhine to the North Sea, he crossed into Roman Britain (A.D. 122), pacified it with benefits, and, at its northern reach, arranged for the building of "Hadrian's Wall" against the un-conquered and incalculable Scots.

After a winter's rest in Rome, he sailed to North Africa to regulate its flourishing cities. In 124 he visited the Hellenized Near East; at al-most every stop he listened to complaints and petitions, and provided funds for temples, theaters, and baths. In 125 and 128 he spent the winters in Athens, mingling happily with scholars and philosophers, and building so wisely that the aging metropolis of the mind became cleaner, more beautiful, and more prosperous than ever before in known history. In 130 he toured Egypt, felt the winds of theological or scholastic doctrine in Alexandria, and then moved leisurely up the Nile with his wife Sabina and his handsome and devoted boyfriend Anti-nous. On that trip the youth drowned. Hadrian, inconsolable, returned to Rome.

There he devoted himself to the further advancement of the capital: The Pantheon that Agrippa had built in 27 B.C. had been mostly de-stroyed by fires in A.D. 80 and 110; Hadrian had his architects and en-gineers replace it (120–24) with a circular temple whose interior, 132 feet in diameter, dispensed with internal supports, and received its sole and sufficient light from a twenty-six-foot-wide oculus in the dome. From that graceful cupola an architectural lineage descended to St. Peter's in Rome—and to our Capitol in Washington.

The revolt of Judea in 135 embittered him; he mourned that it broke the long peace of his reign. In that year he was stricken by a lin-gering illness which broke his health and darkened his mind, even to occasional cruelty. To end an incipient war of succession he adopted his friend Lucius Verus as his heir. Verus soon died. Hadrian replaced him with a man of national reputation for integrity and wisdom, Titus Au-relius Antoninus, and advised him to adopt and train two youths then at the court. One of these died before Antoninus; the other became

Marcus Aurelius. Hadrian died in the year 138, after only sixty-two years of life, but twenty-one of rule, and having provided the Empire, in action and foresight, with three reigns, all among the most beneficient in history.

Titus Aurelius Antoninus was named Pius by the Senate because he excelled in the virtues honored by the old Roman Republic: filial devotion, patriotism, loyalty to friends, generosity with time and purse. He began his reign by pouring his substantial personal fortune into the Imperial Treasury. He canceled arrears of taxes, paid for festival games, and relieved scarcities of oil, wheat, and wine by buying these and distributing them without charge. He gave a public accounting of all his receipts and expenditures. He equalized the penalties for adultery for men and women, and deprived ruthless masters of their slaves. He provided state funds for the extension of education, especially to the poor, and extended to recognized teachers and philosophers many privileges of the senatorial class.

All provinces but Egypt and Dacia flourished during his reign and were happy to be parts of an empire that gave them social order and internal peace. Provincial authors—Strabo, Philo, Plutarch, Appian, Epictetus—praised the *Pax Romana*, and Appian assures us that he had seen at Rome the envoys of foreign states vainly seeking admission for their countries to the Roman yoke. Never had monarchy left men so free, or had so respected the rights of its subjects. "The world's ideal," wrote Renan, "seemed to have been attained. Wisdom reigned, and for twenty-three years the [Roman] world was governed by a father."

In the seventy-fourth year of his life Antoninus fell seriously ill. He called his adopted son Marcus to his bedside and transmitted to him the care of the Empire. To the officer of the day he gave the watchword—*aeguanimitas*. Then he turned as if to sleep, and died (161). All classes and cities vied in honoring his memory.

Antoninus, said Renan, "would have been without competition for the reputation of being the best of sovereigns had he not designated Marcus Aurelius as his successor." Marcus seemed to inherit all the virtues of his predecessor, plus others for which he credited his "good grandparents, good parents, good sisters, good kinsmen." Time struck a balance by giving him a wife of questionable fidelity and morals, whom he never failed to honor, and a fatally unworthy son, whom he never ceased to love. He thanks his books for sparing him logic and astrology, for freeing him from superstition, and for teaching him to live simply and in conformity with nature.

At the age of twelve he adopted the rude cloak of a philosopher, slept on a little straw strewn upon the floor, and long resisted the entreaties of his mother to use a couch. He was a Stoic before he was a man. He offers thanks "that I preserved the flower of my youth; that I took not upon me to be a man before my time, but rather put it off longer than I needed, . . . that I never had to be with Benedicta." He thanked his brother Severus for teaching him "the idea of a state in which there is the same law for all, . . . equal rights, and freedom of speech, and the idea of a kingly government that most of all respects the freedom of the governed"; for two reigns the Stoic idea of monarchy held the throne. He decided to rule by example rather than by law. He allowed himself no luxury, took on all the tasks of administration, and wore himself out by being easy of access. Soon the whole Empire welcomed him as Plato's dream come true: a philosopher was king.

His reputation as a philosopher encouraged the barbarians to try another sortie against the Roman line. In 167 the tribes north of the Danube crossed the river in a surprise attack upon legions depleted by war and pestilence. Marcus put aside his books, organized a new army by enrolling policemen, gladiators, brigands, and slaves, trained it to discipline and strength, led it with strategy and skill through a hard campaign to victory, and returned to Rome to face the problems of succession. He had hoped to train his son Commodus in philosophy and government, but the youth fled from studies to gladiators and soon surpassed his reckless associates in violent action and coarse speech.

Meanwhile indigenous Romans were losing number and vigor through sterility and ease, while the barbarians multiplied through fertility and an arduous life. In the seven years between 168 and 176 the Empire was attacked at one point after another by the Chatti, the Marcomanni, the Mauri (Moors), the Sarmatians, the Quadi, the Iazyges; some invaded Greece to within fourteen miles of Athens; others raided Roman Spain; some crossed the Alps, threatened Venice and Verona, and laid waste the rich fields of northern Italy.

On and off, in those years, Marcus was attacked by a painful stomach ailment that resisted every diagnosis, and even Galen's remedies. Ema-

ciated, his beard untended, his eyes weary with anxiety and sleeplessness, the lonely emperor turned again from domestic cares to the uncongenial tasks of war.

It was in that campaign along the Danube that Marcus, in the intervals of action, composed, in Greek, the little book known as *Meditations*
or *Thoughts,* but which he entitled *Ta eis heuton* (To Himself). He proposed to summarize the conclusions he had reached about the first and
last things in life. He had lost the official Roman religious faith and
had not adopted any of the new creeds that had come from the East; but
he found too many signs and forms of order in nature to doubt that
some mysterious intelligence infused the universe. All things are determined, he felt, by the universal reason—the inherent logic of the
whole; and every part must cheerfully accept its modest fate. "Equa-
nimity" (Antoninus' watchword) "is the voluntary acceptance of what
is assigned to thee by the nature of the whole." Everything "harmonizes with me that harmonizes with thee; O universe. Nothing for me
is too early or too late which is in due time for thee."

He reluctantly concedes that there are bad men in the world. The
way to deal with them is to remember that they, too, are men, the helpless victims of their own faults by the determinism of circumstance. "If
any man has done thee wrong, the harm is his own; . . . forgive him."
Does this seem an impracticable philosophy? On the contrary, nothing
is so invincible as a good disposition, if it be sincere. A really good man
is immune to misfortune, for whatever evil befalls him leaves him still
his own soul. Philosophy is not logic or learning, but understanding
and acceptance.

As for death, accept this, too, as a natural and necessary thing:

> For as the mutation and dissolution of bodies makes room for other
> bodies doomed to die, so the souls that are removed into the air after
> life's existence are transmuted and diffused . . . into the seminal in-
> telligence of the universe, and make room for new souls. . . . Thou
> hast existed as a part, thou shalt disappear in that which produced
> thee. . . . This, too, nature wills. . . . Pass, then, through this little
> space of time comfortably to nature, and end thy journey in content,
> just as an olive falls when it is ripe, blessing the nature that produced
> it, and thanking the tree on which it grew.

He faced death with no hope of happiness beyond the grave and no confidence in the son who expected to succeed him. He continued, through six years, his campaigns in the north, and with such success that when he returned to Rome in 176 he was accorded a triumph as the savior of the Empire. He knew that his victory was only temporary, and two years later he set out again to check the German flood. Amid that campaign he died (180), having forfeited the principle of adoption to love for his son.

Commodus proceeded to inaugurate the long fall of the Roman Empire, while fearful Christians, hidden in the mass, waited patiently for the triumph of Christ.

Chapter Thirteen

ⅿⅿⅿ

THE HUMAN CHRIST

THE SOURCES

Did Jesus exist? Are the first three Gospels of the New Testament merely the loving transmission of a myth? Early in the eighteenth century, Viscount Bolingbroke startled Voltaire by suggesting the possibility that Jesus had never lived. Volney revised the question in his famous *Ruins of Empire* in 1791. When Napoleon met the scholar Wieland in 1808, he asked him no question of politics or war, but did he believe in the historicity of Christ? In 1840 the German historian Ferdinand Christian Baur began to publish a series of passionately controversial volumes aiming to picture Christ as a myth in a class with Osiris, Dionysus, and Mithras.

I do not know of any recognized scholar who still holds these views, though it is generally agreed that many stories told of pagan gods— like that of the Three Wise Men—were popularly added, without ecclesiastical sanction, to the accounts transmitted by Matthew, Mark, and Luke. The Gospel of St. Mark, now ascribed to between A.D. 65 and 70, was apparently circulated while some of the Apostles were still alive and able to contradict him. It is not likely that St. Paul would have preached the religion of Christ if he had ever doubted the existence of the crucified preacher to whom the Apostles were dedicating their lives. That a few simple men should in a few years have invented so powerful and appealing a personality as Jesus would be a miracle far more incredible than any recorded in the Gospels. After two centuries of higher criticism, the outlines of the life, character, and teaching of Christ remain reasonably clear, and constitute the most fascinating feature in the panorama of Western man.

THE SON OF MAN

One must try to feel the place and time of Jesus' birth, the relation of his land and people to the Roman Empire that had engulfed them, the bitterness of the conquered nation, its proud heritage of religion, law, literature, and philosophy, its passionate hope for liberation, its dream of a coming kingdom of freedom, justice, and glory. It took all of these acting upon a sensitive and understanding spirit—to form the carpenter's son, and lead him to the cross.

By the humor of history he was born three or four years "Before Christ"; i.e., according to the Gospel of St. Matthew (Matt. 2:15), before the death of King Herod the Great, who died in 4 B.C. He was a native of Bethlehem in Judea, or, some said, of Nazareth in Galilee. The same Gospel derives his ancestry from King David down to "Joseph the husband of Mary"—which seemed to fit well with the Jewish belief that the Messiah who would redeem Israel and restore her glory would be descended from David; but Matthew adds that "when Mary was espoused to Joseph, before they came together, she was found with child of the Holy Spirit" (Matt. 1:18). The Gospel of Luke expands the miracle into great literature: "The angel Gabriel came in unto her, and said: "Hail, Mary, full of grace; the Lord is with thee; blessed art though amongst women"; to which her cousin Elizabeth, hearing of this, added, "and blessed is the fruit of thy womb"—which became the loveliest of Catholic prayers. Mary answered with that magnificent *Magnificat* which has inspired so much great music: "My soul doth magnify the Lord, and my spirit hath rejoiced in God my Savior. For he hath regarded the low estate of his handmaiden; for behold, henceforth all generations shall call me blessed" (Luke 1:46–48).

I think of the lovely hymns that the Middle Ages composed to Mary, and the joyful songs that I sang to her in my youth; she was my first love. To have conceived and adored her, and raised a thousand temples in her honor, is one of the redeeming features of the human race. After all, there is not much to be said for the absurd athletics with which we generate a soul today.

Jesus was apparently one of a large family, for his neighbors spoke of "his brothers James, Joseph, Simon, and Judas" (Matt. 13:55). Presumably he practiced his father's pleasant trade of carpentry, but he must have absorbed with delight the natural beauties of the countryside, for he later noted sensitively the grace and color of flowers, and the silent fruitfulness of trees.

The story of his questioning the scholars in the Temple is not incredible; he had an alert and curious mind, and in the Near East a boy of twelve already touches maturity. He attended the synagogue, and heard the Scriptures with evident delight; the Prophets and the Psalms helped to mold him and sank deeply into his memory. Perhaps he read also the books of Daniel and Enoch, for his later teaching was shot through with their visions of the Messiah, the Last Judgment, and the coming Kingdom of God.

The air he breathed was tense with religious excitement. Thousands of Jews awaited anxiously the Redeemer of Israel. Magic and witchcraft, demons and angels, "possessions" and exorcism, miracles and prophecies, divination and astrology, were taken for granted everywhere. Thaumaturgists—wonder-workers—toured the towns. On the annual journeys that all good Palestinian Jews made to Jerusalem for the Passover festival, Jesus may have learned something of the Essenes and of their half-monastic life; perhaps the Hindu King Ashoka's Buddhistic missionaries had reached Palestine. But the experience that aroused him to religious fervor was the preaching of John, the son of Mary's cousin Elizabeth.

Matthew and Mark describe John as garbed in haircloth, living on dead locusts and honey, standing by the Jordan, calling people to repentance, and baptizing penitents to a spiritual rebirth. He warned sinners to prepare themselves for the Last Judgment and proclaimed the early coming of the Kingdom of God. If all Judea should repent and be cleansed of sin, said John, the Messiah and the Kingdom would come.

When John the Baptist was imprisoned, Jesus took up his work, and began to preach of the coming of the Kingdom. He "returned to Galilee," says Luke, "and taught in the synagogues." "The spirit of the

Lord is upon me," he said, "because he has anointed me to preach glad tidings to the poor; he hath sent me to heal the broken-hearted, to preach deliverance to captives and recovery of sight to the blind, to set the downtrodden free" (Isa. 56:1–2). "The eyes of everyone in the synagogue," Luke adds, "were fixed upon him. . . . And they all spoke well of him, and were astonished at the winning words that fell from his lips" (Isa. 4:19).

The words were not always pleasant. Jesus accepted and proclaimed some of the harsh doctrines that were developing among his people. He spoke of sinners condemned to a "hell, the fire that never shall be extinguished; where the worm dieth not, and the fire is not extinguished" (Mark 9:43–44); and in the thirteenth chapter of Matthew he spoke of a Last Judgment when "the Son of Man" (i.e., Christ) "shall send forth his angels, and they shall gather out of his kingdom all things that offend, and them that do inequity; and cast them into a furnace of fire; there shall be wailing and gnashing of teeth. Then shall the righteous shine forth as the sun in the kingdom of their Father" (Matt. 13:41–43).

He told without recorded protest how the poor man in heaven would not be permitted to let a single drop of water fall upon the tongue of the rich man in hell (Luke 16:25). Perhaps, like his followers, he felt that some severity and terror were indispensable in preaching to a world addicted to violence, adultery, and greed. His more characteristic side appeared when some Pharisees—conservative elders—asked him to condemn a woman taken in adultery. He said to them: "He that is without sin among you, let him first cast a stone at her" (John 8:7).

Usually, we are told, he was the most lovable of men. Many women sensed in him a sympathetic tenderness that inspired an unswerving devotion. So we read of the prostitute who, moved by his ready acceptance of repentant sinners, knelt before him, anointed his feet, let her tears fall upon them, and dried them with her hair. When some bystanders protested, he answered them, "Her sins, which are many, are forgiven, for she loved much" (Luke 7:37–38, 47).

I believe that most of the miracles ascribed to him were the natural result of suggestion—of the influence of a strong and confident spirit upon impressionable souls; similar phenomena may be observed any week at Lourdes. His presence and his faith were themselves a tonic; at his optimistic touch the weak grew strong and the sick were made well. We cannot set any certain limit to the powers that lie in the thought and will of a strong and believing woman or man.

THE GLAD TIDINGS

What was the gospel—which in English meant "good tidings"— that Jesus brought to his people? His starting point was the Gospel of John the Baptist, which itself went back to Daniel and Enoch; *historia non facit saltum*. The Kingdom of Heaven was at hand, said Jesus; soon God would put an end to the reign of wickedness on earth; the Son of Man (as he called himself) would come "on the clouds of the sky" to judge all humanity, living or dead. The time for repentance was running out; those who repented, lived justly, loved God, and put their trust in his messenger would inherit the Kingdom, and would be raised to power and glory in a world at last freed from all evil, suffering, and death.

Jesus did not clearly define these ideas, and many difficulties still obscure his conception. What did he mean by "the Kingdom?" A supernatural heaven? Apparently not, for the Apostles and the early Christians unanimously expected an earthly kingdom. This was the Jewish tradition that Christ inherited, and he taught his followers to pray to the Father: "Thy Kingdom come, thy will be done, on earth as it is in heaven." Only after that hope had failed did the Gospel of John make Jesus say, "My kingdom is not of this world" (John 18:36). Did he mean a spiritual condition, or a material utopia? At times he spoke of the Kingdom as a state of soul, reached by the pure and sinless—"the kingdom of God is within you" (Luke 17:20); at other times he pictured it as a happy future society in which the apostles would be rulers, and those who had given or suffered for Christ's sake would receive a hundredfold reward (Matt. 19:29).

Many have interpreted the Kingdom as a communist utopia, and have seen in Christ a social revolutionist. The Gospels provide some evidence for this view. Christ promised hunger and woe to the rich and filled, and comforted the poor with Beatitudes that pledged them the Kingdom. To the rich youth who asked what he should do besides keeping the Commandments, Jesus answered: "Sell your property, give your money to the poor, and . . . follow me" (Matt. 19:15). Apparently the Apostles interpreted the Kingdom as a revolutionary inversion of the existing relationships between the rich and the poor; we shall find them and the early Christians forming a communistic band which "had all things in common" (Acts 2:44–45).

But a conservative also can quote the New Testament to his purpose. Christ made a friend of Matthew, who continued to be an agent of the Roman power; he uttered no criticism of the civil government, took no known part in the Jewish movement for national liberation, and counseled a submissive gentleness hardly smacking of political revolution. He advised the Pharisees to "render unto Caesar the things that are Caesar's, and to God the things that are God's." He approved of the slave who invested the 10 minas ($600) that his master had entrusted to him, and made ten more; he disapproved of the slave who, entrusted with one mina, held it in unproductive safekeeping for the master's return; and he put into the master's mouth the hard saying that "to him who has, more will be given; and from him who has nothing even that which he has will be taken away" (Luke 19:26)—an excellent summary of market operations, if not of world history.

He made no attack upon existing economic institutions; on the contrary he condemned those ardent souls who "would take the Kingdom by storm" (Matt. 11:12). The revolution he sought was a far deeper one, without which reforms could only be superficial and transitory. If he could cleanse the human heart of selfish desire, cruelty, and lust, utopia would come of itself. Since this would be the profoundest of all revolutions, beside which all others would be merely coups d'état of class ousting class and exploiting in its turn, Christ was in this spiritual sense the greatest revolutionist in history.

His achievement lay not in ushering in a new state, but in outlining a new morality. His ethical code was predicated on the early coming of the Kingdom and was designed to make men worthy of entering it. Hence the Beatitudes, with their unprecedented exaltation of humility, gentleness, and peace; the counsel to turn the other cheek; hence his indifference to economic provision, property, government; the preferment of celibacy to marriage; the command to abandon all family ties—his were not rules for family life or social order, they were a semimonastic regimen to fit men and women for election by God into an imminent Kingdom in which there would be no law, no marriage, no sexual relations, no property, and no war.

Were these moral ideas new? Nothing is new except arrangement. The central theme of Christ's preaching—the coming Judgment and Kingdom—was already a century old among the Jews. The Mosaic Code had already inculcated human brotherhood. "Thou shalt love thy neighbor as thyself," according to the book of Leviticus; "the stranger that dwelleth with you shall be unto you as one born among you, and thou shalt love him as thyself" (Lev. 19:17–18, 34). The Prophets had ranked a good life above all ritual; and Isaiah and Hosea had begun to change Yahweh from a Lord of Hosts—i.e., Armies—into a God of love. Hillel, like Confucius, had formulated the Golden Rule. We must not hold it against Jesus that he inherited and used the rich moral lore of his people.

For a long time he thought of himself purely as a Jew, sharing the ideas of the Prophets, continuing their work, and preaching like them only to Jews. In dispatching his disciples to spread his Gospel, he sent them only to Jewish cities. "Go not into the way of the Gentiles" (Matt. 10:5), for that would raise the problem of the Mosaic Law. "I came not to destroy the Law of Moses but to fulfill it" (Matt. 5:17). He told the leper whom he had cured to "go to the priest and . . . offer the gift that Moses prescribed" (Matt. 8:4). Nevertheless he offered some modifications in the law. He hardened it in matters of sex and divorce, but softened it toward a readier forgiveness; and he reminded the Pharisees that the Sabbath was made for man, not man for the Sabbath. He relaxed the code of diet and cleanliness, and omitted certain fasts. He condemned conspicuous prayers, showy charities, and ornate funerals.

Jews of all sects except the Essenes opposed his innovations, and especially resented his assumption of authority to forgive sins and speak in the name of God. They were shocked to see him maintain friendly relations with women of dubious morals. The priests of the Temple and the members of the administrative Sanhedrin saw in his growing followers a disguised revolt against Rome, and feared lest the procurator should accuse them of neglecting their responsibility for maintaining social order. Jesus denounced them recklessly:

Alas for you hypocritical Scribes and Pharisees, . . . you blind guides
. . . blind fools! . . . You are like whitewashed tombs! . . . Outwardly you appear to be upright, but within you are full of hypocrisy
and wickedness. . . . You are descended from the murderers of the
Prophets. . . . You serpents! You brood of snakes! How can you escape being sentenced to the pit? . . . The publicans and the harlots
go into the Kingdom of God before you. (Matt. 23:1–34; 21:31)

The final crisis came when the Apostles openly proclaimed that
Jesus was the promised Messiah who would raise Israel out of Roman
bondage and establish the reign of God on earth. When, on the last
Monday before his death, he entered Jerusalem to bring his gospel
from the towns to the capital, "the whole throng of his disciples"
greeted him with the words "Blessed is the *king* who comes in the name
of the Lord" (Luke 19:37). Some Pharisees asked him to repel this salutation; he answered, "If they keep silence the stones will cry out." The
Gospel of John reports that the crowd hailed Jesus as "King of Israel."
Apparently his followers thought of him as a political Messiah who
would overthrow the Roman power and make Judea free.

Perhaps it was these acclamations that mistakenly doomed Christ to
a revolutionist's death.

DEATH AND TRANSFIGURATION

The Feast of the Passover was at hand, and a great number of Jews
were gathering in Jerusalem to offer sacrifice in the Temple. The outer
court of the shrine was noisy with vendors selling doves and other sac-
rificial animals, and with money-changers offering locally acceptable
currency for the idolatrous coins of the Roman realm.

Visiting the Temple on the day after his entry into Jerusalem, Jesus
was shocked by the clamor and commercialism of the booths; in a burst
of indignation that made influential enemies, he and his followers overthrew the tables of the money-changers and the dove merchants, scattered their coins on the ground, and with "a scourge of rods" drove the
traders from the court.

For several days thereafter Jesus taught in the Temple, unhindered;
but at night he left Jerusalem and stayed on the Mount of Olives, fear-

ing arrest or assassination. The agents of the government—civil and ecclesiastical, Roman and Jewish—had long kept watch on him. His failure to secure a large following had inclined them to ignore him; but his enthusiastic reception in Jerusalem set the Jewish leaders wondering whether this excitement, working upon the emotional and patriotic Passover throngs, might flare into an untimely and futile revolt against the Roman power, and result in the suppression of all self-government and religious freedom in Judea. The high priest Caiaphas called a meeting of the Sanhedrin, and expressed the opinion "that one man should die for the people, instead of the whole nation being destroyed" (John 15:15). The majority agreed with him, and the council ordered Jesus' arrest.

Some news of this decision seems to have reached Jesus. On the fourteenth day of the Jewish month of *Nisan* (our April 3), probably in the year 30, Jesus and his disciples ate the Seder, or Passover Supper, in the home of a friend in Jerusalem. They looked to the Master to free himself by some miraculous power; on the contrary he accepted his fate. In accord with Jewish ritual he blessed (in the Greek of the New Testament, *eucharistisae*) the wine that he gave the apostles to drink, and then they sang together the Jewish ritual song "Hallel." He told them, according to the Gospel of John, that he would be with them "only a little longer. . . . I give you a new command: Love one another. . . . Let not your hearts be troubled. Believe in God and believe in me. In my Father's house there are many mansions. . . . I go to prepare a place for you."

That night, we are told, the little band hid in the Garden of Gethsemane, outside of Jerusalem. There a detachment of Temple police found them and arrested Jesus. He was taken first to the house of Annas, a former high priest, then to that of the high priest Caiaphas, where a "Council"—probably a committee of the Sanhedrin—had gathered. Various witnesses testified against Jesus, especially recalling his threat to destroy the Temple. When Caiaphas asked him whether he was "the Messiah, the Son of God," Jesus is reported to have answered, "I am he" (Mark 14:61; Matt. 26:63). In the morning, the Sanhedrin met, found him guilty of blasphemy (then a capital crime), and decided to bring him before the Roman procurator.

It did not seem to Pontius Pilate that this mild-mannered preacher was a real danger to the state. "Are you the King of the Jews?" he asked. According to the Gospel of Matthew, Jesus replied, *"Su eipas"*—"Thou hast said it." The Fourth Gospel quotes Jesus as adding, "For this I was born . . . to give testimony to the truth." "What is truth?" asked the procurator—a question revealing the chasm between the sophisticated and cynical culture of the Roman and the trustful idealism of the Jew. Pilate reluctantly sentenced him to death.

Crucifixion was a Roman, not a Jewish, form of punishment. It was usually preceded by scourging, which, carried out thoroughly, left the body a mass of swollen and bloody flesh. The Roman soldiers crowned Christ with a wreath of thorns, mocking his royalty as "King of the Jews," and placed upon his cross an inscription in Aramaic, Greek, and Latin: *Iesus Nazarathaeus Rex Ioudaeorum.*

Whether or not Christ was a revolutionist, he was obviously condemned as one by Rome; Tacitus understood the matter so (*Annals* 15.44). A small crowd, such as could gather in Pilate's courtyard, had called for Christ's execution; now, however, as he climbed the hill of Golgotha, "he was followed," says Luke, "by a great crowd of people," and of women who beat their breasts in grief. Clearly the condemnation did not have the approval of the Jewish people.

The cross, we are told, was raised at the "third hour"; i.e., at nine in the morning. Mark reports that two robbers were crucified with Jesus, and "reviled him"; Luke says that one of the two prayed to him. Of all the Apostles, only John was present. With him were three Marys— Christ's mother, her sister Mary, and Mary Magdalene; and "there were also some women watching from a distance." Following Roman custom, the soldiers divided the garments of the dying men; and as Christ had only one, they cast lots for it. Possibly we have here an interpolated remembrance of Psalm 22:18: "They part my garments among them, and cast lots upon my vesture." The same Psalm begins with the words "My God, my God, why hast thou forsaken me?"—and this is the desperately human utterance that Mark and Matthew attribute to the dying Christ. Can it be that in those bitter moments the great faith that had sustained him before Pilate faded into a heartbreaking doubt?

A soldier, pitying Christ's thirst, held up to his mouth a sponge soaked in sour wine. Jesus drank, and, we are told, said, "It is consummated." At the "ninth hour"—i.e., three in the afternoon—he cried out with a loud voice and gave up the ghost. Luke's gospel adds: "All the people that came together to that sight . . . smote their breasts and returned to the town." Two kindly and influential Jews, having secured Pilate's permission, took the body down from the cross and placed it in a tomb.

The two robbers crucified with him were still alive; some such victims had suffered three days before dying. To end the agony, soldiers broke the legs of Christ's cosufferers, so that the weight of the body would hang upon the hands, soon stopping the heart. Pilate expressed surprise that a man should die after only six hours of crucifixion; he gave his consent to Christ's removal from the cross only when the centurion in charge had assured him of Christ's death.

Two days after the burial, Mary Magdalene visited the tomb with "Mary the mother of James" (one of the Apostles). They found it empty. "Frightened, yet overjoyed," they ran to tell the news to the disciples. On the way they met a man whom they thought to be Jesus; they bowed before him and clasped his feet. On the same day, we are told, Christ appeared to two disciples on the road to Emmaus, talked with them, ate with them; for a long time "they were prevented from recognizing him"; but when "he took the bread and blessed it, . . . their eyes were opened, and they knew him, and he vanished from them" (Luke 14:13–32).

The disciples went back to Galilee, and soon thereafter "saw him and bowed down before him, though some were in doubt." Forty days after his appearance to Mary Magdalene, says the beginning of the Acts of the Apostles, Christ ascended physically into heaven. The idea of a saint being so "translated" into the sky in body and life was familiar to the Jews; they told it of Moses, Enoch, Elijah, and Isaiah. The Master went as mystically as he had come, but most of the disciples seem to have been sincerely convinced that he had, after his crucifixion, been with them in the flesh.

"They went back with great joy to Jerusalem," says the Gospel of Luke, "and were constantly in the Temple, blessing God" (Luke 24:52).

Chapter Fourteen

॥॥॥॥

THE GROWTH
OF THE CHURCH

For some time the Jewish authorities tolerated the sect as small and harmless, but as the "Nazarenes" multiplied in a few years from 120 to 8,000, the priests became alarmed.

Peter and others were arrested and questioned by the Sanhedrin; some were flogged, then all were released. A year later (A.D. 30?) Stephen, one of the disciples, was summoned before the Sanhedrin and charged with using "abusive language about Moses and God"; he defended himself so vehemently that the enraged priests had him stoned to death. In the year 41 Peter was again arrested, but escaped.

In A.D. 65 the Jews revolted against Rome; the Christian Jews, uninterested in politics, retired to Pella, on the eastern bank of the Jordan. The Jews accused the Christians of cowardice and treason, and the Christians hailed the destruction of the Temple in A.D. 70 as fulfilling one of Jesus' prophecies. Mutual hatred enflamed the two faiths and wrote some of their most pious literature.

Peter went forth to preach the new religion in Syria and points west until he reached Rome, where he founded the See (seat) of Peter, became the first pope, and was crucified in the persecutions under Nero in A.D. 64. Catholic tradition holds that the famous basilica of St. Peter's was built over the spot where Peter died, and that the great altar covers his bones.

As Peter established the Church, so Paul established the creed. He was born in the Hellenized city of Tarsus, in the Roman colony of Cilicia in Asia Minor. His father, who named him Saul, transmitted to him two proud distinctions as both a leading Pharisee and a Roman citizen. Sent to Jerusalem for fuller Jewish instruction, Paul, as the Romans named him, supported the Sanhedrin in its condemnation of Stephen, and undertook a trip to Damascus to eradicate the Christian community there. You know the story: On the road he suffered a stroke, apparently from the heat and blare of the desert sun. He fell blinded to the earth and thought he heard a voice saying, "Saul, why persecutest thou me?" He was led into the city and was three days without sight; "neither did he eat nor drink." Then a recent convert came to him,

and putting his hands on him, said, "Brother Saul, the Lord, even Jesus that appeared unto thee in the way as thou camest, hath sent me, that thou mightest recover thy sight, and be filled with the Holy Spirit." And immediately there fell from his eyes as it were scales, and he received sight forthwith and rose and was baptized. Then was Saul seven days with the disciples which were in Damascus, and straightway he preached Christ in the synagogue. (Acts 9:17–20)

So began the historic mission of the most famous of the disciples. With another recent convert, Barnabas, Paul left to preach his new faith in northern cities. In Antioch their gospel was well received by the Jewish community and by some non-Jews. These last, however, raised a question vital to the spread of Christianity: Must every convert accept the Mosaic Code, with its 613 laws? And circumcision? Paul and Barnabas did not insist on this, and they were soon challenged for violating the example of Christ. They went back to Jerusalem and fought out the matter with the Apostles. Peter sympathized with them, for he, too, had accepted uncircumcised converts. Most of the Apostles objected, feeling that circumcision was part of Abraham's covenant with God. Paul answered that unless non-Jewish converts were spared from this covenant, Christianity would be merely a branch of Judaism ("a Jewish heresy," Heine was to call it), and would fade out in a century. The Apostles yielded. Paul resumed his mission as "Apostle to the Gentiles," and carried the Gospel from Ephesus to Athens to

Rome. The fate of a great religion had for a moment depended on a fragment of flesh.

Paul was crucified in Rome, probably in that same year, 64, that saw Peter's death. Through their labors, and those of a thousand other carriers of the "Glad Tidings," the Christian Church took form and began its historic task of giving the dying Empire and its barbarian invaders a living faith, a sustaining hope, and a moral code based upon an omnipresent, all-powerful God.

THE CATHOLIC CHURCH

The weakening of respect for the established religion had given rise, as in our time, to a hundred net forms of supernatural belief and ritual. Among these were diverse Christian sects; and among these, the creed of the Apostles Peter and Paul proved ablest to survive and spread. By the year 300 the Christians in the Near East numbered a fourth of the population; in Rome the Christians were 100,000. Their stern theology supported a group morality that won the attention and praise of pagan philosophers: So Pliny the Younger reported to the emperor Trajan that the Christians led peaceful and exemplary lives (Pliny *Letters* 10.997); and the learned physician Galen described them as "far advanced in self-discipline and an intense desire to attain moral excellence." In 311, after three centuries of brutal persecutions, the Emperor Galerius, noting their futility, issued an edict of toleration, recognizing Christianity as a lawful religion, and asking prayers of the Christians in return for "our most gentle clemency."

In 312, Constantine, leading an army from Gaul to Turin to face rival claimants to the throne of Rome, saw in the sky (says a legend) a flaming cross adorned with the Greek words EN TOUTOI NIKA (By this conquer). On the next day he announced his acceptance of Christianity and won a decisive battle. He marched east, defeated a rival, and made Byzantium—later renamed Constantinople—the capital of an Eastern Roman Empire that soon displaced Rome as the center of political power.

Gradually thereafter, as the barbarian invasions unsettled secular authority, the protection and administration of social order fell from the pagan officials of towns in Western Europe into the hands of Christian bishops, abbots, and priests under the leadership of the pope at Rome; and the Church, rather than the State, became the source and guardian of civilization. Many of the so-called "barbarians" had already accepted Christianity and were more amenable to popes than to emperors.

The people of Western Europe settled down under warrior kings like Alfred the Great in England, Charlemagne in France, and imperial Ottos and Henrys in Germany; but these rulers sought consecration by the pope as a necessary prop and confirmation of their power—they could at any moment lose that power if the pope excommunicated them. Year by year the papacy grew in influence, until the kings recognized it as the supreme authority in all matters of morals—which might mean almost any major issue. So the emperor Henry IV came to Canossa (1077) to do penance and ask forgiveness and restoration by Pope Gregory VII, Hildebrand.

This "Christian Republic" or papal superstate reached its zenith under Pope Innocent III. In a rule of eighteen years (1198–1216) he forced all the monarchs of Latin Europe except Sverre of Norway to acknowledge his sovereignty in matters of faith, morals, and justice, including the power to free whole peoples from their oath of obedience to their kings. Some states—Portugal, Hungary, Serbia, Bulgaria, Armenia, even England under King John—acknowledged themselves as feudal fiefs of the papacy. In 1204 the conquest of Constantinople by the crusaders led the Greek Church to submit to the Roman papacy, and Innocent could proudly speak of the now "seamless garment of Christ." A Byzantine visitor to Rome described him as not merely the heir of Peter, but the successor of Constantine.

THE DARK SIDE

The victory of the word over the sword, and of the center over the parts of Christendom, was tarnished by the failure of the Crusades and the terrors of the Inquisition.

The Crusades, summoned into action by Pope Urban II in 1098, were the romantic effort of Europe, East and West, to recapture the Near East from Islam for Christendom in commerce and creed. They failed of either aim, for the Near East remained in Moslem hands, and the wealth, science, art, and scholarship of the Moors aroused in the defeated Crusaders a skepticism that soon afflicted Christian orthodoxy with a hundred heresies.

Innocent III, like any ruler, looked upon heresy as treason, as the divisive secession of the part from the order and peace of the whole. He was alarmed most of all by a new faith coming from the Balkans into France, forming powerful minorities in Montpellier, Narbonne, Marseille, Toulouse, Orléans—even in far north Soissons and Reims. These Albigensians divided the universe between God—representing spirit and the good—and Satan—representing matter and evil. They held all flesh to be satanic and all sexual relations to be impure. They accepted Christ's Sermon on the Mount as their ethic, and denounced war or any use of force, even against infidels. They rejected hell and purgatory, and announced that all men would be saved.

They denied that the Church was the Church of Christ; St. Peter had never come to Rome, had never founded the papacy; the popes were successors to the emperors, not to the Apostles. Christ had had no place to lay his head, but the pope lived in a palace. These lordly archbishops and bishops, these wordly priests and fat monks, were the Pharisees of old, returned to life. The Roman Church was the whore of Babylon, and the pope was the Antichrist.

For some time the Albigensians received a broad toleration, as extremists who were refuting themselves by their exaggerations. In 1167 they held a council of their clergy, attended by representatives from several countries; it discussed and regulated their doctrine, discipline, and administration, and adjourned without having been disturbed. Some of the nobility found it desirable to weaken the Church in Languedoc; the Church was rich, the nobles were relatively poor; a few began to seize Church property.

Innocent III, coming to the papacy in 1198, saw in these developments a threat to both the Church and the State. He recognized some excuse for criticism of the Church, but he felt that he could hardly remain idle when the great organization which he headed, and which seemed to him the chief bulwark against violence, social chaos, and royal iniquity, was attacked in its very foundation, robbed of its material support, and mocked with blasphemous travesties. How could any continuing social order be built upon principles that forbade parentage and defended suicide? Could the relations of the sexes, and the rearing of children, be rescued from a consuming disorder except by some such institution as marriage? What was the sense of a crusade against infidels in Palestine when these Albigensian infidels were multiplying in the heart of Christendom?

Two months after his accession, Innocent wrote to the archbishop of Auch in Gascony:

> The little boat of St. Peter is beaten by many storms, and tossed about on the sea. But it grieves me most of all . . . that . . . there are now arising more unrestrainedly and injuriously than ever before, ministers of diabolical error who are ensnaring the souls of the simple. With their superstitions and false inventions they are perverting the meaning of the Holy Catholic Scriptures, and trying to destroy the unity of the Catholic Church. Since . . . this pestilential error is growing in Gascony and the neighboring territories, we wish you and your follow bishops to resist it with all your might. . . . We give you a strict command that, by whatever means you can, you destroy all these heresies, and repel from your diocese all who are polluted by them. . . . If necessary, you may cause the princes and people to suppress them with the sword.

This edict was welcomed by orthodox rulers and prosperous ecclesiastics. Raymond VI of Toulouse agreed to use persuasion on the heretics, but refused to join a war against them. Innocent excommunicated him; Raymond promised to comply, was absolved, and proved negligent again. "How can we do it?" asked a knight who had been commanded by a papal legate to expel the Albigensians from their lands. "We have been brought up with these people, we have kindred among them, and we see them living righteously."

After six years of waiting, Innocent gave to Arnaud of Citeaux, head of the Cistercian monks, full power to establish an inquisition throughout France and to offer a plenary indulgence to kings and nobles who should join in the new crusade. When this, too, seemed inadequate, he laid under edict all lands subject to Count Raymond and offered them to any Christian who would seize them. He summoned the faithful from all over Europe to a crusade against the Albigensians and their protectors; and to all participants he offered a plenary indul-

gence relieving them from penalties for any past sins. Thousands
flocked to the holy war. When the crusaders approached Béziers, they
offered to spare it the horrors of war if it would surrender all heretics
listed by its bishop. The city leaders refused, saying that they would
rather stand siege till they should be reduced to eating their children.
The crusaders scaled the walls, captured the town, and slew 20,000
men, women, and children in indiscriminate massacre.

The most ruthless of the crusaders was Simon de Montfort. Like
many men of this swashbuckling age, he was famous for his chastity,
and had served with honor in Palestine. With his small army of 4,500
men, and urged on by the papal legate, he now assaulted town after
town, overcame all resistance, and gave the population a choice between swearing allegiance to the Roman faith or suffering death as
heretics. Thousands swore, hundreds chose death. For four years Simon
continued his campaigns, devastating nearly all the territory of Raymond VI except Toulouse. In 1215, Toulouse itself surrendered; Raymond was deposed by a council of prelates in Montpellier and Simon
succeeded to his title and most of his lands. In 1227, Raymond VII,
pledging to suppress a heresy, signed a treaty with Pope Gregory IX,
and the Albigensian wars came to an end. Orthodoxy triumphed, toleration ceased, and the Inquisition spread its power over Europe.

The Inquisition had no difficulty in finding biblical texts authoriz-
ing death for heresy—as in Deuteronomy 13:1–9; Exodus 22:18, and
in the Gospel of St. John 15:6. Nearly every Christian professed belief
that the Church had been established by the Son of God. On this assumption any attack upon the Catholic faith was an offense against
God Himself; the contumacious heretic could only be viewed as an
agent of Satan, sent to undo the work of Christ; and any man or government that tolerated heresy was serving Lucifer. Feeling herself an
inseparable part of the moral and political government of Europe, the
Church looked upon heresy precisely as the state looked upon treason;
it was an attack upon the foundations of social order. The most rigorous
code of suppression was enacted by Frederick II in 1220–39. Heretics
condemned by the Church were to be delivered to the "secular arm"—
the local authorities—and burned to death. If they recanted, they were
to be let off with imprisonment for life. All their property was to be

confiscated, their heirs were to be disinherited, their children were to be ineligible to any position of emolument or dignity unless they atoned for their parents' sin by denouncing other heretics. The houses of heretics were to be destroyed and were never to be rebuilt. The saintly King Louis IX placed similar laws among the statutes of France. In 1231, Gregory IX adopted into the laws of the Church Frederick II's legislation of 1224; henceforth Church and State agreed that impenitent heresy was treason, and should be punished with death.

State and Church united in a frightened attack upon heresies that would, in their view, undermine the complex structure of law and morals which kept men from reverting to moral and political anarchy. Nearly every challenged government had turned to inquisition, and punished opinions and conduct considered dangerous to the state.

Freedom is a luxury of security.

MEDIEVAL SONG

The Middle Ages adorned their millennium with literature often delightful, sometimes supreme in its kind. Unique were the troubadours who flourished in eleventh-century France, then in German lands and Spain, dressed like lords, brandishing swords as well as pens, and dreaming of delicate adulteries with noble ladies who—at most—allowed them to kiss a hand.

Presumably it was this inaccessibility that stimulated the verses; it is hard to romanticize desire fulfilled, and where there are no impediments, there is no poetry. The troubadours excelled in the aubade, or song of dawn, and the serena, or evening song; they courted the night and deplored the day.

In Germany the troubadours were Minnesingers—"singers of love"; so Walther von der Vogelweide ("of the bird-pasture") composed the famous ballad *Unter den Linden,* on the function of trees as umbrellas for romance. The late twelfth and early thirteenth centuries saw the composition of the chivalric romances about the quest for the Holy Grail— the sacred bowl from which Jesus had drunk at the Last Supper, and in which Joseph of Arimathea had caught some of the blood dripping from the crucified Christ. Around that legend grew the story of Parzival, most famously told by Wolfram von Eschenbach. Gottfried of Strasbourg provided another libretto for Richard Wagner by composing, in fluid German verse, the story of Tristan and Isolde. Meanwhile, Iceland and Scandinavia were unwinding endless sagas of Norse mythology.

More interesting to a wandering scholar are the "Wandering Scholars" who traveled from university to university, singing songs of rebellion or revelry. Here, most delicately scandalous, is a lover's explanation why he was in heaven:

> *When she recklessly*
> *Gave herself wholly unto Love and me,*
> *Beauty in heaven afar*
> *Laughed from her joyous star.*
> *Too great desire hath overwhelmed me;*
> *My heart's not great enough*
> *For this huge joy that overmastered me,*
> *What time my love*
> *Made in her arms another man of me,*
> *And all the gathered honey of her lips*
> *Drained in one yielded kiss.*
> *Again, again I dream the freedom given*
> *Of her soft breast;*
> *And so am come, another god, to heaven*
> *Among the rest;*
> *Yea, and serene would govern gods and men*
> *If I might find again*
> *My hand upon her breast.*

Wherever the wandering scholars went, they might be confident they would meet the same language of instruction—Latin. However, one of the pivotal events of the Middle Ages—almost marking their end—was Dante's choice of Italian instead of Latin as the vehicle of his trip through hell and purgatory to heaven. We may believe that Italian is the most beautiful of languages, and it seems so when it tells the story of Francesca da Rimini, or when, beginning the final canto, it addresses Mary:

Vergine Madre, figlia del tuo Figlio,
Umile ed alta più che creatura—(Dante Inferno 5.121f)

Virgin Mother, daughter of your son,
Humble and exalted beyond any creature—

But where else shall we find a line of greater power than that which the poet thought he saw inscribed over the gates of hell: *"Lasciate ogni speranza, voi ch'entrate!"*—"All hope abandon, ye who enter here!" *The Divine Comedy* of Dante is the strangest, the most terrible, and at times the most beautiful poem in all the literature of Christianity.

ABÉLARD AND HÉLOÏSE

Héloïse was an orphan girl of uncertain parentage, niece of Fulbert, a canon or clergyman on the staff of the cathedral of Paris (not yet the Notre Dame that was built a century later). He sent her to a nunnery famous for its school and library. When he learned that she could converse in Latin almost as readily as in French, and was studying Hebrew, he took pride in her and brought her to live in his quarters near the cathedral. To tutor her in philosophy and other advanced studies, he sought the idol and paragon of all the scholars of Paris.

Pierre Abélard had begun life in Brittany in or near 1079, as first son of a prosperous farmer. Brilliant at school, he was excited to hear of men called philosophers, who proposed to prove by reason alone the articles of their religious faith. Abandoning his rights of inheritance, he set out to study philosophy wherever he could find it.

His quest soon led him to Paris, and its cathedral school, where William of Champeaux (by Abélard's account) was teaching realism—which then meant that universal or class names—such as "man," "crowd," "stone," "woman," "book"—had an objective existence and reality additional to the reality of any individual member of the class; so "man" was as real as "Socrates"; the crowd was as real as any individual in it, and had its own logic and character. No, said Abélard; nothing exists outside of our minds, except specific individual men, specific things; all general ideas are conceptions formed as tools of classification and thought.

Abélard organized his own school, first at Melun, then at Mon Geneviève, just outside Paris. There his eloquence and brilliance and joy in the intellect attracted more students than he could house. They called themselves *moderni,* and founded a *schola moderna,* or modern school. Abélard's fame had spread through France when Fulbert invited him to tutor Héloïse.

The year was 1117; he was thirty-eight, she seventeen. He admits that his first feeling for her was physical attraction, but this was soon transformed by Héloïse's delicacy into what he described as a "tenderness surpassing in sweetness the most fragrant balm." She seems to have yielded to him with almost childish trust; soon she was pregnant.

He sent her to his sister's home in Brittany, and calmed Fulbert by offering to marry her, on condition that the canon should keep the union secret. Héloïse long refused to marry him, for this would bar him from the priesthood unless she should give up her husband and her child and enter a nunnery. If we may believe Abélard's autobiographical *Historia Calamitatum,* she told him that "it would be far sweeter for her to be called 'my mistress' than be known as 'my wife'; nay, this would be more honorable for me as well."

She finally consented, and she, Abélard, and Fulbert agreed to keep the marriage secret. Soon Fulbert, to quiet scandal, revealed the legal union. Héloïse denied it; Fulbert beat her; Abélard sent her to a nunnery, bidding her accept the garb, but not the vows, of a nun.

Fulbert hired ruffians to castrate Abélard. His emasculation did not immediately disgrace him, though it did disqualify him for the priesthood; all Paris, including the clergy, sympathized with him; students flocked to comfort him—but Abélard realized that he was ruined. He bade Héloïse take the veil and the vows, and he himself took the vows of a monk. Allowed to teach again, he and his pupils built, near Troyes, a hermitage for shelter and an oratory for prayer, which he called the Paraclete—"God as the Consoler"—as if to say that the loyal affection of his disciples had come like a divine comforter into his life amid his solitude and despair.

Slowly recovering his health and courage, Abélard gave himself now to writing some of the most important books in medieval philosophy. In his massive *Dialectica* he reformulated the rules of reasoning for the renascent mind of Western Europe. In his *Dialogue Between a Philoso-*

pher, a Jew, and a Christian, he allowed each of the three to expose weaknesses in the doctrines of the other two. In *Sic et Non*—i.e., *Yes and No*—he posed 157 questions, under each of which he gave an argument for the affirmative and one for the negative. In the prologue he argued that "the first key to wisdom is assiduous and frequent questioning. . . . For by doubting we come to inquiry, and by inquiring we arrive at truth." In *Theologia christiana* he rejected as unreasonable the claim that only a Christian could be saved; God, he argued, gives his love to all peoples. Heretics should be restrained by reason, not by force.

In 1140, St. Bernard, zealous for the Catholic faith, persuaded a Church council at Sens to condemn several of Abélard's views. The philosopher, though now infirm with age and tribulation, set out for Rome to lay his case before the pope. He reached the monastery of Cluny in Burgundy and was well received by its abbot, the saintly Peter the Venerable. There he learned that Innocent II had already confirmed the verdict of the Council of Sens, and had imposed upon him perpetual silence and monastic confinement.

Weary to physical and spiritual exhaustion, Abélard hid himself in the obscurity of Cluny's cells and ritual. He edified his fellow monks by his piety, his silence, and his prayers. He wrote to Héloïse—whom he never saw again—and reaffirmed his faith in the teachings of the Church. He composed, perhaps for her eyes, some of the most beautiful hymns in medieval literature.

Soon he fell ill, and his kindly abbot sent him to the priory of St. Marcel near Chalons. There, on April 21, 1142, he died, age sixty-three. He was buried in the priory chapel, but Héloïse, who was now abbess at the Paraclete, reminded Peter the Venerable that Abélard had asked to be interred there. The good abbot took the body to her himself, tried to comfort her by speaking of Abélard as the Socrates, Plato, and Aristotle of his time, and left with her a letter rich in Christian tenderness:

> Thus, dear and venerable sister in God, him to whom you were united, after your tie in the flesh, by the better and stronger bond of divine love, . . . the Lord now takes in your stead, or as another you, and warms in his bosom; and for the day of His coming, . . . keeps him to restore him to you by His grace.

She joined her dead lover in 1164, having lived to equal his age, and almost his fame. She was buried beside him in the gardens of the Paraclete. That oratory was destroyed in the Revolution, and the graves were disturbed, and perhaps confused. What were reasonably believed to be the remains of Abélard and Héloïse were transferred to Père Lachaise Cemetery in Paris in 1817. There, even in our time, men and women might be seen, on a summer Sunday, bringing flowers to adorn the tomb.

THE MEDIEVAL ACHIEVEMENT

First of all was the transformation of medieval Europe—north of the Rhône, the Rhine, and the Danube—from a wilderness of forest, jungle, and marsh into the earthly basis of new and enduring civilizations. Men and women cleared roads, cut canals, dug wells and mines, built habitations, domesticated themselves and useful animals, organized villages, towns, and cities, developed laws, juries, parliaments, and disciplined youth through parental authority, schools, and religion.

Medieval man risked all on religion. He had seen, or had been told of, a Roman civilization dying with the death of its gods, or the lapse of human fear thereof; he knew, from his own youth, the power and persistence of unsocial habits and desires; and he welcomed in maturity the theological beliefs, moral commandments, priestly exhortations, and theological terrors that might in some measure check the pride and insolence of youths, the crimes of adults, and the wars and sins of states.

He welcomed a Church that taught barbarians to be citizens, that encouraged chastity and chivalry, and persuaded some warriors to be gentlemen. He resented the laziness of monks, was grateful for the devotion of nuns, and appreciated the ecclesiastical organization of charity. He gloried in the cathedrals, smiled at their bright windows, laughed with their gargoyles, and might see in their flying buttresses fountain jets petrified in their flow. He was proud to belong to a Church whose popes could regulate states and chasten kings.

Time strengthened the Church by increasing her wealth and spread; it weakened her by promoting secular affluence, disruptive individualism, political chicanery, and skeptical intellect. The Church had shared vitally in developing universities that rivaled the cathedrals in splendor and influence; she had provided and trained most of the teachers and had dignified them with religious garb; but increasingly these men pursued knowledge and secular advancement rather than faith and ecclesiastical careers. Clergy and laity who joined in searching, preserving, and editing classical manuscripts discovered the charm and depth of ancient literature and philosophy, and began to talk of Plato with greater zest than of Christ.

The medieval soul, like a swelling cell, burst into two historical organisms: the classical, Epicurean, pagan Renaissance in the south, and the patristic, Stoic, puritan Reformation in the north. It became two powerful cultures, and through them fulfilled its historic task of saving and transmitting civilization.

Its death was its fulfillment.

THE RENAISSANCE I:
AROUND LEONARDO

PETRARCH AND BOCCACCIO

The Middle Ages passed into the Renaissance when, on Good Friday 1327, in a church at papal Avignon, Francesco Petrarca saw Laura di Sade, whose delicate beauty, doubled by modesty, made him forget all other divinity but hers.

She received the poet's adoration calmly, and gave his passion all the stimulus of denial. Through the next twenty-six years he composed 207 poems—all about her—in the most exquisite music that the most exquisite of languages had yet known. Listen:

> *In qual parte del ciel, in quale idea*
> *Era l'essempio, onde Natura tolse*
> *Quel bel viso leggiadro, in ch'ella volse*
> *Mostrar qua giú quanto lassú potea?*
> *Qual ninfa in fonti, in solve mai qual dea,*
> *D'pro si fino a l'aura sciolse?*
> *Quando un cor tante in sé vertuti accolse?*
> *Benché la somma è di mia morte rea.*
> *Per divina bellezza indarno mira*
> *Chi gli occhi de costei già mai non vide*
> *Come soavemente ella gli gira,*

Non sa come Amor sana, a come ancide,
Chi non sa come dolce ella sospira,
E come dolce parla, e dolce ride.

Who shall translate that melody? In Italian and Spanish the vowel has conquered the consonant; in English and German the vowel is overcome by the consonants. Nevertheless, Joseph Auslander's translation is bravely good:

In what bright realm, what sphere of radiant thought,
Did Nature find the model whence she drew
That delicate dazzling image where we view
Here on this earth what she in heaven wrought?
What fountain-haunting nymph, what dryad sought
In groves, such golden tresses ever threw
Upon the gust? What heart such virtues knew?—
Though her chief virtue with my death is fraught
He looks in vain for heavenly beauty, he
Who never looked upon her perfect eyes,
The vivid blue eyes burning brilliantly—
He does not know how Love yields and denies;
He only knows who knows how sweetly she
Can talk and laugh, the sweetness of her sighs.

Petrarch's poems, his sensitivity to beauty in woman, nature, literature, and art gave voice to a basic Italian mood, and his passionate pursuit and translation of classic manuscripts endeared him to poets and prelates throughout Western Europe.

In Rome, on April 8, 1341, a colorful procession of youths and senators escorted Petrarch to the steps of the Capitol, and there laid a laurel crown upon his head. From that day kings and popes gladly received him at their courts as the reigning prince of European letters. Boccaccio ranked him with "the illustrious ancients," and Italy proclaimed that Virgil had been born again.

Boccaccio himself was then twenty-eight years old. He had begun life in Paris as the unpremeditated result of an entente cordiale between his father, a Florentine merchant, and a French lass of libertarian principles. Perhaps his unscheduled birth and semi-Gallic origin influenced his character and style.

In 1331—four years after Petrarch's ecstasy—Boccaccio fell in love while worshiping in a Neapolitan church. The lady was Maria d' Aquino, known for her attractive piety and golden hair. He called her *Fiametta*—Little Flame—and longed to singe himself in her fire. For five years he pursued her with poetry and prose. She let him wait till other purses ran dry, and then accepted him till his purse ran dry. Boccaccio left Naples and settled in Florence.

There, in 1348, the Great Plague of the Black Death came, and killed half the 100,000 population. Boccaccio's *Decameron* begins with a frightful description of the mortality: almost every family in Florence doomed to see member after member dying, watching the infected one leaving home to go and die nameless in the street. Boccaccio made his *Decameron* take its plan from the plague: seven young ladies, related or neighbors, meet in church and agree to leave Florence together, with their servants, and to stay at some country villa till the plague should wear itself out. As a pleasant way to mitigate boredom, they invite three of their male friends to accompany them. They settle in a spacious country chateau, and plan to wile away the hours by having each tell a story on each day. As they remained together ten days, they told a hundred tales. Hence, Boccaccio entitled his collection *Decameron*, which was Greek for "ten days" (*deka hemerai*). Some of these novelle are crudely sensual, like that of the virile Masetto, who took care of an entire nunnery; some are stories of virtuous love, like that of the patient Griselda; some have a philosophical import, like the legend of the three equally precious rings, symbolizing the Jewish, Christian, and Mohammedan creeds. We gather that Boccaccio represented a middle class which was losing faith in a literal Christianity, even in the Christian moral code.

So, in its very infancy, the Renaissance was voting for delights and challenges of this earthly world instead of the hypothetical pleasures of a postmortem paradise. The Renaissance restored not only the literature of classical antiquity, but equally its pursuit of a hedonistic freedom. It was in part a pagan liberation of the senses after a thousand years of moral discipline resting on supernatural beliefs.

FLORENCE UNDER THE MEDICI: 1378–1492

The Economic Base

But it took more than a revival of antiquity to make the Renaissance. First of all it took money—smelly, bourgeois money: the profits of skillful managers and lowly labor; of hazardous voyages to the East, and arduous crossings of the Alps, to buy goods cheap and sell them dear; of careful calculations, investments, and loans; of interest and dividends accumulated until enough surplus could be spared from the pleasures of the flesh, from the purchase of senates, signories, and mistresses, to pay a Michelangelo or a Titian to transmute wealth into beauty, and perfume a fortune with the breath of art.

Money is the root of all civilization. The funds of merchants, bankers, and the Church paid for the manuscripts that revived antiquity. Nor was it chiefly those manuscripts that freed the mind and senses of the Renaissance; it was the secularism that came from the rise of the middle classes; it was the growth of the universities, of knowledge and philosophy, the realistic sharpening of minds by the study of history and law, the broadening of minds by wider acquaintance with the world. Doubting the dogmas of the transmitted creed, and seeing the clergy as being as epicurean as the laity, the educated Italian shook himself loose from intellectual and ethical restraints; his liberated senses took unabashed delight in all embodiments of beauty in nature, woman, man, and art; and his new freedom made him creative for an amazing century (1434–1534) before it destroyed him with moral chaos, disintegrative individualism, and national subjection. The interlude between two disciplines was the Renaissance.

Why was northern Italy the first to experience this spring awakening? There the old Roman wells had never been quite destroyed; the towns had kept their ancient structure and memories, and now renewed their Roman law.

Classic art survived in Rome, Verona, Mantua, Padua; Agrippa's Pantheon still functioned as a place of worship, though it was fourteen hundred years old; and in the Forum one could almost hear Cicero and Caesar debating the fate of Catiline. The Latin language was still a living tongue, of which Italian was merely a melodious variant. Pagan deities, myths, and rites lingered in popular memory, or under Christian forms. Italy stood athwart the Mediterranean, commanding that basin of classic civilization and trade.

Northern Italy was more urban and industrial than any other region of Europe except Flanders. It had never suffered a full feudalism, but had subjected its nobles to its cities and its merchant class. It was the avenue of trade between the rest of Italy and Transalpine Europe, and between Western Europe and the Levant; its commerce and industry made it the richest region in Christendom. Its adventurous traders were everywhere, from the fairs of France to the farthest ports of the Black Sea. Accustomed to dealing with Greeks, Arabs, Jews, Egyptians, Persians, Hindus, and Chinese, they lost the edge of their dogmas, and brought into the literate classes of Italy that same indifference to creeds which in nineteenth-century Europe came—a second time—from widening contact with alien faiths.

So Italy advanced, in wealth and art and thought, a century ahead of the rest of Europe; and it was only in the sixteenth century, when the Renaissance faded in Italy, that it blossomed in France, Germany, Holland, England, and Spain. The Renaissance was not a period in time, but a mode of life and thought, moving from Italy through Europe with the course of commerce, war, and ideas.

It made its first home in Florence for much the same reasons that gave it birth in Italy. Through the organization of industry, the extension of her commerce, and the operation of her financiers, Florence, the city of flowers, was in the fourteenth century the richest town in the peninsula, excepting Venice. While the Venetians in that age gave their energies almost entirely to the pursuit of pleasure and wealth, the Florentines, possibly through the stimulus of a turbulent semidemocracy, developed a keenness of mind and wit, and a skill in every art that made their city, by common consent, the cultural capital of Italy. The quarrels of the factions raised the temperature of life and thought; rival families contended in the patronage of art as well as in the pursuit of power.

A happy stimulus was added when Cosimo de' Medici offered the resources of his own and other fortunes and palaces to house and entertain the delegates to the Council of Florence (1439). The Greek prelates and scholars who came to that assembly to discuss the union of Eastern and Western Christianity had a far better knowledge of Greek literature than any Florentine could then possess; some of them lectured in Florence, and the elite of the city crowded to hear them. When Constantinople fell to the Turks (1453), many Greeks left it to make their home in the city where they had found such hospitality fourteen years before. Several of them brought additional manuscripts of ancient texts. So, by the concourse of diverse streams of influence, the Renaissance took form in Florence, and made it the Athens of Italy.

Behind the cultural primacy of Florence lay its industry, commerce, and finance. About a fourth of its population was engaged in industry. As early as 1300, Florence had two textile factories, employing some 30,000 men and women; it had reached the stage of large investment, central provision of materials and machines, systematic specialization of labor, and control of production by suppliers of capital.

To finance this industrial revolution, Florence had eighty banking houses, which performed almost all the functions of a modern bank; issuing letters of credit, lending substantial sums to individuals, businesses, and governments—e.g., 1,365,000 florins to Edward III of England; cashing checks, inverting the savings of their depositors, stabilizing peace, financing war. From the thirteenth through the fifteenth century Florence was the financial capital of Europe; there the rates of exchange were fixed. In 1345 the Florentine state issued negotiable bonds paying 5 percent interest, and redeemable in gold at maturity. In 1400 the revenues of the government of Florence exceeded the total governmental revenue of Elizabethan England.

The bankers, merchants, manufacturers, professional men, and skilled workers of Florence and its realm—and of Western Europe generally—were organized in twenty-one guilds called, in Italy, *arti,* or "trades"; the word "art" was applied to every skilled work, and had not yet received an esthetic connotation.

Every voter had to be a member of a recognized guild. Below the twenty-one guilds were seventy-two unions of voteless workers; below these, thousands of day laborers forbidden to organize; below these, a few slaves. The formal government of Florence was headed by the Signoria, or council of *signori,* or gentlemen, chosen by lot from the leaders of the guilds, and checked occasionally by a Consiglio del Popolo chosen from guild members in general. But the actual government was usually a banker who could organize florins into influence subtler and stronger than electoral power. In Florence's golden age this was Cosimo de' Medici.

Cosimo de' Medici

The name is a puzzle: we find no medicos in his ancestry. In 1428, at age thirty-nine, he fell heir to the largest fortune in Tuscany, controlling a bank, extensive farms, some silk and woolen factories, and a varied trade with Russia, Syria, Scotland, and Spain. He was on cordial terms with cardinals and sultans. He contributed so heavily to public works and charities that the populace quietly accepted his indirect dictatorship of Florentine affairs.

History also gives him its vote because he found money enough to finance a score of scholars, artists, poets, and philosophers. He spent part of his fortune collecting classic texts. When Niccolò de' Niccoli ruined himself in buying ancient manuscripts, Cosimo opened for him unlisted credit at the Medici bank, and supported him till Niccolò's death.

He engaged forty-five copyists to transcribe such manuscripts as could not be bought. He placed his "precious minims" (as Walt Whitman described them) in the monastery of San Marco, or in an abbey at nearby Fiesole, or in his own library, and opened these collections to teachers and students without charge.

He established in Florence (1445) a Platonic Academy for the study of Plato, and enabled Marsilio Ficino to give half a lifetime to the translation and exposition of Plato's works. Now, after a reign of four hundred years, scholasticism lost its sovereignty over philosophy in the West, and the exhilarating spirit of Plato entered like energizing yeast into the rising body of European thought.

We are not attempting here a history of the Renaissance, of all its intellectual explorations and artistic splendors, but we must note in passing that, in this Florentine zenith, Filippo Brunelleschi raised over the cathedral of Santa Maria del Fiore a precarious cupola rising 133 feet above its supporting walls and dominating, for leagues around, the panorama of a red-roofed Florence nestling like a bed of roses in the lap of Tuscan hills. In that same age Lorenzo Ghiberti designed, and carved in bronze, those paneled portals that made the Baptistery of Florence one of the lasting glories of the Renaissance.

Donatello, a pupil of Ghiberti, thought those doors too feminine in the grace of their line; his own spirit was masculine and boldly innovative. In 1430 he cast for Cosimo a bronze *David* that must have stirred Michelangelo to rivalry; here the nude figure in the round made its unblushing debut in Renaissance sculpture. In Padua's Piazza San Antonio, the ambitious sculptor, after six years of labor, raised the first important equestrian statue of modern times, representing the wily Venetian general nicknamed Gattamelata—the "honeyed cat." Cosimo called Donatello back to Florence and gave him commission after commission.

Donatello not only produced a succession of masterpieces; he persuaded Cosimo to buy choice relics of ancient sculpture, and to place them in the Medici gardens for young artists to study. Patron and artist grew old together, and Cosimo took such care of the sculptor that Donatello rarely thought of money. He kept his funds (says Vasari) in a basket suspended from the ceiling of his studio, and bade his aides and friends to take from it according to their needs, without consulting him. He lived in simplicity, content, to the age of eighty. All the artists—nearly all the people—of Florence joined in the funeral that laid him to rest, as he had asked, in the crypt of San Lorenzo, beside Cosimo's own tomb (1466).

Lorenzo

Cosimo had died in 1464. His son Piero inherited his father's wealth, authority, and gout, and earned the name Il Gottoso. He ruled unhappily for five years, died in 1469, and left his power to his son Lorenzo, the future Il Magnifico.

Cosimo had done his best to prepare the bright youth for the management of money and men. Lorenzo was tutored in Greek and philosophy, and absorbed a dozen disciplines by hearing the conversation of poets, statesmen, artists, humanists, and generals. He wrote passionate sonnets to highbrow ladies. Piero, thinking marriage a good cure for romance, persuaded him to marry Clarice Orsini, so allying the Medici with one of the two most powerful families in Rome. From that union would come Popes Leo X and Clement VII.

Two days after Piero's death, a deputation of leading citizens came to Lorenzo and asked him to assume the guidance of the state. Circum-

stances convinced him. The finances of the Medici firm were so entan-
gled with those of the city that he feared ruin if the enemies or rivals of
his house should capture political power. To quiet criticism of his consent, he appointed a council of experienced citizens to advise him on all
matters of major importance.

He consulted the council throughout his career, but he soon showed
such good judgment that it rarely questioned his leadership. He ruled
as Cosimo and Piero had done, remaining (till 1490) a private citizen,
but recommending policies to a *balia* (council) in which the supporters
of his house had a safe majority.

The citizens acquiesced because prosperity continued. When Galeazzo Maria Sforza, duke of Milan, visited Florence in 1471, he was
amazed at the signs of wealth in the city, and still more at art that
Cosimo, Piero, and Lorenzo had gathered in the Medici palace and gardens. Here already was a museum of statuary, vases, gems, paintings,
illuminated manuscripts, and architectural remains and models.
Galeazzo declared that he had seen a greater number of fine paintings
in this one collection than in all the rest of Italy.

Amid the general prosperity, old factions kept their peace, crime
abated, order prospered, though liberty declined. "We have here,"
wrote a contemporary, "no robberies, no nocturnal commotions, no as-
sassinations. By night or day every person may transact his affairs in
perfect safety." "If Florence was to have a despot," said the judicious
historian Guicciardini, "she could never have found a more delightful
one." The merchants preferred prosperity to freedom, the proletariat
was quieted with public works ensuring employment, tournaments al-
lured the elite, horse races thrilled the bourgeoisie, pageants amused
the populace.

It was the custom of the Florentines in Carnival days to promenade
the streets in gay or frightful masks, singing satirical or erotic songs.
Lorenzo relished the jollity, but distrusted its tendency to disorder and
so ultimately resolved to bring it under control by lending it the approval and order of government; under his rule the pageants became
the most popular feature of Florentine life. He engaged leading artists
to design and paint the chariots, banners, and costumes; he and his
friends composed lyrics to be sung from the *carri;* and these songs reflected the moral relaxation of the carnival.

The most famous of Lorenzo's pageants was the "Triumph of Bacchus," wherein a procession of floats carrying lovely maidens, and a cavalcade of richly garbed youths on prancing steeds, came over the Ponte Vecchio to the spacious square before the cathedral, while voices in polyphonic harmony, to the accompaniment of cymbals and lutes, sang a poem composed by Lorenzo himself, and hardly becoming a cathedral:

1. *Quanto e bella giovinezza,* 1. Fair is youth and void of sorrow,
   Che si fuge tutta via!   But it hourly flies away.
   Chi vuol esser lieto sia!   Youths and maids, enjoy today;
   Di doman non c'e certezza. Nought ye know about tomorrow.

2. This is Bacchus and the bright Ariadne, lovers true!
   They, in flying time's despite,
   Each with each finds pleasures new;

3. These, their nymphs, and all their crew
   Keep perpetual holiday.
   Youths and maids, enjoy today;
   Nought ye know about tomorrow . . .

14. Ladies and gay lovers young!
    Long live Bacchus, live Desire!
    Dance and play, let songs be sung;
    Let sweet love your bosoms fire.

15. In the future come what may
    Youths and maids enjoy today;
    Nought ye know about tomorrow.

Such poems and pageants lend some pale color to the charge that Lorenzo corrupted Florentine youth. Probably it would have been "corrupt" without him; morals in Venice, Ferrara, and Milan were no better than in Florence; they were better in Florence under the Medici bankers than later in Rome under the Medici popes.

Lorenzo's esthetic sensibilities were too keen for his morals. Poetry was one of his prime devotions, and his compositions rivaled the best of his time. While his only superior, Politian, still hesitated between Latin and Italian, Lorenzo's verses restored to the vernacular the literary primacy that Dante had established and the humanists had overthrown. He preferred Petrarch's sonnets to the love poetry of the Latin classics, though he could read these easily in the original; and more than once he himself composed a sonnet that might have graced Petrarch's *Canzoniere*. But he did not take poetic love too seriously. He wrote with finer sincerity about the rural scenes that gave exercise to his limbs and peace to his mind; his best poems celebrate the woods and streams, trees and flowers, flocks and shepherds, of the countryside. Sometimes he wrote humorous pieces in terza rima that lifted the simple language of the peasantry into sprightly verse; sometimes he composed satirical farces Rabelaisianly free; then again, a religious play for his children, and some hymns that catch here and there a note of honest piety. But his most characteristic poems were the *Canti carnascialeschi*—Carnival Songs—written to be sung in festival time and mood, and expressing the legitimacy of pleasure and the discourtesy of maidenly prudence. Nothing could better illustrate the morals and manners, the complexity and diversity of the Italian Renaissance than the picture of its most central character ruling a state, managing a fortune, jousting in tournament, writing excellent poetry, supporting artists and authors with discriminating patronage, mingling at ease with scholars and philosophers, peasants and buffoons, marching in pageants, singing bawdy songs, composing tender hymns, playing with mistresses, begetting a pope, and honored throughout Europe as the greatest and noblest Italian of his time.

THE AGE OF POLITIAN

Encouraged by his aid and example, Florentine men of letters now wrote more and more of their works in Italian. Slowly they formed that literary Tuscan which became the model and standard of the whole peninsula—"the sweetest, richest, and most cultured, not only of all the languages of Italy," said the patriotic Varchi, "but of all the tongues that are known today."

But while reviving Italian literature, Lorenzo carried on zealously his grandfather's enterprise of gathering for the use of scholars in Florence all the classics of Greece and Rome. He sent Politian and John

Lascaris to various cities in Italy and abroad to buy manuscripts; from one monastery at Mt. Athos Lascaris brought two hundred, of which eighty were as yet unknown to Western Europe. According to Politian, Lorenzo wished that he might be allowed to spend his entire fortune, even to pledge his furniture, in the purchase of books. He paid scribes to make copies for him of manuscripts that could not be purchased, and in return he allowed other collectors, like King Matthias Corvinus of Hungary and Duke Federigo of Urbino, to send their copyists to transcribe manuscripts in the Medicean Library. After Lorenzo's death this collection was united with that which Cosimo had placed in the convent of San Marco; together, in 1495, they included 1,039 volumes, of which 460 were Greek. Michelangelo later designed a lordly home for these books, and posterity gave it Lorenzo's name—Bibliotheca Laurentiana, the Laurentian Library. When Bernardo Cennini set up a printing press in Florence (1471) Lorenzo did not, like his friend Politian or Federigo of Urbino, turn up his nose at the new art; he seems to have recognized at once the revolutionary possibilities of movable type; and he engaged scholars to collate diverse texts in order that the classics might be printed with the greatest accuracy possible at that time. So encouraged, Bartolommeo di Libri printed the *editio priceps* of Homer (1488) under the careful scholarship of Demetrius Chatcondyles; John Lascaris issued the *editiones principes* of Euripides (1494), the *Greek Anthology* (1494), and Lucian (1496); and Cristoforo Landino edited Horace (1482), Virgil, Pliny the Elder, and Dante, whose language and allusions already required elucidation. We catch the spirit of the time when we learn that Florence rewarded Cristoforo, for these labors of scholarship, with the gift of a splendid home.

Lured by the reputation of the Medici and other Florentines for generous patronage, scholars flocked to Florence and made it the capital of literary learning. To develop and transmit the intellectual legacy of the race, Lorenzo restored and enlarged the old University of Pisa, and the Platonic Academy at Florence. The latter was no formal college but an association of men interested in Plato, meeting at irregular intervals in Lorenzo's city palace or in Ficino's villa at Careggi, dining together, reading aloud part or all of a Platonic dialogue, and discussing its philosophy. November 7, the supposed anniversary of Plato's birth and death, was celebrated by the Academy with almost religious solemnity; a bust believed to be of Plato was crowned with flowers, and a lamp was burned before it as before the image of a deity.

Among those who attended the discussions of the Platonic Academy were Politian, Pico della Mirandola, Michelangelo, and Marsilio Ficino. Marsilio had been so faithful to Cosimo's commission as to devote almost all his life to translating Plato into Latin and to studying, teaching, and writing about Platonism. In youth he was so handsome that the maidens of Florence eyed him possessively, but he cared less for them than for his books. For a time he lost his religious faith; Platonism seemed superior; he addressed his students as "beloved in Plato" rather than "beloved in Christ"; "he burned candles before a bust of Plato, and adored him as a saint." Christianity appeared to him, in this mood, as but one of the many religions that hid elements of truth behind their allegorical dogmas and symbolic rites. St. Augustine's writings, and gratitude for recovery from a critical illness, won him back to the Christian faith. At forty he became a priest, but he remained an enthusiastic Platonist. Socrates and Plato, he argued, had expounded a monotheism as noble as that of the Prophets; they, too, in their minor way, had received a divine revelation; so, indeed, had all men in whom reason ruled. Following his lead, Lorenzo and most of the humanists sought not to replace Christianity with another faith, but to reinterpret it in terms that a philosopher could accept. For a generation or two (1447–1534) the Church smiled tolerantly on the enterprise.

Next to Lorenzo himself, Count Giovanni Pico della Mirandola was the most fascinating personality in the Platonic Academy. Born in the town (near Modena) made famous by his name, he studied at Bologna and Paris, and was received with honor at almost every court in Europe; finally Lorenzo persuaded him to make Florence his home. His eager mind took up one study after another—poetry, philosophy, architecture, music—and achieved in each some outstanding excellence. Politian described him as a paragon in whom Nature had united all her gifts: "tall and finely molded, with something of divinity shining in his face"; a man of penetrating glance, indefatigable study, miraculous memory, and ecumenical erudition, eloquent in several languages, a favorite with women and philosophers, and as lovable in character as he was handsome in person and eminent in all qualities of intellect. His mind was open to every philosophy and every faith; he could not find it in him to reject any system, any man; and though in his final years he spurned astrology, he welcomed mysticism and magic as readily as he accepted Plato and Christ. He had a good word to say for the Scholastic philosophers, whom most other humanists repudiated as having barbarously expressed absurdities. He found much to admire in Arabic and Jewish thought, and numbered several Jews among his teachers and honored friends. He studied the Hebrew Cabala, innocently accepted its alleged antiquity, and announced that he had found in it full proofs for the divinity of Christ. As one of his feudal titles was Count of Concordia, he assumed the high duty of reconciling all the great religions of the West—Judaism, Christianity, and Islam—and these with Plato, and Plato with Aristotle. Though flattered by all, he retained to the end of his brief life a charming modesty that was impaired only by his ingenuous trust in the accuracy of his learning and the power of human reason.

Going to Rome at the age of twenty-four (1486), he startled priests and pundits by publishing a list of nine hundred propositions, covering logic, metaphysics, theology, ethics, mathematics, physics, magic, and the Cabala, and including the generous heresy that even the greatest mortal sin, being finite, could not merit eternal punishment. Pico proclaimed his readiness to defend any or all of these propositions in public debate against any person, and offered to pay the traveling expenses of any challenger from whatever land he might come. As a preface to this proposed tournament of philosophy he prepared a famous oration, later entitled *De hominis dignitate* (On the Dignity of Man), which expressed with youthful ardor the high opinion that the humanists—contradicting most medieval views—held of the human species. "It is a commonplace of the schools," wrote Pico, "that man is a little world, in which we may discern a body mingled of earthly elements, and a heavenly spirit, and the vegetable soul of plants, and the senses of the lower animals, and reason, and the mind of angels, and the likeness of God." And then Pico put into the mouth of God Himself, as words spoken to Adam, a divine testimony to the limitless potentialities of man: "I created thee as being neither heavenly nor earthly—that thou mightest be free to shape and to overcome thyself. Thou mayest sink into a beast, or be born anew to the divine likeness." To which Pico added, in the high spirit of the young Renaissance:

> This is the culminating gift of God, this is the supreme and marvelous felicity of man . . . that he can be that which he wills to be. Animals, from the moment of their birth, carry with them, from their mothers' bodies, all that they are destined to have or be; the highest spirits [angels] are from the beginning . . . what they will be forever. But God the Father endowed man, from birth, with the seeds of every possibility and every life.

No one cared to accept Pico's multifarious challenge, but Pope Innocent VIII condemned three of the propositions as heretical. Since these formed so tiny a proportion of the whole, Pico might have expected mercy, and indeed, Innocent did not press the matter. But Pico issued a cautious retraction, and departed for Paris, where the University offered him protection. In 1493 Alexander VI, with his wonted geniality, notified Pico that all was forgiven. Back in Florence, Pico became a devout follower of Savonarola, abandoned his pursuit of omniscience, burned his five volumes of love poetry, gave his fortune to provide marriage dowries for poor girls, and himself adopted a semimonastic life. He thought of joining the Dominican order, but died before he could make up his mind—still a youth of thirty-one. His influence survived his brief career, and inspired Reuchlin to continue, in Germany, those Hebrew studies which had been among the passions of Pico's life.

LORENZO PASSES

For some time before his death Lorenzo perceived that he, who had preached the gospel of joy, had not much longer to live.

His wife died in 1488; and though he had been unfaithful to her he sincerely mourned her loss and missed her helping hand. She had given him numerous progeny, of whom seven survived. He had sedulously supervised their education, and in his later years he labored to guide them into marriages that might redound to the happiness of Florence as well as their own.

Lorenzo retired from active participation in the government of Florence, delegated more and more of his public and private business to his son Piero, and sought comfort in the peace of the countryside and the conversation of his friends. He excused himself in a characteristic letter.

> What can be more desirable to a well-regulated mind than the enjoyment of leisure with dignity? This is what all good men wish to obtain, but which great men alone accomplish. In the midst of public affairs we may indeed be allowed to look forward to a day of rest; but no rest should totally seclude us from an attention to the concerns of our country. I cannot deny that the path which it has been my lot to tread has been arduous and rugged, full of dangers, and beset with treachery; but I console myself in having contributed to the welfare of my country, the prosperity of which may now rival that of any other state, however flourishing. Nor have I been inattentive to the interests and advancement of my own family, having always proposed to my imitation the example of my grandfather Cosimo, who watched over his public and private concerns with equal vigilance. Having now obtained the object of my cares, I trust I may be allowed to enjoy the sweets of leisure, to share the reputation of my fellow-citizens, and to exult in the glory of my native place.

But little time was left him to enjoy his unaccustomed peace. He had hardly moved to his villa at Careggi (March 21, 1492) when his stomach pains became alarmingly intense. Specialist physicians were summoned, who made him drink a mixture of jewels. He became rapidly worse, and reconciled himself to death. He expressed to Pico and Politian his sorrow that he could not live long enough to complete his collection of manuscripts for their accommodation and the use of students. As the end approached he sent for a priest, and with his last strength insisted on leaving his bed to receive the sacrament on his knees. He thought now of the uncompromising preacher who had denounced him as a destroyer of liberty and a corrupter of youth, and he longed to have that man's forgiveness before he died. He despatched a friend to beg Savonarola to come to him to hear his confession and give him a more precious absolution. Savonarola came. According to Politian he offered absolution on three conditions: that Lorenzo should have a lively faith in God's mercy, should promise to mend his life if he recovered, and should meet death with fortitude; Lorenzo agreed, and was absolved. According to Savonarola's early biographer, G. F. Pico (not the humanist), the third condition was that Lorenzo should promise "to restore liberty to Florence"; in Pico's account Lorenzo made no response to this demand, and the friar left him unabsolved. On April 9, 1492, Lorenzo died, aged forty-three.

When the news of this premature death reached Florence almost the entire city mourned, and even Lorenzo's opponents wondered how social order could now be maintained in Florence, or peace in Italy, without his guiding hand. Europe recognized his stature as a statesman, and sensed in him the characteristic qualities of the time; he was "the man of the Renaissance" in everything but his aversion to violence. His slowly acquired prudence in policy, his simple but persuasive eloquence in debate, his firmness and courage in action, had made all but a few Florentines forget the liberty that his family had destroyed; and many who had not forgotten remembered it as the freedom of rich clans to compete in force and chicanery for an exploitive dominance in a "democracy" where only a thirtieth of the population could vote. Lorenzo had used his power with moderation and for the good of the state, even to the neglect of his private fortune. He had been guilty of sexual looseness, and had given a bad example to Florentine youth. He had given a good example in literature, had restored the Italian language to literary standing, and had rivaled his protégés in poetry. He had supported the arts with a discriminating taste that set a standard for Europe. Of all the "despots" he was the gentlest and the best. "This man," said King Ferdinand of Naples, "lived long enough for his glory, but too short a time for Italy." After him Florence declined, and Italy knew no peace.

Leonardo da Vinci

The most fascinating figure of the Renaissance was born on April 15, 1452, near the village of Vinci, some sixty miles from Florence. His mother was a peasant girl, Caterina, who had not bothered to marry his father. Her seducer, Piero d'Antonio, was a Florentine attorney of some means. In the year of Leonardo's birth Piero married a woman of his own rank. Caterina had to be content with a peasant husband; she yielded her pretty love child to Piero and his wife; and Leonardo was brought up in semiaristocratic comfort without maternal love. Perhaps in that early environment he acquired his taste for fine clothing, and his aversion to women.

He went to a neighborhood school, took fondly to mathematics, music, and drawing, and delighted his father by his singing and his playing of the lute. Yet Leonardo in his prime was known for his strength, bending a horseshoe with his hands; he was an expert fencer, and skilled in riding and managing horses, which he loved as the noblest and fairest of animals. Apparently he drew, painted, and wrote with his left hand; this, rather than a desire to be illegible, made him write from right to left.

In order to draw well he studied all things in nature with curiosity, patience, and care; science and art, so remarkably united in his mind, had there one origin—detailed observation. When he was turning fifteen his father took him to Verrocchio's studio in Florence, and persuaded that versatile artist to accept him as an apprentice. All the educated world knows Vasari's story of how Leonardo painted the angel at the left in Verrocchio's *Baptism of Christ,* and how the master was so overwhelmed by the beauty of the figure that he gave up painting and devoted himself to sculpture. Probably this abdication is a postmortem legend; Verrocchio made several pictures after the *Baptism.* Perhaps in these apprentice days Leonardo painted the *Annunciation* in the Louvre, with its awkward angel and its startled maid. He could hardly have learned grace from Verrocchio.

In 1472 he was admitted to membership in the Company of St. Luke. This guild, composed chiefly of apothecaries, physicians, and artists, had its headquarters in the hospital of Santa Maria Nuova. Presumably Leonardo found there some opportunities to study internal as well as external anatomy. A week before his twenty-fourth birthday Leonardo and three other youths were summoned before a committee of the Florentine Signory to answer a charge of having had homosexual relations. The result of this summons is unknown. On June 7, 1476, the accusation was repeated; the committee imprisoned Leonardo briefly, released him, and dismissed the charge as unproved. Unquestionably he was a homosexual. As soon as he could afford to have his own studio he gathered handsome young men about him; he took some of them with him on his migrations from city to city; he referred to one

or another of them in his manuscripts as *amantissimo* or *carissimo*—
"most beloved," "dearest." What his intimate relations with these
youths were we do not know; some passages in his notes suggest a dis-
taste for sexual congress in any form. Leonardo might reasonably doubt
why he and a few others had been singled out for public accusation
when homosexuality was so widespread in the Italy of the time. He
never forgave Florence for the indignity of his arrest.

Apparently he took the matter more seriously than the city did. A
year after the accusation he was invited, and agreed to accept a studio in
the Medici gardens; and in 1478 the Signory itself asked him to paint
an altarpiece for the chapel of St. Bernard in the Palazzo Vecchio. For
some reason he did not carry out the assignment; Ghirlandaio took it
over; Filippino Lippi completed it. Nevertheless the Signory soon gave
him—and Botticelli—another commission: to paint full-length portraits of two men hanged for the conspiracy of the Pazzi against
Lorenzo and Giuliano de' Medici. Leonardo, with his half-morbid interest in human deformity and suffering, may have felt some fascination in the gruesome task.

But indeed he was interested in everything. All postures and actions
of the human body, all expressions of the face in young and old, all the
organs and movements of animals and plants from the waving of wheat
in the field to the flight of birds in the air, all the cyclical erosion and elevation of mountains, all the currents and eddies of water and wind, the
moods of weather, the shades of the atmosphere, and the inexhaustible
kaleidoscope of the sky—all these seemed endlessly wonderful to him;
repetition never dulled for him their marvel and mystery; he filled
thousands of pages with observations concerning them, and drawings
of their myriad forms. When the monks of San Scopeto asked him to
paint a picture for their chapel (1481), he made so many sketches for so
many features and forms of it that he lost himself in the details, and
never finished *The Adoration of the Magi*.

Nevertheless it is one of his greatest paintings. The plan from which
he developed it was drawn on a strictly geometrical pattern of perspective, with the whole space divided into diminishing squares; the mathematician in Leonardo always competed—often cooperated—with the
artist. But the artist was already developed; the Virgin had the pose and
features that she would keep in Leonardo's work to the end; the Magi

were drawn with a remarkable understanding for a youth—of character and expression in old men; and the "Philosopher" at the left was literally a brown study of half-skeptical meditation, as if the painter had so soon come to view the Christian story with a spirit unwillingly incredulous and still devout. And around these figures half a hundred others gathered, as if every kind of man and woman had hurried to this crib seeking hungrily the meaning of life and some Light of the World, and finding the answer in a stream of births.

The unfinished masterpiece, almost erased by time, hangs in the Uffizi at Florence, but it was Filippino Lippi who executed the painting accepted by the Scopetini brotherhood. To begin, to conceive too richly, to lose himself in experimenting with details—to see beyond his subject a boundless perspective of human, animal, plant, and architectural forms, of rocks and mountains, streams and clouds and trees, in a mystic chiaroscuro light; to be absorbed in the philosophy of the picture rather than in its technical accomplishment, to leave to others the lesser task of coloring the figures so drawn and placed, for revealing significance; to turn in despair, after long labor of mind and body, from the imperfection with which the hand and the materials had embodied the dream: this was to be Leonardo's character and fate, with a few exceptions, to the end.

Perhaps he entered upon each work of art with a view to solve a technical problem of composition, color, or design, and lost interest in the work when the solution had been found. Art, he said, lies in conceiving and designing, not in the actual execution; this was labor for lesser minds. Or he pictured to himself some subtlety, significance, or perfection that his patient, and at last impatient, hand could not realize, and he abandoned the effort in despair. He passed too quickly from one task or subject to another; he was interested in too many things; he lacked a unifying purpose, a dominating idea; this "universal man" was a medley of brilliant fragments; he was possessed of and by too many abilities to harness them to one goal.

He wrote five thousand pages, but never completed one book. Quantitatively he was more an author than an artist. He aspired to be a good writer; made several attempts at eloquence, as in his repeated descriptions of a flood; "and wrote vivid accounts of a tempest and a battle." He clearly intended to publish some of his writings, and often began to put his notes into order for this purpose. So far as we know he published nothing during his lifetime; but he must have allowed some friends to see selected manuscripts, for there are references to his writings in Flavio Biondo, Jerome Cardan, and Cellini. He wrote equally well on science and art, and divided his time almost evenly between them. The most substantial of his manuscripts is the *Trattato della pittura,* or *Treatise on Painting,* first published in 1651. Despite devoted modern editing, it is still a loose aggregation of fragments, in poor array, and often repetitious. Leonardo anticipates those who argue that painting can be learned only by painting; he thinks a sound knowledge of theory helps; and he laughs off his critics as being like "those of whom Demetrius declared that he took no more account of the wind that came from their mouths than of that which they expelled from their lower parts." His basic precept is that the student of art should study nature rather than copy the works of other artists. "See to it, O painter, that when you go into the fields you give your attention to the various objects, looking carefully in turn first at one object then at another, making a bundle of different things selected among those of less value." Of course the painter must study anatomy, perspective, modeling by light and shade; boundaries sharply defined make a picture seem wooden. "Always make the figure so that the bosom is not turned in the same direction as the head"; here is one secret of the grace in Leonardo's own compositions. Finally he urges: "Make figures with such action as may suffice to show what the figure has in mind." Did he forget to do this with Mona Lisa or did he exaggerate our ability to read the soul in the eyes and the lips?

He made portraits of Lodovico, regent of Milan, and his pretty bride Beatrice d'Este, and their children, of Lodovico's mistresses Cecilia Gaflerani and Lucrezia Crivelli; these paintings are lost, unless *La Belle Ferroniere* of the Louvre is Lucrezia. Vasari speaks of the family portraits as "marvelous," and the picture of Lucrezia inspired a poet to a fervid eulogy of the lady's beauty and the artist's skill.

Perhaps Cecilia was Leonardo's model for *The Virgin of the Rocks.* The painting was contracted for (1483) by the Confraternity of the Conception as the central part of an altarpiece for the church of San Francesco. The original was later bought by Francis I and is in the Louvre. Standing before it, we note the softly maternal face that Leonardo would use a dozen times in later works; an angel recalling the one in Verrocchio's *Baptism of Christ;* two infants exquisitely drawn; and a background of jutting, overhanging rocks that only Leonardo could have conceived as Mary's habitat. The colors have been darkened by time, but possibly the artist intended a darkling effect, and suffused his pictures with a hazy atmosphere that Italy calls *sfumato*—"smoked." This is one of Leonardo's greatest pictures, surpassed only by *The Last Supper, Mona Lisa,* and *The Virgin, Child, and St. Anne.*

The Last Supper and *Mona Lisa* are the world's most famous paintings. Hour after hour, day after day, year after year, pilgrims enter the refectory that holds Leonardo's most ambitious work. In that simple rectangular building the Dominican friars who were attached to Lodovico's favorite church—Santa Maria delle Grazie—took their meals. Soon after the artist arrived in Milan, Lodovico asked him to represent the Last Supper on the farthest wall of this refectory. For three years (1495–98), on and off, Leonardo labored or dallied at the task, while duke and friars fretted over his incalculable delays. The prior (if we may believe Vasari) complained to Lodovico of Leonardo's apparent sloth, and wondered why he would sometimes sit before the wall for hours without painting a stroke. Leonardo had no trouble explaining to the duke—who had some trouble explaining to the prior—that an artist's most important work lies in conception rather than in execution, and (as Vasari put it) "men of genius do most when they work least." There were in this case, said Leonardo to Lodovico, two special difficulties—to conceive features worthy of the Son of God, and to picture a man as heartless as Judas; perhaps, he slyly suggested, he might use the too frequently seen face of the prior as a model for Iscariot. Leonardo hunted throughout Milan for heads and faces that might serve him in representing the Apostles; from a hundred such quarries he chose the features that were melted in the mintage of his art into those astonishingly individualized heads that make the wonder of the dying masterpiece. Sometimes he would rush from the streets or his studio to the refectory, add a stroke or two to the picture, and depart.

The subject was superb, but from a painter's point of view it was pitted with hazards. It had to confine itself to male figures and a modest table in a simple room; there could be only the dimmest landscape or vista; no grace of women might serve as foil to the strength of the men;

no vivid action could be brought in to set the figures into motion and convey the sense of life. Leonardo let in a glimpse of landscape through the three windows behind Christ. As a substitute for action he portrayed the gathering at the tense moment Christ has prophesied that one of the Apostles will betray Him, and each is asking, in fear or horror or amazement, "Is it I?" The institution of the Eucharist might have been chosen, but that would have frozen all thirteen faces into an immobile and stereotyped solemnity. Here, on the contrary, there is more than violent physical action; there is a searching and revelation of spirit; never again, so profoundly, has an artist revealed in one picture so many souls. For the Apostles Leonardo made numberless preliminary sketches; some of these—for James the Greater, Philip, Judas— are drawings of such finesse and power as only Rembrandt and Michelangelo have matched. When he tried to conceive the features of Christ, Leonardo found that the Apostles had exhausted his inspiration. According to Lomazzo (writing in 1557), Leonardo's old friend Zenale advised him to leave the face of Christ unfinished, saying, "Of a truth it would be impossible to imagine faces lovelier or gentler than those of James the Greater or James the Less. Accept your misfortune, then, and leave your Christ incomplete; for otherwise, when compared with the Apostles, He would not be their Savior or their Master." Leonardo took the advice. He or a pupil made a famous sketch (now in the Brera Gallery) for the head of Christ, but it pictured an effeminate sadness and resignation rather than the heroic resolve that calmly entered Gethsemane. Perhaps Leonardo lacked the reverent piety that, had it been added to his sensitivity, his depth, and his skill, might have brought the picture nearer to perfection.

Because he was a thinker as well as an artist, Leonardo shunned fresco painting as an enemy to thought; such painting on wet and freshly laid plaster had to be done rapidly before the plaster dried. Leonardo preferred to paint on a dry wall with tempera colors mixed in a gelatinous substance, for this method allowed him to ponder and experiment. But these colors did not adhere firmly to the surface; even in Leonardo's lifetime—what with the usual dampness of the refectory and its occasional flooding in heavy rains—the paint began to flake and fall; when Vasari saw the picture (1536) it was already blurred; when Lomazzo saw it, sixty years after its completion, it was already ruined beyond repair. The friars later helped decay by cutting a door through the legs of the Apostles into the kitchen (1656). The engraving by which the painting has been reproduced throughout the world was taken not from the spoiled original but from an imperfect copy made by one of Leonardo's pupils, Marco d'Oggiono. Today we can study only the composition and the general outlines, hardly the shades or subtleties. But whatever were the defects of the work when Leonardo left it, some realized at once that it was the greatest painting that Renaissance art had yet produced.

On and off, during the years 1503–6, Leonardo painted the portrait of Mona Lisa—i.e., Madonna Elisabetta, third wife of Francesco del Giocondo, who in 1512 was to be a member of the Signory.

Presumably a child of Francesco, buried in 1499, was one of Elisabetta's children, and this loss may have helped to mold the serious features behind La Gioconda's smile. That Leonardo should call her back to his studio so many times during those three years; that he should spend upon her portrait all the secrets and nuances of his art—modeling her softly with light and shade, framing her in a fanciful vista of trees and waters, mountains and sky; clothing her in raiment of velvet and satin woven into folds whose every wrinkle is a masterpiece; studying with passionate care the subtle muscles that form and move the mouth, bringing musicians to play for her and to evoke upon her features the disillusioned tenderness of a mother remembering a departed child: these are inklings of the spirit in which he came to this engaging merger of painting and philosophy. A thousand interruptions, a hundred distracting interests, the simultaneous struggle with the Anghiari design, left unbroken the unity of his conception, the unwonted pertinacity of his zeal.

This, then, is the face that launched a thousand reams upon a sea of ink. Not an unusually lovely face; a shorter nose would have launched more reams; and many a lass in oil or marble—as in any Correggio— would by comparison make Lisa only moderately fair. It is her smile that has made her fortune through the centuries—a nascent twinkle in her eyes, an amused and checked upcurving of her lips.

What is she smiling at? The efforts of the musicians to entertain her? The leisurely diligence of an artist who paints her through a thousand days and never makes an end? Or is it not just Mona Lisa smiling, but all women, saying to all men: "Poor impassioned lovers! A Nature blindly commanding continuance burns your nerves with an absurd hunger for our flesh, softens your brains with a quite unreasonable idealization of our charms, lifts you to lyrics that subside with consummation—and all that you may be precipitated into parentage! Could anything be more ridiculous? But we too are snared; we women pay a heavier price than you for your infatuation. And yet, sweet fools, it is pleasant to be desired, and life is redeemed when we are loved."

Or was it only the smile of Leonardo himself that Lisa wore—of the inverted spirit that could hardly recall the tender touch of a woman's hand, and could believe in no other destiny for love or genius than obscene decomposition, and a little fame flickering out in man's forgetfulness?

When at last the sittings ended, Leonardo kept the picture, claiming that this most finished of all portraits was still incomplete. Perhaps the husband did not like the prospect of having his wife curl up her lips at him and his guests, hour after hour from his walls. Many years later, Francis I bought it for 4,000 crowns ($50,000), and framed it in his palace at Fontainebleau. Today, after time and restorations have blurred its subtleties, it hangs in the majestic Salon Carré of the Louvre, daily amused by a thousand worshipers, and waiting for time to efface and confirm Mona Lisa's smile.

THE INVENTOR

It is hard for us to realize that to Lodovico, as to Caesar Borgia, Leonardo was primarily an engineer. Even the pageants that he planned for the Duke of Milan included ingenious automata. "Every day," says Vasari, "he made models and designs for the removal of mountains with ease, and to pierce them to pass from one place to another; and by means of levers, cranes, and winches to raise and draw heavy weights; he devised methods for cleaning harbors, and for raising water from great depths." He developed a machine for cutting threads in screws; he worked along correct lines toward a water wheel; he devised frictionless roller-bearing band brakes. He designed the first machine gun, and mortars with cog gears to elevate their range; a multiple-belt drive; three-speed transmission gears; an adjustable monkey wrench; a machine for rolling metal; a movable bed for a printing press; a self-locking worm gear for raising a ladder. He had a plan for underwater navigation, but refused to explain it. He revived the idea of Hero of Alexandria for a steam engine, and showed how steam pressure in a gun could propel an iron bolt twelve hundred yards. He invented a device for winding and evenly distributing yarn on a revolving spindle, and scissors that would open and close with one movement of the hand. Often he let his fancy bemuse him, as when he suggested inflated skis for walking on water, or a water mill that would simultaneously play several musical instruments. He described a parachute: "If a man have a tent made of linen, of which the apertures have all been stopped up, and it be twelve cubits across and twelve in depth, he will be able to throw himself down from any great height without sustaining any injury."

Through half his life he pondered the problem of human flight. Like Tolstoi he envied the birds as a species in many ways superior to man. He studied in detail the operation of their wings and tails, the mechanics of their rising, gliding, turning, and descending. His sharp eye noted these movements with passionate curiosity, and his swift pencil drew and recorded them. He observed how birds avail themselves of air currents and pressures. He made several drawings of a screw mechanism by which a man, through the action of his feet, might cause wings to beat fast enough to raise him into the air. In a brief essay *Sul volo* (*On Flight*) he described a flying machine made by him with strong starched linen, leather joints, and thongs of raw silk. He called this "the bird," and wrote detailed instructions for flying it.

Did he actually try to fly? A note in the *Codice Atlantico* says: "Tomorrow morning, on the second day of January, 1496, I will make the thong and the attempt"; we do not know what this means. Fazio Cardano, father of the physicist Jerome Cardan (1501–76), told his son that Leonardo himself had essayed flight. Some have thought that when Antonio, one of Leonardo's aides, broke his leg in 1510, it was in trying to fly one of Leonardo's machines. We do not know.

Leonardo was on the wrong track; human flight came not by imitating the bird, except in gliding, but by applying the internal combustion engine to a propeller that could beat the air not downward but backward; forward speed made possible upward flight. But the noblest distinction of man is his passion for knowledge. Shocked by the wars and crimes of mankind, disheartened by the selfishness of ability and the perpetuity of poverty, saddened by the superstitions and credulities with which the nations and generations gild the brevity and indignities of life, we feel our race in some part redeemed when we see that it can hold a soaring dream in its mind and heart for three thousand years, from the legend of Daedalus and Icarus, through the baffled groping of Leonardo and a thousand others, to the glorious and tragic victory of our time.

THE SCIENTIST

Side by side with his drawings, sometimes on the same page, sometimes scrawled across a sketch of a man or a woman, a landscape or a machine, are the notes in which this insatiable mind puzzled over the laws and operations of Nature. Perhaps the scientist grew out of the artist: Leonardo's painting compelled him to study anatomy, the laws of proportion and perspective the composition and reflection of light, the chemistry of pigments and oils; from these researches he was drawn to a more intimate investigation of structure and function in plants and animals; and from these inquiries he rose to a philosophical conception of universal and invariable natural law. Often the artist peered out again in the scientist; the scientific drawing might be itself a thing of beauty, or terminate in a graceful arabesque. He tried his hand at almost every science. He took enthusiastically to mathematics as the purest form of reasoning; he felt a certain beauty in geometrical figures, and drew some on the same page with a study for *The Last Supper.* He expressed vigorously one of the fundamental principles of science: "There is no certainty where one can neither apply any of the mathematical sciences nor any of those that are not based upon them." And he proudly echoed Plato: "Let no man who is not a mathematician read the elements of my work."

Armed with the great text of Theophrastus on plants, he turned his alert mind to "natural history." He examined the system on which leaves are arranged about their stalks, and formulated its laws. He observed that the rings in a cross section of a tree trunk record the years of its growth by their number, and the moisture of the year by their width. He seems to have shared several delusions of his time as to the power of certain animals to heal some human diseases by their presence or their touch. He atoned for this uncharacteristic lapse into superstition by investigating the anatomy of the horse with a thoroughness to which recorded history had no precedent. He prepared a special treatise on the subject, but it was lost in the French occupation of Milan. He almost inaugurated modern comparative anatomy by studying the limbs of men and animals in juxtaposition. He set aside the superannuated authority of Galen, and worked with actual bodies. The anatomy of man he described not only in words but in drawings that excelled anything yet done in that field. He planned a book on the subject, and left for it hundreds of illustrations and notes. He claimed to "have dissected more than thirty human cadavers," and his countless drawings of the fetus, the heart, lungs, skeleton, musculature, viscera, eye, skull, and brain, and the principal organs in women, support his claim. He was the first to give—in remarkable drawings and notes—a scientific representation of the uterus, and he described accurately the three membranes enclosing the fetus. He was the first to delineate the cavity of the bone that supports the cheek, now known as the antrum of Highmore. He poured wax into the valves of the heart of a dead bull to get an exact impression of the chambers. He was the first to characterize the moderator band (*catena*) of the right ventricle. He was fascinated by the network of blood vessels; he divined the circulation of the blood, but did not quite grasp its mechanism. "The heart," he wrote, "is much stronger than the other muscles. . . . The blood that returns when the heart opens is not the same as that which closes the valves." He traced the blood vessels, nerves, and muscles of the body with fair accuracy. He attributed old age to arteriosclerosis, and this to lack of exercise. He began a volume, *De figure umana,* on the proper proportions of the human figure as an aid to artists, and some of his ideas were incorporated in his friend Pacioli's *De divina proportione.* He analyzed the physical life of man from birth to decay, and then planned a survey of mental life. "Oh, that it may please God to let me also expound the psychology of the habits of man in such fashion as I am describing his body!"

From his studies in so many fields, Leonardo rose at times to philosophy. "O marvelous Necessity! Thou with supreme reason constrainest all effects to be the direct result of their causes, and by a supreme and irrevocable law every natural action obeys thee by the shortest possible process." This has all the proud ring of nineteenth-century science, and suggests that Leonardo had shed some theology. Vasari, in the first edition of his life of the artist, wrote that he was of "so heretical a cast of

mind that he conformed to no religion whatever, accounting it per-
chance better to be a philosopher than a Christian"—but Vasari omitted this passage in later editions. Like many Christians of the time,
Leonardo took a fling now and then at the clergy; he called them Pharisees, accused them of deceiving the simple with bogus miracles, and
smiled at the "false coin" of celestial promissory notes which they exchanged for the coinage of this world. On one Good Friday he wrote:
"Today all the world is in mourning because one man died in the Ori-
ent." He seems to have thought that dead saints were incapable of hearing the prayers addressed to them. "I could wish that I had such power
of language as should avail me to censure those who would extol the
worship of men above that of the sun . . . Those who have wished to
worship men as gods have made a very grave error." He took more liberties with Christian iconography than any other Renaissance artist: he
suppressed halos, put the Virgin across her mother's knee, and made
the infant Jesus try to bestride the symbolic lamb. He saw mind in
matter, and believed in a spiritual soul, but apparently thought that
the soul could act only through matter, and only in harmony with invariable laws. He addressed the Deity with humility and fervor in some
passages; but at other times he identified God with Nature, Natural
Law, and "Necessity." A mystic pantheism was his religion until his
final years.

Probably he did little painting after 1517, for in that year he suffered a paralytic stroke that immobilized his right side; he painted
with his left hand, but needed both hands for careful work. He was now
a wrinkled wreck of the youth whose repute for beauty of body and face
came down to Vasari across half a century. His once proud self-
confidence faded, his serenity of spirit yielded to the pains of decay, his
love of life gave place to religious hope. He made a simple will, but he
asked for all the services of the Church at his funeral. Once he had written: "As a day well spent makes it sweet to sleep, so a life well used
makes it sweet to die." Vasari tells a touching story of how Leonardo
died, on May 2, 1519, in the arms of King Francis I (Leonardo had arrived in France in 1516 under contract to Francis as "painter, engineer,
and architect of the King, and state mechanician"); but apparently
Francis was elsewhere at the time. The body was buried in the cloister
of the Collegiate Church of St. Florentin in Amboise.

How shall we rank him?—which of us commands the variety of knowledge and skills required to judge so multiple a man? The fascination of his polymorphous mind lures us into exaggerating his actual achievement; for he was more fertile in conception than in execution. He was not the greatest scientist or engineer or painter or sculptor or thinker of his time; he was merely the man who was all of these together and in each field rivaled the best. There must have been men in the medical schools who knew more of anatomy than he; the most notable works of engineering in the territory of Milan had been accomplished before Leonardo came; both Raphael and Titian left a more impressive total of fine paintings than has survived from Leonardo's brush; Michelangelo was a greater sculptor; Machiavelli and Guicciardini were profounder minds. And yet Leonardo's studies of the horse were probably the best work done in the anatomy of that age; Lodovico and Cesare Borgia chose him, from all Italy, as their engineer; nothing in the paintings of Raphael or Titian or Michelangelo equals *The Last Supper*; no painter has matched Leonardo in subtlety of nuance, or in the delicate portrayal of feeling and thought and pensive tenderness; no statue of the time was so highly rated as Leonardo's plaster *Sforza*; no drawing has ever surpassed *The Virgin, Child, and St. Anne*; and nothing in Renaissance philosophy soared above Leonardo's conception of natural law.

He was not "the man of the Renaissance," for he was too gentle, introverted, and refined to typify an age so violent and powerful in action and speech. He was not quite "the universal man," since the qualities of statesman or administrator found no place in his variety. But, with all his limitations and incompletions, he was *the fullest man* of the Renaissance, perhaps of all time. Contemplating his achievement we marvel at the distance that man has come from his origins, and renew our faith in the possibilities of mankind.

Chapter Sixteen

ᴍᴍ

THE RENAISSANCE II: ROME

THE WANDERING PAPACY (1309–1417)

In 1309 the papacy had abandoned Rome as ungovernable, and had established itself in Avignon, where it became, to the anguish of most Christians, a captive of the French kings.

After 1377 the papacy divided itself into hostile camps, with rival popes at Rome and Avignon, while, across the Mediterranean, in Africa and Asia, a virile and warlike Mohammedanism spread and multiplied, threatening the life of Christianity. This Papal Schism continued until prelates, princes, and scholars assembled at Constance in 1414, and, after three years of debate and negotiation, chose as pope Cardinal Odonne Colonna, who took the name of Martin V. He restored the supremacy of the papacy over the councils and rapidly replenished the papal treasury, much to the discomfort of Catholics north of the Alps. In 1430 a German envoy to Rome sounded the tocsin of the Reformation of 1517:

> Greed reigns supreme in the Roman court, and day by day finds new devices . . . for extorting money from Germany under pretext of ecclesiastical fees. . . . Hence much outcry . . . and heartburnings; also many questions in regard to the papacy will arise, or else obedience will at last be entirely renounced, to escape from these outrageous

exactions of the Italians; and this latter course, as I perceive, would be acceptable to many countries.

There ensued a half-hidden contest, between the nascent Reformation and the maturing Renaissance, for control of the income and mind of the Roman Church. Martin himself had appointed as a papal secretary one of the outstanding humanists—Poggio Bracciolini. Martin's successor, Eugenius IV (r. 1431–47), was already won to the Renaissance, and helped it wherever his embattled pontificate led him. Driven from Rome by a Colonna-managed uprising of the populace, he fled with his curiate to Ferrara and summoned to it a new council of bishops and cardinals.

An epochal event in military history cooperated with his views. As the onrushing Turks neared Constantinople, bringing Islam with them, the leaders of Eastern Christianity fled from their ancient capital to Italy, and offered to confer with Western prelates for the union of Greek and Latin Christianity. Eugenius welcomed them at Ferrara and called a Roman Catholic council to confer with them. There, for eight months, the theologians debated the beloved minima of their faiths. When plague broke out at Ferrara, Cosimo de' Medici invited the theologians to transfer their consultations to Florence; they came, Eugenius with them; Cosimo and his friends honored them, fed them, and bought their classic texts. Eugenius added to his secretariat Flavio Biondo, Leonardo Bruni, and other Italian humanists who could negotiate with the Greeks in Greek. The homeless theologians agreed to unite the Greek and Roman churches and creeds. But the priests and populace of the Christian East repudiated the agreement; the Turks took Constantinople; the great schism of Eastern from Western Christianity continued; but Pope Eugenius, fortified by the classical experts, carried the Renaissance to Rome.

THE SCHOLAR POPES

Among the fervent students whom Eugenius had admired in Florence was Tommaso Parentucelli, a young priest who spent all his money on books, borrowed to buy more, and aspired to gather into one library all the great books in the world.

In 1443, Eugenius made him an archbishop, in 1446 a cardinal; in 1447 the conclave made him pope. "Who would have thought," he exclaimed, "that a poor bellringer of a priest would be made pope, to the confusion of the proud?" It was one of the democratic features of Catholicism that any normal youth could rise to the papacy. The humanists of Italy rejoiced, and one of them proclaimed that Plato's vision had come true: a philosopher had become king.

Nicholas V, as he now called himself, had three aims: to be a good pope, to rebuild Rome, and to restore classical literature, learning, and art. Dowered with all the revenues of the papacy, he sent agents to Athens, Constantinople, Germany, and England to seek and buy—or copy—Greek or Latin manuscripts, pagan or Christian; he installed a large corps of copyists and editors in the Vatican; he called almost every prominent humanist in Italy to Rome; and he paid his scholars with a liberality that alarmed his financiers and grieved the provinces; bold critics charged that the contributions of the pious were spent on the vanities of pagan literature and the luxuries of skeptical cardinals.

When Nicholas called for a tenth of all the revenue of Western Europe to be devoted to a crusade to recover Constantinople from the Turks (1453), Europe hardly listened. Nicholas bowed to reality, and the lust of life cooled in his veins. He died in 1455, at fifty-eight. He had been extravagant in his generosity, but he had restored peace in the Church and had brought back order and splendor to Rome; he had founded the Vatican Library and had united the Catholic and the classical world, the Church and the Renaissance.

The mating seemed complete in Pope Pius II. Born in Siena in 1405, of the prominent Piccolomini family, he was christened Enea Silvio; but he signed most of his many writings (nearly all Latin) "Aeneas Silvius," after the Aeneas of Virgil's *Aeneid*; and even his papal name echoed Virgil's favorite adjective for his hero—*pius,* which meant "reverent" and faithful toward one's parents or native land. The word fitted the pope more than the man, for in his fifty-three prepapal years he had availed himself of all the moral laxity of the age. He sampled a dozen women, and wrote for a friend a love letter designed to melt the obstinacy of a girl who preferred marriage to fornication. Amid his wanderings he remained faithful only to literature, loving the ancient classics and writing the best Latin of his time. As Latin was the language of diplomacy, he readily found diverse employments, from lovers to kings.

In 1445, Frederick III, secular head of the Holy Roman Empire, sent him as envoy to Eugenius IV. Silvius, who had attacked Eugenius in numerous tracts, apologized so eloquently that the humanist pontiff readily forgave him, and from that time the wandering scholar belonged to the pope. He became a priest (1446), and at forty-one resigned himself to chastity; henceforth he lived an exemplary life. In 1449 he was made bishop of Siena; in 1456 he became Cardinal Piccolomini; in 1458 he was chosen pope.

He was now fifty-three, and his adventurous life had taken such toll of his strength that he seemed already old. He made no attempt to hide his youthful errors and amours; on the contrary, he issued publicly a Bull of Retraction, asking God and the Church to forgive him. He had become a humanist in Florence, and now he included the scholars Platina and Biondo in his secretariat; but he did not pay them intoxicating fees. Greater issues absorbed him: the Turks, bringing a rival religion with them, were advancing toward Vienna and into Serbia and Bosnia; soon they might reach the Adriatic; what could stop them from crossing that sea into divided, quarreling Italy?

Pius II proclaimed another crusade; he begged the northern Powers to send fleets to join his own—only Venice complied. Pius led a squadron around Italy, reached Ancona, and waited hopefully for the Venetians. He succumbed to exhaustion just as they arrived. He was given a stately funeral in Rome, but his crusade died with him.

I pass over Pope Sixtus IV, who governed the Church from 1471 to 1484, brought it near bankruptcy through nepotism and war, built the Sistine Chapel that bears his name, rebuilt the Vatican Library, added 1,100 classical manuscripts to the 2,527 already there, and appointed Torquemada to direct the Inquisition in Spain. I should have enjoyed saying a kind word for Pope Alexander VI, and even for his unscrupulous son Caesar Borgia; but I hurry on to Pope Julius II and the summit of the Roman Renaissance.

JULIUS II

Julius was an able and undiscourageable general who led or assigned one army after another to recapture the Papal States for the papacy as necessary buffers against environing principalities eager to control the Church. He was a powerful administrator of affairs and men. We can still feel the depth and force of his character from Raphael's profound portrait in the Pitti Palace at Florence. Under him, Raphael and Michelangelo came to their fulfillment.

Raphael

Raphael was born in 1483 to Giovanni Santi, the leading painter of Urbino. He was named after the fairest of the archangels and grew up in the odor of art. From that happy youth he passed to Perugia, where, in three years under Perugino, he learned to paint pious Madonnas. Then Pinturicchio lured him to Siena and taught him that a woman could be a goddess of beauty without being the Mother of God. The pagan side of Raphael—which would later enliven the bathroom of a cardinal with rosy nudes—developed in the amiable artist along with the piety that would produce *The Sistine Madonna*.

In 1508 he received at Florence a call from Julius II to come and work for him in Rome. He was glad to go, for Rome, not Florence, was now the exciting and stimulating center of the Renaissance. Julius had found in the Vatican some administrative rooms whose walls seemed to call for fresh decoration. In consultation with theologians and scholars, a plan was devised to illustrate the union of religion and philosophy, of classic culture and Christianity, of Church and State, in the civilization of the Renaissance.

Raphael worked on the project for four-and-a-half years, with almost religious care and dedication. On one wall, he pictured the persons of the Christian Trinity, with Mary near them; in a cloud around them Adam, Abraham, Moses, David, Peter, and Paul, and other heroes of the Testaments, binding them in all illuminating continuity of the two religions; cherubim and seraphim weaving through space as if on the wings of song; below them theologians and philosophers debating the doctrine of the Eucharist; and the human characters so individualized as to make each figure a biography. All this *Disputa del Sacra-mento* by a youth of twenty-eight.

But could this happy condottiere of the brush represent with equal force and grandeur the role of science and philosophy among men? We have no evidence that Raphael had ever done much reading; he spoke with his brush and listened with his eyes; he lived in a world of form and color in which words were trivial things unless they issued in the signif-icant actions of men and women. He must have prepared himself by hurried study, by dipping into Plato and Diogenes Laertius and Mar-silio Ficino, and by humble conversation with learned men, to rise now to his supreme conception. *The School of Athens*—half a hundred figures summing up rich centuries of Greek thought, and all gathered in an im-mortal moment under the coffered arch of a massive pagan portico.

There, on the wall directly facing the apotheosis of theology in the *Disputa,* is the glorification of philosophy: Plato of the Jovelike brow, deep eyes, flowing white hair and beard, with a finger pointing upward to his perfect state; Aristotle walking quietly beside him, thirty years younger, handsome and cheerful, holding out his hand with downward palm, as if to bring his master's soaring idealism back to earth and the possible; Socrates counting off his arguments on his fingers, with armed Alcibiades listening to him lovingly; Pythagoras trying to im-prison in harmonic tables the music of the spheres; a fair lady who might be Aspasia; Heracleitus writing Ephesian riddles; Diogenes lying carelessly disrobed on the marble steps; Archimedes drawing geometries on a slate for four absorbed youths; Ptolemy and Zoroaster bandying globes; a boy at the left running up eagerly with books, surely seeking an autograph; an assiduous lad seated in a corner taking notes; peeking out at the left, little Federigo of Mantua, Julius' pet; Bramante again; and hiding modestly, almost unseen, Raphael him-self, now sprouting a mustache. There are many more, about whose identity we shall let leisurely pundits dispute; all in all, such a parlia-ment of wisdom had never been painted, perhaps never been conceived before. And not a word about heresy, no philosophers burned at the stake; here, under the protection of a pope too great to fuss about the difference between one error and another, the young Christian has sud-denly brought all these pagans together, painted them in their own character and with remarkable understanding and sympathy, and placed them where the theologians could see them and exchange fallibilities, and where the pope, between one document and another, might contemplate the cooperative process and creation of human thought.

This painting and the *Disputa* are the ideal of the Renaissance—pagan antiquity and Christian faith living together in one room and harmony. These rival panels, in the sum of their conception, composition, and harmony, were to be surpassed only by Michelangelo, Tintoretto, and Veronese, and equaled by none in representing the marriage of Pericles' Greece and Leo's Rome. Almost at the same time (1508–12) as Raphael's work for Julius II (1505–12), the culminating figure of the Renaissance, under the same papal scrutiny, painted the ceiling of the Sistine Chapel.

Michelangelo

Michelangelo, named like Raphael after an archangel, was born in 1475, second son of Lodovico Buonarotti Simone, mayor of the little town of Caprese, on the road from Florence to Arezzo.

Michelangelo prided himself on having in him a drop or two of noble blood; research has proved him mistaken, but perhaps it had misdefined its terms. He received some schooling in Florence, but he learned no Latin and never felt the calming hypnosis of the classical mood; he was Hebraic, not classic, more Protestant than Catholic, though he designed the Church's overpowering citadel.

He preferred drawing to writing, which is a corruption of drawing. He preferred sculpture to painting, and soon won admission to the gardens in which the Medici displayed their collections of ancient statuary and architecture. Pleased with the youth's zeal and products, Lorenzo took him into his house, treated him as a son, and regularly seated him at the same table with Politian, Ficino, Pico della Mirandola, and Lorenzo himself. There, Michelangelo heard the most enlightened talk about government, literature, philosophy, and art.

But that aristocratic circle had lost the Christian ethic as well as the Christian creed, and thought the garden of Epicurus more pleasant than Gethsemane. In those years, Savonarola was preaching his fiery gospel of puritan, almost ascetic, reform; Michelangelo went often to hear him, and never forgot him. When Savonarola died (1498), something of his spirit lingered in the somber artist—a scorn of the moral decay in the Italian capitals, a fierce resentment of despotism, a dark presentiment of doom. When he painted *The Last Judgment*, he hurled the friar's fulminations down the centuries.

In 1496 he accepted the invitation of a cardinal to visit Rome. There, on a contract with the French ambassador, he carved the *Pietà* which still startles us in St. Peter's: the Virgin Mother holding her crucified son in her lap. Michelangelo was only twenty-three, and the group shows defects that his youth might excuse—the excessive drapery, the Mother's hand too small for her body, her left hand hanging inexplicably in the air, her face that of a woman younger than her son. But the figure of Christ, limp and almost reduced to bone, the drapery of flowing stone, the little group containing the essence of human history as a race between motherhood and mortality: this, like Raphael's *stanze* (rooms), reveals how rapidly an artist had to mature in the heat and race of the Renaissance.

The call of impoverished relatives brought the now-famous sculptor back to Florence. There, in 1501, the cathedral's Board of Works challenged him to chisel into a human figure a block of marble thirteen-and-a-half feet tall, and so irregularly shaped that it had lain unused for a century. Michelangelo toiled on the refractory material for two-and-a-half years, using every inch of its height, and drew from it the proudly virile *David*—which stood for centuries as the city's defiance of its enemies. Giorgio Vasari, famous historian of art, thought this proudly naked youth "surpassed all other statues, ancient or modern, Latin or Greek."

Meanwhile, Pope Julius II itched for a tomb of such size and beauty as would remind even a distant posterity of his triumphs in politics and war. He sent for Michelangelo, who came despite fear that he would be miserable with Julius; they were so much alike. He proposed a colossal monument twenty-seven feet long and eighteen wide, with forty attendant statues surrounding a coffined Julius dominant though dead. The pope gave the artist 2,000 ducats, sent him off to Carrara to pick the finest veins of marble, and took himself to war for Perugia and Bologna. The war was costly and left no ducats for art; Michelangelo, seeking audience and ducats, was refused entry to the pope. He left

Rome after sending this note to Julius: "Most beloved Father, I have been turned out of the Palace today by your orders; wherefore I give you notice that from this day forward, if you want me, look for me elsewhere than at Rome."

Two years later (1508), his anger cooling and his purse thinned, Michelangelo heeded Julius' summons and returned to Rome, hoping to finish the tomb. He was alarmed to learn that the pope wanted him to paint the ceiling of the Sistine Chapel; he protested that he was a sculptor, not a painter, and recommended Raphael as a better man for the task. Julius insisted, and offered a fee of 3,000 ducats ($50,000). Michelangelo yielded, and began, in May 1508, his four-and-a-half years of toil on the supreme painting of the Renaissance.

Picture the old pope mounting the frail frame, aided to the platform by the artist, and asking, impatiently, "When will it be finished?" The reply, as reported by Vasari, was a lesson in integrity: "When I shall have done all that I believe required to satisfy art." When for the last time Michelangelo descended from the scaffold, he was exhausted, emaciated, and prematurely old. He was only thirty-seven, and had fifty-one years yet to live. Julius died (February 21, 1513) four months later.

Michelangelo mourned the passing of the great pope and wondered if the next pontiff would have as sure an instinct as Julius for great art. He retired to his humble lodgings and bided his time.

LEO X

The pope who gave his name to one of the most brilliant and immoral ages in history owed his ecclesiastical career to the political strategy of his father. Lorenzo de' Medici had been almost destroyed by Sixtus IV; he hoped that the power of the Medici family, and the security of his progeny in Florence, would be helped by having a Medici sitting in the college of cardinals. He destined his second son for the ecclesiastical state almost from Giovanni's infancy.

At seven the boy was tonsured; at eight he was appointed protonotary apostolic; at fourteen he was made a cardinal. (One might become a cardinal without becoming a priest; cardinals were then chosen for political ability and family connections rather than for religious zeal.)

All who met Cardinal de' Medici liked him. He was affable, modest, and unostentatiously generous. Even his ample income hardly sufficed for his aid to poets, artists, musicians, and scholars. He enjoyed all the arts and graces of life; nevertheless the historian Guicciardini, who lost no love on popes, described him as "having the reputation of a chaste person, and unblamable of manners"; and Aldus Manutius complimented him on his "pious and irreproachable life."

In 1513 he was called to Rome to take part in choosing a successor to Julius. He was still only thirty-seven and could hardly have expected that he would be chosen pope. He entered the conclave in a litter, suffering from an anal fistula. After a week of debate, and apparently without simony, Giovanni de' Medici was elected (March 11, 1513), and took the name Leo X.

He was not yet a priest, but this defect was remedied on March 15. Everybody was surprised and pleased. After the dark intrigues of Alexander and Caesar Borgia, and the wars and turbulence of Julius, it was a relief that a young man already distinguished for his good nature was now to lead the Church, presumably in the ways of peace. Poets, sculptors, painters, goldsmiths rejoiced; humanists promised themselves a revival of the Augustan Age.

Leo's court became the center of the intellect and wit of Rome; the place where scholars, poets, artists, and musicians were welcomed, paid, and, in many cases, housed. It was without question the most refined and moneyed court in the world of its time.

Rome prospered and expanded as the gathered tribute of Europe's piety flowed into its economic and cultural arteries. Prelates and poets, panderers and parasites, couriers and courtesans, hurried to Rome to drink the golden rain. Some cardinals had an income of 30,000 ducats a year ($500,000). They lived in stately palaces manned by as many as three hundred servants and adorned with every art and luxury known at the time. They did not quite think of themselves as ecclesiastics; they were statesmen, diplomats, administrators; they were the Roman Senate of the Roman Church and proposed to live like senators. They smiled at those foreigners who expected of them the continence and piety of priests. The Roman Empire was restored.

Luther came and saw it and was shocked; Erasmus came and saw it and was charmed. Michelangelo agreed with Luther; he preferred the commoner to the baron, the letterless to the intellectual, the toil of the worker to the luxuries of the rich. He gave most of his earnings to maintain his shiftless relatives.

He was a bear of a man—bent but powerful, with grizzly hair and beard, sharp, small eyes, crushed nose, protruding ears; he was naturally uncomfortable at court, happy alone with his tools and his visions of manly force in character and frame. He cared little for women; he painted them, but always in their maternal maturity, not in the charm of their youth. He lived precariously, penuriously, often lunching on a crust of bread, or sleeping with his working clothes on, "as if," says Vasari, "he had no mind to undress that he might dress again."

Leo, accustomed to every courtesy of speech and dress, learned to avoid Michelangelo, and left him to his work on Julius' tomb, or some muscular *Captives,* or a seated *Moses* of beard and horn and wrinkled brow, presenting ominously the Tables of the Law. The happy pope naturally took to Raphael, who agreed with him in temperament and taste. Both were amiable epicureans who made Christianity a pleasure and took their heaven here; but both worked as hard as they played.

Leo plied the happy artist with tasks: to complete the *stanze,* to design cartoons (outline drawings for prospective paintings or tapestries), to share in the building of St. Peter's, to arrange for the preservation of classical art. Raphael accepted these commissions with good cheer and appetite, and found time, besides, to produce a score of religious pictures, several series of pagan frescoes, and half a hundred Madonnas or portraits any one of which would have assured him wealth and fame. Now (1515) he painted the *Sistine Madonna* for the convent of San Sisto at Piacenza. In him, as often in Christian history, the Virgin fought a losing battle with young women of accessible beauty, as in *La Fornarina* at the Borghese Gallery. In the end Raphael gave more of his time and vigor to unveiled charms, and died at the age of thirty-seven (1520). All the artists in Rome followed his cortege to the grave.

His beloved pope survived him by a year. Leo was bedded, in August 1521, by the first stages of malaria, the persistent pain of his fistula, and the mounting worries of war. Like Julius II he had turned more and more from the enjoyment of art to the pursuit of martial power. On December 1 he was cheered by learning that Piacenza and Parma had been taken by papal forces; once, he had declared that he would gladly give his life if those cities might be added to the states of the Church. On the night of December 1–2, 1521, he died, ten days short of forty-five.

He was a good man ruined by his love of beauty and his habituation to wealth. Raised in a palace, he had learned luxury as well as art; and when the revenues of the papacy were placed in his trust, they slipped through his careless fingers while he basked in the happiness of recipients or the triumphs of expensive wars. He made the Papal States stronger than ever, but lost Germany by his exactions and extravagances. He was a glory and a misfortune to the Church.

DEBACLE

The Besieged Intellect

We should exalt Renaissance Italy beyond its due if we did not note that there, as elsewhere, civilization was of the few, by the few, and for the few.

The simple common man tilled the earth, pulled the carts, or bore the burdens, toiled from dawn to dusk and at evening had no muscle left for thought; he let others think for him as others made him work for them. He took his opinions, his religion, his answers to the riddles of life from the air about him, or from the ancestral cottage. He accepted not only the fascinating, comforting, inspiring, terrifying marvels by which were daily conveyed to him the traditional theology, but he added to them the demonology, sorcery, portents, magic, divination, and astrology that composed a popular metaphysics which the Church deprecated as more troublesome than heresy. Machiavelli, though skeptical of religion, suggested the possibility that "the air is peopled with spirits," and declared his belief that great events are heralded by prodigies, prophecies, revelations, and "signs in the sky."

Particularly widespread among the people was the notion that Satan, and any number of minor devils, hovered in the air, and might use supernatural powers to help their faithful worshipers. A class of women professed to have access to such devils, and through them to supernatural knowledge and powers. In 1484 a bull of Pope Innocent VIII forbade resort to such witches, and bade the Inquisition be on the alert against such practices. He specified no particular punishment, but the Inquisition, following the Old Testament's command "Thou shalt not suffer a witch to live," made witchcraft a capital crime; and in 1485, in Como alone, forty-one women were burned to death for witchcraft. Such executions multiplied: 140 in Brescia in 1486, and 300 more at Como in 1514, in the pontificate of the refined and gentle Leo X.

In such an environment science marked time; indeed it fell below the level it had reached under Albertus Magnus in the thirteenth century. It could not enjoy, as art did, the united support of laity and the Church. The only prosperous science was medicine, for men will sacrifice for health anything but appetite. Physicians were condemned for their high fees, and envied for their high social standing and their startling scarlet robes. They broke down the medieval hostility to the dissection of cadavers; sometimes ecclesiastics helped them. In 1319 medical students at Bologna stole a corpse from a cemetery and brought it to a teacher at the university, who dissected it for their instruction; they were prosecuted but acquitted; and from that time the civil authorities winked an eye at the use of executed and unclaimed criminals in "anatomies." Soon dissection was practiced in all the medical schools of Italy, including papal schools in Rome. Even so, by A.D. 1500 anatomy had only reached the knowledge possessed by Hippocrates and Galen in Greek and Roman antiquity.

Surgery rose rapidly in repute as its repertoire of operations and instruments approached the variety and competence of ancient Egyptian practice. By 1500 many European physicians had realized the Hippocratic ideal of adding philosophy to medicine; they passed with ease from one subject to the other in their study and teaching; and some of them, being also gentlemen, were part of the elixir of their time.

Renaissance Philosophy

At first glance the Renaissance offers no memorable name in philosophy; none comparable with the lusty luminaries whom Raphael was picturing as *The School of Athens,* or even with the heyday of Scholasticism from Abélard to Aquinas. Even so, it has one too-forgotten figure—Pietro Pomponazzi—so diminutive that his familiars called him Peretto—"little Peter"; and as he covered his heresies by ascribing them to the generally accepted Aristotle, he likened himself to an ant exploring an elephant. Professor of philosophy at the University of

Padua from 1495 to 1509, and then at the University of Bologna from 1512 to his death in 1525, he escaped the Inquisition because he had unburnable friends.

In his major work *Tractatus de immortalitate animae* (1516) he interpreted Aristotle as teaching that the individual's soul is inextricably bound up with his body, and dies with it; only the soul or mind of the universe is indestructible. Pomponazzi concluded that as a philosopher he agreed with Aristotle, but as a Christian he accepted the teaching of the Church. This was a hoary dodge, at which all cognoscenti smiled; and as Aristotle's view had just been condemned by the Fifth Lateran Council (1513) under the presidency of Leo X himself, many of Pomponazzi's friends expected his arrest by the Inquisition. But the humanists Bembo and Bibbiena, then high in Leo's councils, interceded with the genial pontiff, who contented himself with ordering the philosopher to write an assurance of submission to the Church. In *Apologiae libri tres* (1518) Pomponazzi assured the world that as a good Christian he accepted all the teachings of the Church.

In two minor works, wisely postmortem, Pomponazzi rejected many superstitions, magical incantations, and mysterious cures; all worldly events, he announced, have natural causes. Miracles are manifestations of natural forces only partly known to us. He conceded much to astrology: the lives of men and the history of states—even of religions—are affected by the actions of the stars. He defended the freedom of the human will; not only because we seem conscious of such freedom, but because without it there could be no moral responsibility and all social order would rest precariously on fear of the police or of divine punishment. Hence, he concluded, great legislators have taught belief in a future state of reward and suffering as an indispensable aid to government. "These things," he said of his own speculations, "are not to be communicated to common people, for they are incapable of receiving these secrets."

The lower classes kept the beloved faith despite the philosophers. The thousands who heard Savonarola must have believed, and the example of Vittoria Colonna shows that piety could survive education. But the soul of the great creed had been pierced with the arrows of doubt, and the Gothic splendor of the medieval myth had been tarnished by its accumulated gold.

Machiavelli

One man remains, hard to classify or place: diplomat, historian, dramatist, philosopher; the most cynical thinker of his time, and yet a patriot fired with an ideal; a man who failed in almost everything that he undertook, but left upon history a deeper mark than almost any other figure of the age.

Niccolò Machiavelli was the son of a Florentine lawyer—a man of moderate means, who held a minor post in the government and owned a small rural villa at San Casciano, ten miles out of the city. The boy received the ordinary literary education, learning to read Latin readily, but not Greek. He took a fancy to Roman history, became enamored of Livy, and found for almost every political institution and event of his day an illuminating analogue in the history of Rome.

He began, but seems never to have completed, the study of law. He cared little for the art of the Renaissance, and expressed no interest in the discovery of America; perhaps he felt that merely the theater of politics was now enlarged, while the plot and characters would remain unchanged. His one absorbing interest was politics, the technique of influence, the chess of power. In 1498, at twenty-nine, he was appointed secretary to the Dieci della Guerra—a Council of Ten for War—and held that post for fourteen years.

In 1500 he accompanied—and soon led—a mission to Louis XII of France. He followed the French court from château to château, and transmitted to the Florentine Signoria such alert "intelligence," such keen analyses, that on his return his friends acclaimed him as a graduate diplomat.

The turning point in his development was his mission to Caesar Borgia (1502). At Senigallia he noted Borgia's happiness at having ensnared, and then strangled or caged, the adventurers who had conspired against him. These were events that stirred all Italy; to Machiavelli they were lessons in philosophy. Here was a man, six years younger than himself, who in two years had overthrown a dozen tyrants, given order to a dozen cities, and made himself the very meteor of his time; how weak seemed words before this youth who used them with such lordly economy! From that moment, Caesar Borgia became the hero of Machiavelli's thought, as Bismarck would be Nietzsche's;

here, in this embodied "will to power," was a morality beyond good and evil, a model for supermen.

In 1512, Julius II overthrew the Florentine republic and restored the Medici to power. Machiavelli lost his diplomatic post, was accused of plotting to restore the government, was arrested, tortured, freed, and retired, with a wife and four children, to the villa at San Casciano. There he spent the rest of his life, writing *Discourses on the First Ten Books of Livy* and a summary of his conclusions, called *Il Principe.* It circulated in manuscript, but was not published till five years after his death. Thereafter it was among the most frequently reprinted volumes in the history of philosophy.

It is the most honest and immoral of books. It expounds, clearly and frankly, the doctrine that a state need not, must not, practice the moral code which it recommends to its citizens. It may justly punish perjury, fraud, theft, cruelty, and murder, but it may rightly practice any or all of these if it considers them necessary to the protection of the state. Machiavelli interprets the old Roman rule *salus populi suprema lex* to mean that the safety of the state—that is, the people organized—is the supreme law. Moreover (Machiavelli proceeds) the Christian ideal of peace may enervate a citizenry; an occasional war is a national tonic, restoring discipline, unity, and strength. Virtue, in the Roman Republic, was not humility or gentleness, but manliness, virility, courage armed with energy and intelligence. A war that strengthens a nation is good. When a state ceases to expand, it begins to die.

In his *Discourses,* Machiavelli extended his argument from the ethics of government to what seemed to him the miserable fragmentation of Italy into petty states warring upon one another with purchasable armies allergic to combat, under condottieri open to any liberal offer from any enemy. He knew that northern rulers coveted the fruitful lands and brilliant art of Italy. He dallied a while with the hope that Caesar Borgia, so regularly victorious, would master all Italy and then lead a patriotic army to the defense of the peninsula. But Caesar Borgia died in 1507, and Machiavelli, tired of politics, tired of his rural retreat, tired even of his tavern friends, gave up his life in 1527. In that year a predominantly German army conquered and devastated Rome, and put an end to the Roman Renaissance.

Adrian VI

The population of the capital, from princes to populace, was shocked to learn, on January 2, 1522, that the conclave of cardinals had elected to the papacy a non-Italian (the first since 1378)—and, worse yet, a Teuton (the first since 1161), at the very time when Martin Luther was leading Germany into open revolt against the Church of Rome.

Adrian Dedel was a Hollander, born of lowly folk in Utrecht in 1459; educated at Louvain; made chancellor of that university at the age of thirty-four; tutor at forty-seven to the dour and resolute youth who was to be Charles V, emperor of the Holy Roman Empire. In 1515, Adrian was sent on a mission to Spain, and so impressed King Ferdinand with his administrative ability that he was made bishop of Tortosa. Through all this progress he remained modest in everything but theology, and persecuted heresies with a zeal that endeared him to the people of Spain. Perhaps it was through the influence of Charles V that he was made pope by a conclave of cardinals overwhelmingly Italian.

Adrian VI felt lost in the Vatican and pronounced it better fit for an emperor than for a successor to fisherman Peter. He sent away all but four of the hundred grooms that Leo had kept for his stable; he reduced his personal servants to two—both Dutch—and bade them bring his household expenses down to 1 ducat ($12.50) a day. He was horrified by the looseness of sex and tongue and pen in Rome, and agreed with Lorenzo and Luther that the capital of Christianity was a sink of iniquity.

He cared nothing for the ancient art that the cardinals showed him; he denounced the statuary as relics of idolatry and walled up the Belvedere Palace, which contained Europe's first collection of classical sculpture. He had a mind to wall up the humanists, too, and the poets, who seemed to him to live and write like pagans who had banished Christ.

To lead the Church back from Leo to Christ became the devout passion of Adrian's pontificate. He set himself with blunt directness to reform such ecclesiastical abuses as he could reach. He suppressed superfluous offices with sometimes inconsiderate and indiscriminate vigor. He canceled the contracts that Leo had signed to pay annuities to those who had bought church offices; 2,550 persons who had purchased these as an investment lost, so to speak, both principal and interest; Rome resounded with their cries that they had been defrauded; and one of the victims tried to kill the pope. Relatives who came to Adrian for sinecures were told to go back and earn an honest living.

He put an end to simony and nepotism, scored the venality of the Curia, enacted severe penalties for bribery and embezzlement, and punished guilty cardinals with the same treatment as the humblest clerk. He bade bishops and cardinals go back to their sees and read the lessons on the morality that he expected of them. The ill repute of Rome, he told them, was the talk of Europe. He would not accuse the cardinals themselves of vice, but he charged them with allowing vice to go unpunished in their palaces. He asked them to put an end to their luxuries and to content themselves with a maximum income of 6,000 ducats ($75,000) a year. All ecclesiastical Rome, wrote the Venetian ambassador, "is beside itself with terror, seeing what the Pope has done in the space of eight days."

But the eight days were not enough, nor the brief thirteen months of Adrian's active pontificate. Vice hid its face for a while, but survived; reforms irked a thousand officials, and met with a sullen resistance and the hope for Adrian's early death. The pope mourned to see how little one man could do to better men—"How much does a man's efficiency," he often said, "depend upon the age in which his work is cast!"—and he remarked wistfully to his old friend Heeze: "Dietrich, how much better it went with us when we were living quietly in Louvain!"

After only thirteen months in Rome, Adrian, broken in body and spirit, fell sick and died (September 14, 1523). He left all his property to the poor and insisted upon a quiet and inexpensive funeral. It was a pity that puritan Teutonic Adrian could not understand the pagan Italian Renaissance, and could not build a bridge between Germany paying, and Italy spending, Peter's pence.

But it was a crime and a folly that Rome could not bear a Christian pope.

The Sack of Rome (1527)

Adrian's successor, who took the name Clement VII, was Giulio de' Medici, the illegitimate son of Lorenzo's brother Giuliano. When Giuliano was killed, Lorenzo took Giulio into his family, and brought him up with his own sons. These included Leo, who, as pope, dispensed Giulio from the canonical impediments of bastardy, made him an archbishop, then a cardinal, then chief administrator of the pontificate. Giulio was tall and handsome, rich and learned, well mannered and of moral life, an admirer and patron of literature, music, and art.

Rome greeted his elevation to the papacy as heralding the return of Leo's gulden age. He distributed among the cardinals all the benefices that he had enjoyed. He won the hearts and dedication of scholars and scribes by drawing them into his service or supporting them with gifts. He dealt out justice justly, gave audiences freely, bestowed charity with less than Leonine, but with wiser generosity, and charmed all by his courtesy to every person and class. No pope ever began so well, or ended so miserably.

The task of steering a safe course between Francis I and Charles V in a war almost to the death, while the Turks were overrunning Hungary and one-third of Europe was in full revolt against the Church, proved too much for Clement's abilities, as for Leo's, too. The magnificent portrait of Clement in his early pontificate, by Sebastiano del Piombo, is deceptive: he did not show in his actions the hard resolution that there seems limned in his face; and even in that picture a certain weak weariness shows in the tired eyelids drooping upon sullen eyes.

Clement made irresolution a policy. He carried thought to excess, and mistook it as a substitute for action instead of its guide. He could find a hundred reasons for a decision, and a hundred against it; it was as if "Buridan's ass" sat on the papal throne. (I should explain that Jean Buridan was a scholastic philosopher who explained the psychology of hesitation by describing a philosophical donkey who, desperately hungry, but placed equidistant between two piles of hay, and unable to find any reason to go to one instead of the other, died of hunger.)

Clement's "haystacks" were Francis, king of France, and Charles I, king of Spain (1516–56), who was also (1519–56) Charles V, emperor of the Holy Roman Empire. When these two fought for control of Italy, Clement oscillated between the Frenchman and the Spaniard, until Charles sent agents to win Clement or depose him.

Meanwhile the Turks under Suleiman the Magnificent captured Budapest (September 10, 1526), Belgrade, and Algiers. Clement feared that Europe would become not merely Protestant but Mohammedan.

Charles, remaining in Spain, and moving his dramatis personae by remote control, commissioned his agents to assemble a new army. They promised a Tirolean condottiere, Georg von Frundsberg, freedom to plunder if he would lead his German mercenaries into Italy and unseat Clement VII. Frundsberg was still nominally Catholic, but he sympathized with Luther and hated Clement as a traitor to the head of the Holy Roman Empire. He raised 38,000 gulden and collected 10,000 mercenaries eager for adventure and pillage, and not averse to hanging a pope. He led them across the Po and allowed them to ravage Lombardy.

Meanwhile another Charles, duke of Bourbon, having personal reasons for opposing Francis I, led his army out of Milan to join Frundsberg's forces near Piacenza. The conglomerate horde, now numbering some 22,000 men, advanced toward Rome, robbing freely as it passed.

When Clement realized that neither Charles V nor Francis I would come to his aid, he mustered 60,000 ducats with which his emissaries persuaded both Frundsberg and Bourbon to keep their men out of the Papal States. But their troops refused to honor this agreement. For four months they had endured a thousand hardships only in the hope of plundering Rome; most of them were now in rags, many were shoeless, all were hungry, none was paid; they refused to be bought off with a miserable 60,000 ducats, of which they knew only a small part would trickle down to them. Fearing that Bourbon would sign the truce, they besieged his tent, crying, "Pay! Pay!" He hid himself elsewhere, and they plundered his tent. Frundsberg tried to calm them, but was stricken with apoplexy in the course of his appeal; he played no further part in the campaign and died a year later. Bourbon took command, but only by agreeing to march on Rome. On March 29 he sent messages to Charles de Lannoy (Viceroy of Naples for Charles) and Clement that he could not hold back his men and that the truce was perforce at an end.

Now at last Rome realized that it was the intended and helpless prey. On Holy Thursday (April 9), when Clement was giving his blessing to a crowd of 10,000 persons before St. Peter's, a fanatic clad only in a leather apron mounted the statue of St. Paul and shouted to the pope: "Thou bastard of Sodom! For thy sins Rome shall be destroyed. Repent and turn thee! If thou wilt not believe me, in fourteen days thou shalt see." On Easter Eve this wild eremite—Bartolommeo Carosi, called Brandano—went through the streets crying, "Rome, do penance! They shall deal with thee as God dealt with Sodom and Gomorrah."

Bourbon, perhaps hoping to satisfy his men with the enlarged sum, sent to Clement a demand for 240,000 ducats; Clement replied that he could not possibly raise such a ransom. He had now some 4,000 soldiers to meet the attack of 20,000 hungry men.

On May 6, Bourbon's multitude approached the walls under cover of fog. They were repelled by a fusillade; Bourbon himself was hit, and died almost instantly. But the assailants could not be deterred from repeated attack; their alternatives were to capture Rome or starve. They found a weakly defended position; they broke through it and poured into the city. Clement, most of the resident cardinals, and hundreds of officials fled to the Castel Sant'Angelo.

As the invaders rushed on through the streets, they killed indiscriminately. They entered the hospital and orphanage of Santo Spirito and slaughtered nearly all the patients. St. Peter's and the Vatican were rifled from top to bottom, and horses were tethered in Raphael's *stanze*. Every palace paid ransom for protection, only to face later attacks from other packs and pay ransom again. Children were flung from high windows to pry parental savings from secrecy. One cardinal was lowered into a grave and was told that he would be buried alive unless ransom was brought.

The number of deaths cannot be calculated. The sack lasted eight days, while Clement looked on from the towers of the Castel Sant'Angelo like tortured Job. Charles, still in Spain, was glad to hear that Rome had been taken, but was shocked when he heard of the savagery of the sack; he disclaimed responsibility for the excesses but took full advantage of the Pope's helplessness. On June 6 his representatives, possibly without his knowledge, compelled Clement to sign a humiliating peace. All those in Sant'Angelo were allowed to depart except Clement and the thirteen cardinals who had accompanied him. The whole edifice of the papacy, material and spiritual, seemed to be collapsing into a tragic ruin that awoke the pity even of those who felt that some punishment was deserved by the infidelities of Clement, the sins of the papacy, the greed and corruption of the Curia, and the iniquity of Rome.

Erasmus mourned the passing of the city's halcyon days: "Rome was not alone the shrine of the Christian faith, the nurse of noble souls, and the abode of the pluses, but the mother of nations. To how many was she not dearer and sweeter and more precious than their own land! . . . In truth this is not the ruin of one city, but of the whole world."

Fearing a league of England and France, and softened by 112,000 ducats from the continuing revenues of the Church, Charles released the imprisoned pope (December 27, 1527), and Clement VII, disguised as a servant, made his way from Rome to Orvieto and thence to Viterbo. After nine months of humiliation and poverty he was allowed to reenter Rome. Needing an ally, Charles made his peace with the pontiff, declared himself a humble servant of Christ, and kissed the papal feet in acknowledgment that his spreading state needed the help of the ailing Church. On February 22–24, 1530, Clement crowned Charles with the iron crown of Lombardy and the crown of the Holy Roman Empire.

Clement died four years later (September 25, 1534) after the most disastrous pontificate in the history of the Roman Church. At his accession Henry VIII was still *defensor fidei* against Luther, and the Protestant revolt had as yet proposed no vital doctrinal changes; at Clement's death, England, Denmark, Sweden, half of Germany, and part of Switzerland had definitely broken away from the Church, and Italy had submitted to a Spanish domination fatal to the thought and life that had, for good or evil, marked the Renaissance. Everyone had rejoiced at Clement's accession; nearly everyone rejoiced at his death; and the rabble of Rome repeatedly defiled his tomb.

But at the other end of Italy, Venice, in the sunset of her glory, was giving the Renaissance another brilliant life.

THE RENAISSANCE III: VENETIAN SUNSET

VENICE AND HER REALM

In 1378, Venice was at its nadir. Her Adriatic trade was bottled up by a victorious Genoese fleet; her communications with her tributaries were blocked by hostile forces; her people were starving; her government contemplated a humiliating surrender.

Half a century later she ruled Padua, Vicenza, Verona, Brescia, Bergamo, both sides of the northern Adriatic, and, beyond it, Lepanto, Patras, and Corinth. Secure in her many-moated citadel, she seemed immune to the political vicissitudes of the mainland; her wealth and power had mounted until she sat like a throned queen at the head of Italy. The annual income of her government—800,000 ducats ($20,000,000) in 1455—exceeded that of any other Italian state and equaled that of all Christian Spain. The proud palaces and fluid promenade of the Grand Canal led the traveled Philippe de Comines to pronounce this "the most beautiful street in the world."

Her wealth came from a hundred industries—shipbuilding, iron, glass, leather, textiles, gems—and a commercial fleet that carried the products of Venice and her dependencies to Greece, Egypt, and Asia, and returned with silks, spices, rugs, drugs, and slaves; her exports in an average year were valued at 10,000,000 ducats; no other city in Europe equaled that trade.

An earthy licentiousness and profanity sat side by side in the Venetian (and Italian) character with orthodox belief and weekly piety. On Sundays and holy days, the populace crowded into St. Mark's and absorbed doses of terror and hope from the mosaics and statues, the icons and sermons. Even the prostitutes came here after a wearing night, to cleanse themselves from men. The great basilica hardly symbolized Venetian civilization, or Venetian art. Built in its present form in 1073, it remained, through every renovation, thoroughly Byzantine in its external ornament and internal gloom; its ritual, sermons, and mosaics conveyed medieval myths and terrors rather than the lusty joy and careless creed of the Italian Renaissance.

Beside that spreading fane, the Palace of the Doges united classic columns, Romanesque arches, and Gothic pinnacles to enclose luxurious chambers for lordly senators, or cover underground dungeons for careless enemies. Facing the Piazza San Marco or the Grand Canal, palaces rose year by year, outwardly modest, inwardly adorned with all the wealth and warmth of Venetian art and luxury. Here Byron reveled and Wagner died. Here, as in the Palazzo dei Dogi, or in a score of churches modest or magnificent, or in the *scuoli* (schools) of the friars, would rise, in a dazzling succession, the paintings of Gentile and Giovanni Bellini, Carpaccio, Giorgione, Titian, Tintoretto, and Veronese. Rome would find it difficult to rival that dynasty.

Even the enemies of Venice admired her government and sent agents to study its structure and functioning. It was controlled by a closed oligarchy of old families, listed in a *Libro d'oro,* who chose a Maggior Consiglio, or Greater Council, which chose sixty men to serve as a legislative Senate, which chose a doge (leader) as executive, who, with six privy councilors, constituted the Signoria. To guard against internal or external conspiracies the Maggior Consilio yearly chose a Council of Ten as a committee of public safety. Through its spies and swift procedure, its secret sessions and trials, this Consiglio dei Dieci became for a time the most powerful arm of the government.

Many legends arose about this council, usually exaggerating its secrecy and severity. All in all, it was an efficient constitution, which maintained the state in a prosperous stability, and was capable of far-calculated policies that might have been difficult to maintain under a government subject to frequent fluctuations of public sentiment.

Venetian life was more attractive in its setting than in its spirit. The autocracy was competent and showed high courage in adversity; but it was sometimes brutal and always selfish; like its neighbors, it never thought of itself as a part of Italy, and cared little what political tragedy might befall that divided land. It developed powerful personalities— self-reliant, shrewd, acquisitive, valiant, proud; we know a hundred of them through portraits by artists whom they were refined enough to patronize. It was a culture that, compared with the Florentine, lacked subtlety and depth; that, compared with the Milanese under Lodovico, lacked finesse and grace. But it was the most colorful, sumptuous, and sensually bewitching civilization that history has ever known.

VENETIAN ART

Before Titian

Sensuous color is the essence of Venetian art, even of its architecture. Many Venetian churches and dwellings, as well as some business buildings, had mosaics or frescoes on their fronts.

The facade of St. Mark's gleamed with gilt and almost haphazard ornament; nearly every decade brought to it new spoils and forms, until the face of the great church became a bizarre medley of architecture, sculpture, and mosaic, in which decoration drowned structure, and the parts forgot the whole. To admire that facade one must stand 576 feet away, at the farther end of the Piazza San Marco; then the brilliant conglomeration of Romanesque portal, Gothic ogees, classic columns, Renaissance railing, and Byzantine domes blends into one exotic phantasm, an Aladdin's magic dream.

Between St. Mark's and the Grand Canal, the Palace of the Doges stands as the proud face of the civic state. Largely rebuilt from 1309 to 1443, its southern facade, fronting the water, and its western facade, opposite the classical *Libreria Vecchia,* or Old Library, which Iacopo Sansovino built in 1536 as an added splendor for the piazza—the graceful Gothic arcades and balconies, the superbly sculptured capitals, of the palace can hold the eye and mind for hours. Ruskin thought one of those capitals the finest in Europe. Within the court Bartolommeo Buon the Younger and Antonio Rizzo raised an ornate arch, adorned with two strange statues—Adam seeming to protest that he had been seduced, and Eve possibly wondering why knowledge should be accounted a sin. From that court the famous Scala dei Giganti, or Stairway of the Giants, led by massive steps to the offices and assembly rooms of the Greater Council, the Senate, and the Ten.

It was a vainglory and yet a glory that the Venetians wanted pictures: individuals to perpetuate their excellences—hence so many masterpieces by Titian; the government to impress its subjects with its power and dignity—hence some of the finest murals in history; the Church to tell the Christian story to the people, of whom only a few could read—hence so many Annunciations, Nativities, Visitations, Massacres of the Innocents, Flights to Egypt, Transfigurations, Last Suppers, Crucifixions, Entombments, Resurrections, Ascensions, Martyrdoms. Even the Greeks had had no such success in perpetuating their creeds.

Some external stimuli helped to beget a Venetian school of painting. Two artists from other cities helped to replace the dark and solemn faces of the Byzantine tradition and the lifeless figures of Giotto's saints. Antonello of Messina, traveling on business in Flanders, noticed the brighter finish and greater permanence of oil paintings, and their finer gradations of color, as compared with the tempera—mixing the colors with some gelatinous substance—still used in Italy. Settling in Venice because "greatly addicted to women and pleasure," he tried his hand at oil painting, and so impressed the tempera painters that a revolution in methods brought the first flowering of the Venetian pictorial art.

Two half-brothers—Gentile and Giovanni Bellini—led the colorful parade. In 1474 the Signoria assigned to them the task of repainting fourteen decaying panels in the hall of the Maggior Consiglio. The results were among the earliest Venetian paintings in oil. Their success may have encouraged Mohammed II, conqueror (1453) of Christian Constantinople, to ask the Venetian government for an able portrait painter. It sent him Gentile Bellini. Gentile enlivened the aged sultan with erotic pictures, and then (1474) painted him as a powerful character accustomed to victory.

In 1480, Gentile returned to Venice; Mohammed died a year later; his successor, obeying the Moslem ban on picturing the human figure, scattered into oblivion all but two of Gentile's Turkish paintings. Gentile continued to produce great pictures till his death (1507).

His brother Giovanni (fondly Gian), younger by one year, survived him by nine, and brought the art of oil painting to its first Venetian peak. He achieved a splendor of color, a grace and accuracy of line, a delicacy of feeling, a depth of interpretation, that—even in the lifetime of his brother—made him the most acclaimed and sought-after painter in Venice. Churches, guilds, and private patrons seemed never to tire of his Madonnas and Christs; and the brilliant Doge Loredano found time to sit for one of the greatest portraits in Venetian art.

Between the labors of the Bellini and the triumphs of Titian, one especially fascinating painter intervened who is still known to us only by his family name, Giorgione da Castelfranco. We do not know his parents, but we see his lineage when we learn that in his thirteenth year he was sent to Venice to serve as apprentice to Gian Bellini. He developed rapidly, won encouraging commissions, bought a house, frescoed its front, and filled it with music and revelry, for he played the lute fetchingly well, and preferred gay women in the flesh to the fairest of them frozen on canvas or wall. Add a touch of quiet woodland and you have his first masterpiece, *The Gypsy and the Soldier:* a casual woman naked except for a shawl around her shoulders, sits on her discarded dress on the bank of a rippling stream and nurses her child, while near her a comely youth is so pleased with the prospect that he ignores the lightning that announces a storm.

In Giorgione's *Sleeping Venus* the passage from Christian to pagan themes and sentiments is complete; Christianity is forgotten to recapture the mood of Ovid's Rome. In another piece—the *Fête champêtre,* or *Pastoral Scene,* of the Louvre—two nude women unconscious of shame, and two men clothed and unhurriedly triumphant, celebrate the union of feminine beauty with woodland charm. Only in his finest, subtlest picture—*Concert champêtre (Pastoral Symphony)*—does Giorgione transcend desire to achieve esthetic sensitivity and realization. A monk sits at a clavichord, his beautifully rendered hands on the keys, his face turned round to a bald cleric on our right; the cleric lays one hand on the monk's shoulder and holds in the other a cello resting on the floor. Has the music ended, or not yet begun? It does not matter; what moves us is the silent depth of feeling in the countenance of the monk, whose every fiber has been refined, and his every sentiment ennobled, by music; who hears it long after all the instruments have been mute. That face, not idealized but profoundly realized, is one of the miracles of Renaissance painting.

Giorgione lived a short life and apparently a merry one. He seems to have had many women and to have healed each broken romance with a new one soon begun. Vasari reports that Giorgione caught the plague from his latest love; all that we know is that he died in the epidemic of 1511 at the age of thirty-four. He left two pupils who were to make a stir in the world: Sebastiano del Piombo, who went off to Rome, and Tiziano Vecelli, the greatest Venetian painter of all.

Titian

He was born at Pieve in the Dolomites (1477), and though he was transferred to Venice in his tenth year, those mountains, like supernatural entities hovering over human absurdities, lingered in his memories and landscapes. He studied under the Bellini, worked beside Giorgione, and deeply felt his influence.

He developed slowly, as if leaving time for all his gifts to mature. In 1515 he reached mastery with three thoughtful pictures. First, *The Three Ages of Man:* infants sleeping in innocent nudity under a tree, while Cupid inoculates them with desire; a young couple in the springtime of love; and a bearded octogenarian contemplating a skull. Second: *Sacred and Profane Love,* where the nude is done with a fond perfection that may have started Rubens on a long tour of unimpeded beauties; here the movement of the Renaissance from the Virgin to Venus seems complete. But in this same year, 1515, Titian painted for the church of the Frari what is perhaps his greatest work, *The Assumption of the Virgin* from the earth toward paradise; to this day the sight of that masterpiece is an unforgettable event in any sensitive wanderer's life. Standing wordless before this powerful evocation, the unwilling skeptic mourns his doubts and acknowledges the power and beauty of the myth.

The favorite friend of this greatest of Venetian painters was the most scurrilous, immoral, shameless, brilliant writer of his time, patron of prostitutes and favored friend of the emperor Charles V. Son of an obscure shoemaker and an unknown mother, he was content to be named Aretino, from his native Arezzo. He did not mind being a bastard, since he found distinguished company in that class.

He passed through various forms of poverty until he amassed ample ducats from his wit and pen; prominent people paid him to be spared from his satire, and thousands read his books to enjoy seeing million-aires mauled and notables pilloried. Moving to Venice in 1521, the "Scourge of Princes" rented comfortable rooms on the Grand Canal, and enjoyed the procession of business and pleasure passing beneath his window with hardly more noise than the signals of the gondoliers and the lapping of their oars.

Now he dressed like a lord, dispersed charity to the poor, supported a succession of mistresses, and entertained a host of friends. Titian was happy to enjoy Aretino's hospitality and to profit from his recommen-dations to titled or moneyed notables. In 1530, Aretino introduced him to Charles V.

The Holy Roman Emperor, having conquered most of Italy, was busy reorganizing it, and fretted impatiently for a portrait which he thought worthy of 1 ducat ($12.50). Federigo, marquis of Mantua, quietly gave Titian 150 ducats more, and assured Charles that he had been sitting for "the best painter now living." By 1532 the emperor was convinced, and during the next sixteen years he sat for Titian so often that the artist must have longed for freedom.

It must have been with some relief that he passed on to paint the pope. Paul III was also "imperial"—a man of virile character and subtle craft, with a face that recorded two generations of history; here was a better opportunity for Titian than he had found in the uncommunica-tive emperor. At Bologna in 1543, Paul faced frankly the realism of Titian's portraiture. Seventy-five years old, weary but indomitable, he sat in his papal robes, the long head and large beard bent over a once-powerful frame, the ring of office conspicuous on his aristocratic hand; this and Raphael's Julius II contest the distinction of being the finest, deepest portrait of the Italian Renaissance.

In 1552, Titian ended his travels and returned to Venice. He had been too busy to find time to die, but now, seventy-five, he may have felt mortality and some summons to return from Grecian deities to the faith of his youth. He painted another series of Christian pictures, but some persisting vitality repeatedly drew him back to pagan themes, and many a Diana or Aphrodite still issued from his brush.

Greater and deeper than these mythological nudes were the portraits that Titian now produced with such abundance that his art seemed a second nature. Astonishing is his representation of Aretino—the evocation of a fascinating scoundrel by a faithful friend. Almost as revealing as Titian's portrait of himself at eighty-nine; a face lined and yet cleansed by the flow of many days, blue eyes a bit somber, seeing death, but a hand grasping a brush—the artistic passion still unspent.

He died in 1576 at age ninety-nine. There were still giants after him, like Tintoretto and Veronese, who glorified with their art the chambers of the government; we leave them to longer works. Venetian art and letters sang the greatness of Venice even as her economy sank to ruin in a Mediterranean dominated at one end by the Turks and deserted at the other by a Europe seeking American gold.

No vicissitudes of trade or war could extinguish the proud memory of a marvelous century—1480–1580—during which the Mocenigi and Priuli and Loredani had made and saved imperial Venice, and the Lombardi and Leopardi had adorned her with statuary, and Sansovino and Palladio had crowned her waters with churches and palaces, and the Bellini and Giorgione and Titian and Tintoretto and Veronese had lifted her to the art leadership of Italy, and Aldus Manutius had poured out, in excellent print and form, to all who cared, the literary heritage of Greece and Rome, and the irrepressible Mephistophelean Scourge of Princes had sat enthroned on the Grand Canal judging and milking mankind.

Lingering in Italy

We have not done justice to Tintoretto, Veronese, and others who embellished the magisterial chambers of the Palace of the Doges; we have neglected Correggio, Cellini, and other dedicated souls who for a time made Italy the "Light of the World"; and we have forgotten the last decade and labors of Michelangelo, who entombed dead Medici with immortal sculpture and crowned St. Peter's with a cupola that is still, in a doubting age, the center and peak of Western civilization.

We honor Michelangelo because through a long and tortured life he continued to create, and produced in each main field, a masterpiece. We see these works torn, so to speak, out of his flesh and blood, out of his mind and heart, leaving him for a time weakened with birth. We see them taking form through a hundred thousand strokes of hammer and chisel, pencil and brush; one after another, like an immortal population, they take their place among the lasting shapes of beauty or significance.

We cannot know what God is, nor understand a universe so mingled of apparent evil and good, of suffering and loveliness, destruction and sublimity; but in the presence of a mother tending her child, or of an informed will giving order to chaos, meaning to matter, nobility to form or thought, we feel as close as we shall ever be to the life and law that constitute the incomprehensible intelligence of the world.

Chapter Eighteen

ﾟﾟﾟﾟﾟ

THE REFORMATION I:
WYCLIF AND ERASMUS

PRELUDE (A.D. 30–1307)

The Roman Catholic Church is one of the most remarkable organizations in history, and an objective study of its origins, purpose, methods, vicissitudes, faults, and achievements would shed more light upon the nature and possibilities of man and government than the study of almost any other subject or institution open to human inquiry.

When the fading belief in Rome's pagan deities could no longer give moral support to a disordered and imperiled state in the task of controlling the native individualism of men and groups, a new faith in a stern, yet forgiving God, and his redeeming and inspiring Son, gave to a growing minority a creed that both fed and calmed human wonder and fear, and developed a moral code and social order that made a new civilization possible.

The old masculine Latin of Roman soldiers was softened to fit hymns and chivalry; literature frolicked and experimented in a hundred forms; art added the joy and exultation of Gothic ornament and spires to the calm nobility of classic colonnades and domes. And the Roman Catholic Church grew to such acceptance and devotion that it could check the natural self-seeking of men and state with the power of the venerated word.

By A.D. 1300 that majestic structure had been eroded by the nature of man. Some administrators of the Church proved human, venal, biased, oppressive, or extortionate; some kings—made stronger by social order and developing economies—rejected papal claims to secular power and mourned the passage of their people's money to a foreign potentate.

In 1303, Philip IV of France successfully challenged the authority of Pope Boniface VIII over the property and activities of the Catholic Church in France. He imprisoned Boniface for three days in Anagni, in central Italy; the pontiff died soon after. In 1305, Philip procured the election of a Frenchman to the papacy as Clement V; and in 1309 he persuaded him to move the papal seat from Rome to Avignon on the Rhone. There, till 1377, the papacy became in some measure a feudal fief of the French king, and was so considered by other rulers who increasingly mourned the export of their people's savings to a foreign papacy.

As if to proclaim their vassalage, the Avignon pontiffs, in a total of 134 nominations to the college of cardinals, named 113 Frenchmen. The electors of the Holy Roman Empire repudiated any further interference of the popes in the election of kings or emperors. In some German cities papal collectors were hunted down, imprisoned, mutilated, or strangled. In 1372 the clergy of Bonn, Cologne, and Mainz bound themselves to refuse payment of papal tithes.

In Italy, the papal capital states, chiefly Ferrara, Bologna, Ravenna, Rimini, Urbino—were seized by condottieri despots who gave the now distant pope a formal obeisance, but kept the revenues. The English government fumed at the loans of the Avignon popes to the king of France during the Hundred Years' War. Harassed on every side, the Avignon popes found it impossible to meet the cost of administration and the demands of cardinals and favorites for their accustomed comforts and delights. "Wolves are in control of the Church," cried the Spanish prelate Alvaro Pelayo, "and feed upon the blood of the Christian flock." In 1311, William Durand, bishop of Mende (in southern France) told the Council of Vienne:

> The whole Church might be reformed if the Church of Rome would begin by removing evil examples from herself . . . by which men are scandalized and the whole people, as it were, infected . . . For in all lands . . . the Church of Rome is in ill repute, and all cry and publish

it abroad that within her bosom all men, from the greatest even unto
the least, have set their hearts upon covetousness . . . That the whole
Christian folk take from the clergy pernicious examples of gluttony
is clear and notorious, since the clergy feasts more luxuriously . . .
than princes and kings.

And, in England, kings and Parliament smiled upon a priest who anticipated Luther and Henry VIII by almost two centuries in assailing
the theology and political claims of the Catholic Church.

JOHN WYCLIF

John Wyclif was born in 1320 near the Yorkshire village which gave
him his name. He studied at Oxford, became a priest, served for a year
as master of Balliol College, accepted various benefices from the popes
and issued several volumes whose graceless Latin obscured and long
protected a merciless predestination theology. By general Christian
consent, God is omnipotent and omniscient; there is no act, event,
thought, or volition, however "free," past, present, or future, unknown
to Him; therefore, none occurs without His implicit consent. It seems
to follow that those unnumbered sinners who had not made their peace
with God and obtained his grace before their death had been condemned to everlasting hell by the Almighty before their birth. Good
works do not win salvation, but they indicate that he who performs
them has received divine grace, and is one of the elect—chosen from all
eternity for eternal bliss.

From the communism and divine inspiration ascribed to the Apostles by the New Testament, Wyclif concluded that their successors and
their ordained delegates were meant to have no property. The reform
most needed in the Church and its clergy is the complete renunciation
of worldly goods. Parliament liked this, refused to pay the expected
tribute to the papacy, and appointed Wyclif to defend the refusal. John
of Gaunt proposed that the English government should confiscate part
of Church property in England; he invited Wyclif to defend the plan in
a series of sermons; Wyclif came, supported by John's armed retinue;
the clergy dared not protest.

Pope Gregory XI issued bulls condemning eighteen propositions found in Wyclif's writings; unless he retracted them, the bishops were to arrest him and keep him in chains. But the Parliament that met in October 1737 was so strongly anticlerical that the king's advisors asked Wyclif to prepare an opinion on the question "Whether the realm of England can legitimately—when the necessity of repelling invasion is imminent—withhold the treasure of the Realm that it be not sent to foreign parts, although the pope demand it under pain of censure and in virtue of obedience to him?" Wyclif answered: "The pope cannot demand this treasure except by way of alms." Against the contention that the English Church was part of, and should obey, the universal or Catholic Church, Wyclif recommended the ecclesiastical independence of England: "The Realm of England, in the words of Scripture, ought to be one body, and clergy, lords, and commonalty members of that body." This anticipation in 1377 of Henry VIII's declaration of ecclesiastical independence seemed so bold that the king's advisors directed Wyclif to make no further statement on the matter.

Nevertheless, in March 1378, Wyclif appeared before the bishops' assembly at Lambeth to defend his views. The mother of King Richard II sent the archbishop a letter deprecating any final condemnation of Wyclif, and in the midst of the proceedings a crowd forced its way in from the street and declared that the English people would not tolerate any Inquisition in England. The bishops deferred decision, and Wyclif went home triumphant.

Now, in books, or tracts, he multiplied his heresies and doubled his denunciations. He described some monasteries as "dens of thieves, nests of serpents, and houses of living devils." "Prelates deceive men by feigned indulgences or pardons, and rob them of their money. . . . Men be great fools that buy these bulls. . . . So dear." If the pope has the power to snatch souls from purgatory, why does he not free them at once? Wyclif alleged that "many-priests . . . defile wives, maidens, widows, and nuns." He excoriated prelates who hunted and hawked and gambled and related fake miracles; who pray only for show, and collect fees for every religious service they perform; who ride fat horses with harness of silver and gold; "they are robbers . . . malicious foxes . . . ravishing wolves . . . gluttons . . . devils . . . apes"—here even Luther's cordial vituperation is forecast. Perhaps, Wyclif suggested, the pope is the Antichrist predicted by the apostle John, the Beast of the Apocalypse, heralding the Second Coming of Christ.

As cures for these frailties, Wyclif proposed that the Church should be deprived of all material possessions and powers, and priests should live in apostolic poverty. Monks should return to the full observance of their rule. If the clergy refuses to surrender its material possessions, the state should confiscate all ecclesiastical property, and "priests should be constrained to keep to the poverty that Christ ordained." Kings may command all this, and compel obedience; they are responsible to God alone, from whom they derive their dominion and authority. Priests should be ordained by the king.

Many notables in the English government were scandalized by Wyclif's denunciations; even some supporters were alarmed. He reaffirmed his views in the *Confessio* of May 10, 1381. A month later, social revolution flared in England and frightened the holders of property; Wyclif now lost most of his parliamentary support. King Richard II, having narrowly escaped dethronement by the uprising, ordered the University of Oxford to expel Wyclif and all his adherents. He retired to his living at Lutterworth, disassociated himself from the rebels, continued his pamphleteering against the Church, organized a body of "Poor Preaching Priests" (later called Lollards), gathered scholars to translate the Bible from Jerome's Latin version, and apparently translated the New Testament himself. The collective product was not a model of English prose, but it was a vital event in English history.

In 1384, Pope Urban VI summoned Wyclif to appear before him in Rome. A sharper summons came in a paralytic stroke on December 28, 1384, as Wyclif was attending mass. Three days later he died. He was buried at Lutterworth, but by a decree of the Council of Constance (May 4, 1415) his bones were dug up and cast into a nearby stream.

THE PAPAL SCHISMS (1378–1417)

Germany and Italy agreed with England in scorning the Avignon papacy. In 1372 the abbots of Cologne publicly agreed that "the Apostolic Sea has fallen into such contempt that the Catholic faith in these parts seems seriously imperiled." In 1362, when Urban V sent two legates to Milan to excommunicate the recalcitrant Visconti, Bernabo compelled them to eat the bulls—parchment, silken cords, and leaden seals (1362). In 1376, Florence, in a quarrel with Pope Gregory XI, demolished the buildings of the Inquisition, jailed or hanged resisting priests, and called upon Italy to end all temporal power of the Church. It became clear that the Avignon popes were losing Europe in their fealty to France. In 1377, Gregory XI returned the papacy to Rome.

However, a rival pope set himself up in Avignon, and Roman Catholic Europe was divided in a "Papal Schism" that lasted thirty-nine years and sometimes saw three rival popes claiming universal religious authority and all papal revenues. The result was a triple financial campaign whose persistence and devices scandalized the Christian world. I quote again a message sent in 1430 by a German envoy in Rome to his prince:

> Greed reigns supreme in the Roman court, and day by day finds new devices . . . for extorting money from Germany. . . . Hence much outcry and heartburnings. . . . Many questions in regard to the papacy will arise, or else obedience will at last be entirely renounced, to escape from these outrageous exactions by the Italians; and this latter course, as I perceive, would be acceptable to many countries.

The flow of ecclesiastical levees into Rome might have been tolerated if these funds had been turned into competent administration of the Church, but it seemed to the North that they were too largely consumed in luxurious living. We must recall the appeal of Pope Pius II to his cardinals in 1643:

> People say that we live for pleasure, accumulate wealth, bear ourselves arrogantly, ride on fat mules and handsome palfreys . . . keep hounds for the chase, spend much on actors and parasites and nothing in defense of the faith. And there is some truth in their words: many among the cardinals and other officials of our court do lead this kind of life. If the truth be confessed, the luxury and pomp of our court is too great. And this is why we are so detested by the people that they will not listen to us, even when we say what is just and reasonable.

Perhaps the Catholic historian Ludwig von Pastor paints too dark a picture:

> A deep-rooted corruption had taken possession of nearly all the officials of the Curia. . . . The inordinate number of gratuities and exactions passed all bounds. Moreover, on all sides deeds were dishonestly manipulated, and even falsified. No wonder that there arose from all parts of Christendom the loudest complaints about the corruption and financial extortions of the papal officials.

And the same historian spreads his verdict indiscriminately:

> It is not surprising, when the highest ranks of the clergy were in such a state, that among the regular orders and secular priests vice and irregularities of all sorts should become more and more common. The salt of the earth had lost its savor. . . . But it is a mistake to suppose that the corruption of the clergy was worse in Rome than elsewhere; there is documentary evidence of the immorality of the priests in almost every town in the Italian peninsula. . . . No wonder, as contemporary writers sadly testify, the influence of the clergy had declined, and in many places hardly any respect was shown for the priesthood. Their immorality was so gross that suggestions in favor of allowing priests to marry began to be heard.

We might suggest two modifications of the indictment. The parish priest seems to have been loved and honored almost everywhere; he was too busy serving his community, or sharing in its labor, to have much time for sin. And though both the secular clergy and the monastic orders may rightly be charged with sexual adventures, often with private or open concubinage, this was partly a revolt against the irksome canon law of 1074 forbidding priestly marriage. Greek and Russian Orthodox Churches had continued to allow such unions; the Roman Catholic clergy itched for the same right, and being denied it took more or less openly to concubinage. Bishop Hardouin of Angers reported in 1428 that the clergy of his diocese did not consider concubinage a sin, and made no attempt to conceal their practice of it.

This recurrent triumph of Magdalene over the Virgin in the history of religion, and a score of other developments, were undermining the moral and doctrinal structure that medieval Christianity had built over the malleable figure of Christ. The spread of education and learning, the exhumation of classical culture, the increasing independence and secularism of the universities, the secret nourishment of Christian doubt by the triumph of Islam over the Crusades, the unwitting liberation of reason by the Scholastic philosophers, the bold skepticism of Duns Scotus and William of Ockham, the liberation of the flesh in every class, the worldliness of cardinals and monks, the passage from pious agriculture to the religious apathy of urban workers, of traveled merchants, of realistic, interest-loving financiers, the rising wealth and growing armies of kings and states, the replacement of clergymen with secular officials in government, the worldliness of cardinals and monks, and now the fragmentation of the papacy: these and other developments threatened the collapse of the whole majestic edifice—doctrinal, administrative, and moral—of the once proudly Catholic, i.e., "Universal," Church.

In 1381, Heinrich von Langenstein, a German theologian at the University of Paris, in the treatise *Concilium pacis,* argued that a crisis had arisen from which only a power outside of the rival popes could rescue the Church and restore moral order to a bewildered Christendom. In 1411, Sigismond, king of Hungary and head of the Holy Roman Empire, compelled John XXIII, then one of the three claimants to the papacy, to call a general council to meet at Constance in southwestern Germany. In November 1414, the longest council in Christian history began to assemble—3 patriarchs, 29 archbishops, 150 bishops, 14 university deputies, 26 princes, 140 nobles, and 4,000 priests. On April 6, 1415, the Council issued a decree which one historian has called "the most revolutionary official document in the history of the world":

This holy synod of Constance, being a general council, and legally assembled in the Holy Spirit for the praise of God and for ending the present Schism, and for the union and reform of the Church of God in its head and its members . . . ordains, declares, and decrees as follows: First, it declares that this synod . . . represents the Church Militant, and has its authority directly from Christ; and everybody, of whatever rank or dignity, including also the pope, is bound to obey this council in those things that pertain to the faith, to the ending of this Schism, and to a general reform of the Church in its head and members. Likewise it declares that if anyone, of whatever rank, condition, or dignity, including also the pope, shall refuse to obey the commands, statutes, ordinances, or orders of this holy council, or of any other holy council properly assembled, in regard to the ending of the Schism or to the reform of the Church, he shall be subject to proper punishment . . . and, if necessary, recourse shall be had to other aids of justice.

On July 6, 1415, the Council condemned the writings of the dead Wyclif and ordered the death of John Huss. On May 30, 1416, it ordered the death of Jerome of Prague. On November 17, 1417, it chose as pope Oddone Colonna, who took the title of Martin V, and ended the Papal Schism. On April 22, 1418, the Council declared itself dissolved.

JOHN HUSS

The second prelude to the Reformation took form in Bohemia. That romantic realm had been settled by the Slavs in the fifth century, had risen to importance in the twelfth as part of the Holy Roman Empire, and had its golden age in the fourteenth under King Charles I (r. 1342–78), who made Prague one of the handsomest cities in Europe. In the twenty-seventh year of that reign, 1369, John Huss was born in the village of Husinetz, whose first syllable became his name.

In 1390 he came to Prague as a poor student, earned his way by serving in the churches, studied for the priesthood, and joined in what Paris would term the "Bohemian" ways of university youth. In 1401 he entered the priesthood and reformed his life to an almost hermetic austerity. As head of the "Bethlehem Chapel" he became the most famous preacher in Prague.

His fate was sealed when some of Wyclif's books fell into his hands. He was so charmed by the author's heresies that he said, "Wyclif, I trust, will be saved; but, could I think he could be damned, I would my soul were with his." The administrative chapter of the Prague cathedral proposed that Wyclif's teachings be banned from the university; Huss continued to support them. In 1409, Archbishop Zbynek excommunicated him and several associates. Huss appealed to Pope John XXIII; John summoned him to appear before the papal court; Huss refused to go. When the pope sent agents to Prague to sell indulgences for a crusade against the king of Naples, Huss and his chief disciple, known to us only as Jerome of Prague, preached against the Church's collection of money to spill Christian blood. Huss, scorning caution, called the pope a money-grubber, Antichrist. The pope excommunicated him and laid an interdict upon any town that should shelter him. For two years Huss secluded himself in rural retreats.

Mostly in those years he wrote his major books, some in Latin, some in Czech, nearly all adopting Wyclif's heresies. He rejected image worship, auricular confession, and papal infallibility, and followed Wyclif on predestination. He accepted the legend that a supposed Pope John VIII had revealed her sex by giving unpremeditated birth to a child.

In 1414, Sigismund, king of Hungary and head of the Holy Roman Empire, anxious to restore unity and vigor to his realm against the advancing Turks and Islam, advised Huss to go to the Council of Constance and seek reconciliation with the Church. He gave Huss an Imperial safe-conduct to Constance, promised him a hearing by the Council, and guaranteed him a safe return to Bohemia. Huss set out in October, escorted by Czech nobles and friends.

Arrived, he was treated courteously by the Council and the Church, and lived in freedom. But when some orthodox Bohemians read to the assemblage the text of Huss's heresies, it summoned him to defend himself. Shocked by his replies, it imprisoned him. He fell ill, and for a time was near death; Pope John XXIII sent papal physicians to treat him. Meanwhile his pupil and fellow heretic, Jerome of Prague, made his way to Constance, and nailed to the city gates, church doors, and the homes of cardinals an appeal that the Council should give Huss a public hearing and let him return safely to his home. Jerome himself tried to get back to Bohemia, but stopped on the way to preach against the Council. He was arrested, brought back to Constance, and jailed.

Sigismund protested that the Council had violated the safe-conduct that he had given to Huss; it answered that his authority did not extend to spiritual concerns. He pleaded with Huss to offer some retraction of his heresies; Huss offered to withdraw any of his views that could be disproved by the Bible. On July 6, 1415, the Council condemned Wyclif and Huss, and delivered Huss to the secular arm. After rejecting a final appeal to save himself by a retraction, he was led out of the city and was burned to death while singing hymns.

On May 30, 1416, after almost a year of imprisonment, and after recanting a recantation, Jerome of Prague was led out to the same spot and the same fate.

THE RENAISSANCE CHURCH (1418–1517)

The Reformation came just when the papacy was having one of its most brilliant periods. The Council of Constance had reduced three popes to one; Martin V restored the centralized administration and finances of the church, and Eugenius IV brought a bevy of classical scholars from Ferrara, Florence, even from Greece, to revitalize a drowsy Rome chaotically clerical, rebelliously feudal, or violently populist.

When Nicholas V came to the papacy in 1447, the flow of Peter's pence from Transalpine Europe was again fertilizing Italy, helping to generate the Renaissance south of the Alps and the Reformation north of them. Nicholas V almost rebankrupted the papacy by his enthusiastic support of scholars who were recovering, translating, or editing classical manuscripts, until the Catholic capital became almost a continuation of Plato's Athens or Seneca's Rome.

Caesar Borgia scattered Christian ethics to the winds and applied the principles of Machiavelli's *Prince* in recapturing for the papacy its lost states and their revenues, while his father, Pope Alexander VI (1492–1503), enriched Roman architecture and his children with the golden flow. Julius II (1503–13) completed the reconquest of central Italy for the popes, and, despite the repeated depletion of his treasury, collected funds enough to pay Raphael and Michelangelo for adorning the papal palace and the Sistine Chapel. Leo X (1513–21), son of the banker Lorenzo de' Medici, scattered gold among poets, artists, scholars, and favorites, and sent out indulgence purveyors to raise money for the completion of St. Peter's.

But the gathered revenues financed political corruption, moral laxity, and sexual license among the clergy as well as the laity, while the Pope himself remained reasonably virtuous and resolutely happy. Luther, visiting Rome in 1510, was awed by its splendor, made then no reported criticism of its morals, and earned so many indulgences that he almost wished his parents dead so that he might deliver them from purgatory into heaven; however, in later retrospect, he described the Rome of 1510 as "an abomination," the popes as worse than pagan emperors, and the papal court as being served at supper by "twelve naked girls."

Erasmus, visiting Rome in 1509, was charmed by the easy life, fine manners, and intellectual cultivation of the cardinals; he was amused by the pagan themes that had entered into the literature and talk of the capital; but he was shocked by the costly martial campaigns of Pope Julius II. Let us tarry with Erasmus, for he was accounted the most brilliant writer of his time.

DESIDERIUS ERASMUS

We do not know how he came by these names, which mean the "desired beloved." He was born in or near Rotterdam in 1466 or 1469, the second and natural son of a clerk in minor orders and of the widowed daughter of a physician.

He was sent for schooling to the Brethren of the Common Life at Deventer, where Latin was the *pièce de resistance;* some pagan classics were used as texts. He became a master of Latin, read more classics, and found them a revealing delight.

About 1484 both parents died. The father left a modest estate to his two sons; their guardians absorbed most of it and steered the youths into a monastic career requiring no patrimony at all. They protested, wishing to go to a university; they yielded, and Desiderius became a monk and, in 1492, a priest, and soon thereafter secretary to Henry, bishop of Cambrai.

He served his master well for several years and was rewarded by being sent to the University of Paris. There he listened impatiently to lectures, preferring to explore ancient literature and young charms. He taught himself Greek; in time the Athens of Plato and Aristotle, Sophocles and Euripides, Zeno and Epicurus, had become as familiar to him as the Rome of Caesar and Cicero, Augustus and Horace, Nero and Seneca. Those friendships ruined the young priest's orthodoxy and left him not much more of Christianity than a heretical admiration for the ethics of Christ.

His addiction to books was as expensive as a vice. To add to his allowance he tutored pupils who admired his familiarity with ancient tongues and lore. One of them, Mountjoy, took him to England and into aristocratic homes. The excitable priest wrote ecstatically to a friend: "There are nymphs here with divine features, so gentle and kind. . . . Wherever you go you are received on all hands with kisses; when you leave you are dismissed with kisses. . . . O Faustus! If you had once tasted how soft and fragrant those lips are, you would wish to be . . . for a whole life in England."

At Mountjoy's house in Greenwich, Erasmus met Thomas More, then only twenty-two, yet distinguished enough to secure the scholar an introduction to the future Henry VIII. At Oxford he was charmed by the informal companionship of students and faculty. He was impressed by the progress of humanism in England and influenced profoundly for his betterment. From a vain and flighty youth, drunk with the wine of the classics and the ambrosia of women, he was transformed into an earnest and painstaking scholar, anxious for some lasting and beneficent achievement. When he left England (January 1500), he had formed his resolve to study and edit the Greek text of the New Testament as the distilled essence of that real Christianity which, in the judgment of reformers and humanists alike, had been overlaid and concealed by the dogmas and accretions of centuries.

Stationing himself in Paris, he prepared and published *Adagia*—818 quotations, chiefly from classical authors. Pleased with its reception, he issued edition after edition, each expanded, until it held 3,260 entries. The book almost supported him, but he gladly accepted (1506) the invitation of a British physician to be "general guide and supervisor" of two sons on a tour of Italy. Roman cardinals welcomed him as already a scholar of European renown.

In 1509 a friend of the English humanists, now King Henry VIII, invited Erasmus to England. Erasmus went, received the revenues of a parish in Kent, and was appointed professor of Greek at Cambridge. While staying with Thomas More, in 1511, he wrote, in seven days, his most famous book—*Encomium moriae (The Praise of Folly)*. Forty editions were published in his lifetime; as late as 1632, Milton found it "in everyone's hands" at Cambridge.

To begin with, said the little book, the human race owes its existence to folly. For what man in his senses would pay for a moment's pleasure with a lifetime of monogamy? What sane woman would pay for a transient ecstasy with the pains of birth and the tribulations of motherhood? Could anyone be happy if he faced the facts of life, or knew the future? If men and women paused to reason, all would be lost. However, science and philosophy are ignored by the people and do little damage to the vital ignorance of the human race.

The little book proceeded to smile at the beliefs and practices of Christians: the creation of the world from nothing, the innocent sin of Eve, the merciless punishment of generation after generation, the virgin birth, transubstantiation; and "What shall I say of such as cry up and maintain the cheat of pardons and indulgences?—that by these compute the time of each soul's stay in purgatory, and assign it a longer or shorter residence there according as the living have bought more or fewer of those paltry pardons from the pontifical pedlars?" (All this six years before Luther's Wittenberg challenges.) The satire runs on at the expense of monks, inquisitors, cardinals, and popes; all ranks and varieties of the clergy agree in pursuing money and witches even to death.

The popes, according to the satirist, have lost every resemblance to the Apostles by "their riches, honors, dispensations, licenses, indulgences, tithes," their worldly policies and bloody wars. How could such an institution exist except for the folly and gullible simplicity of mankind?

Probably, Erasmus' intellectual environment in Cambridge and in the circle of Henry VIII offered a sympathetic audience to satires of the Catholic Church. His next production was so unreasonably merciless that he made every effort to conceal his authorship, but Thomas More listed *Iulius exclusus* (1514) among his friend's works. Pope Julius II died in 1513, after a pontificate distinguished by his labors as general and by his financing Raphael and Michelangelo in their greatest paintings. Erasmus' imaginary dialogue pictured Peter barring Julius from heaven:

PETER: Let me look a little closer.... Priest's cassock, but blood-y armor beneath it; eyes savage, mouth insolent, forehead-brazen, body scarred with sins all over, breath loaded with wine, health broken with adultery. Ay, threaten as you will, I will tell you what you are.... You are Julius the Emperor come back from Hell....

JULIUS: Then you won't open the gates?

PETER: Sooner to anyone else than to such as you.

All in all, as we skim Erasmus' writings before 1517, we can hardly blame Luther and other reformers for reproaching Erasmus for having sounded the tocsin of revolt, and then running to cover when the call to action came.

In July, 1514, Erasmus returned from England to the Continent. Hearing of this, the prior of his forgotten monastery sent him a reminder that his leave of absence had long since expired and it was time for the wanderer to return to his vows and his cell. Horrified by this prospect, Erasmus petitioned his English friends to intercede for him with Pope Leo X. After some delay the amiable pontiff sent to London documents that freed Erasmus not only from his monastic commitments but also from the disabilities legally attaching to bastardy. To these pages Leo added a personal note:

Beloved son, health and apostolic benediction. The good favor of your life and character, your rare erudition and high merits, witnessed not only by the monuments of your studies, which are everywhere celebrated, but also by the general vote of the most learned men, and commended to us finally by the letters of two most illustrious princes, the King of England and the Catholic King [of France], give us reason to distinguish you with special and singular favor. We have therefore willingly granted your request, being ready to declare more abundantly our affection for you when you shall either yourself minister occasion, or accident shall furnish it, deeming it right that your holy industry, assiduously exerted for the public advantage, should be encouraged to higher endeavors by adequate rewards.

Perhaps it was a judicious bribe to good behavior, perhaps a sincere gesture from a tolerant and humanist court; in any case Erasmus never forgot this papal courtesy, and he would always find it hard to break from a church that had so patiently borne the sting of his pen.

GERMANY ON THE EVE OF LUTHER
(1300–1517)

The Economy

In the final century before Luther, all classes in Germany prospered except the poorest peasantry; and probably it was the rising status of most peasants that sharpened their resentment against surviving disabilities.

The great majority were tenant farmers paying rent to a feudal chieftain in produce, services, or money. They complained of the twelve—in some cases sixty—days of payless labor which custom required them to give him yearly; of his withdrawal of land from the *Allgemeine,* or "commons," in which tradition had allowed them to fish, cut timber, and pasture their flocks; of the damage done to their crops by the lord's huntsmen and hounds; of the biased administration of justice in the local courts, which the landlords controlled; and of the death tax laid upon the tenant family when the demise of its head interrupted the care of the land. All classes of tillers grudged the annual tithe levied by the Church on their harvests and broods.

Agrarian revolts broke out sporadically through fifteenth-century Germany. In 1431 the peasants around Worms rose in futile rebellion. In 1476 a cowherd, Hans Bohm, announced that the Mother of God had revealed to him that the Kingdom of Heaven on earth was at hand: there were to be no more emperors, popes, princes, or feudal lords; all men were to be brothers, all women sisters; all were to share alike in the fruits of the earth; land, woods, pastures, and waters were to be common and free. Thousands of peasants came to hear Hans; a priest joined him; the bishop of Würzburg smiled tolerantly. But when Hans told his followers to bring to the next meeting all the weapons they could muster, the bishop had him arrested; the bishop's soldiers fired into the crowd that tried to save him; the movement collapsed.

In 1493 the feudal tenants of the bishop of Strasbourg demanded an end to feudal dues and ecclesiastical tithes, the abolition of all debts, and the death of all Jews. They planned to seize the town of Schlettstadt and thence to spread their power through Alsace. The authorities got wind of the plot, seized the leaders, tortured and hanged them, and frightened the rest into temporary submission. In 1502 the peasants of the bishop of Speyer formed a revolutionary group of 7,000 men pledged to end feudalism, to "hunt out and kill all priests and monks," and to restore what they believed to have been the communism of their ancestors. A peasant revealed the scheme in the confessional; ecclesiastics and nobles united in circumventing it; the main conspirators were tortured and hanged. Similar uprisings were organized in Germany until they culminated in the Peasants' War that threatened all Germany in 1525 and frightened Luther into the arms of the princes.

A more matter-of-fact revolution was proceeding in German industry and commerce. Most industry was still handicraft, increasingly controlled by entrepreneurs, who provided material and capital, and bought and sold the finished product. Mining flourished; great profits were made in turning gold into chalices and monstrances for altars, and making chairs and tables of solid silver; reliable coins of gold and silver eased the passage to a money economy; and Aeneas Silvius, in 1458, marveled to see German women, bridles, helmets, and armor adorned with gold.

Financiers now became a major political power. Jewish moneylenders were displaced by Christian family firms like the Welsers, the Hochstetters, and the Fuggers, all of Augsburg, which, at the end of the fifteenth century, was the financial capital of Christendom. The Fuggers raised their firm to supremacy by advancing money to the princes of Germany, Austria, and Hungary in return for the revenues of mines, lands, and cities. From such speculative investments the Fuggers had become, by 1500, the richest family in Europe.

From Jakob Fugger II (1459–1525) we may date the capitalist era in Germany, the dominance of businessmen controlling money over feudal lords owning land. By the end of the fifteenth century, German mining and textiles were already organized on capitalistic lines—i.e., controlled by providers of capital.

Some merchant capitalists of Augsburg or Nuremberg were worth

5,000,000 francs each ($25,000,000?). Many bought their way into the landed aristocracy and sported coats of arms. Joachim Hochstetter and Franz Baumgartner spent 5,000 florins ($125,000) on a single banquet, or wagered 10,000 florins in one game. The luxuriously furnished and artistically decorated homes of rich businessmen stirred the resentment of nobility, clergy, and proletariat alike. Geiler von Kaiserberg demanded that they "should be driven out like wolves, since they fear neither God nor man, and breed famine, thirst, and poverty." The Cologne Reichstag of 1512 called upon all civic authorities to proceed "with diligence and severity . . . against the usurious, forestalling, capitalistic companies." Such decrees were repeated by other diets, but to no effect. Some legislators themselves had investments in the great merchant firms; agents of the law were pacified with shares of stock, and many cities prospered from the freedom of finance and trade.

Strasbourg, Colmar, Metz, Augsburg, Nuremberg, Ulm, Ratisbon (Regensburg), Mainz, Speyer, Trier, Worms, Cologne, Bremen, Hamburg, Magdeburg, Lübeck, and Breslau were thriving hubs of industry, commerce, letters, and arts. They and seventy-seven others were "free cities"—they made their own laws, and acknowledged no political allegiance except to the emperor, who was usually too indebted to them for men or money to attack their liberties. Though these cities were ruled by guilds dominated by businessmen, nearly every one of them was a paternalistic "welfare state" to the extent that it regulated production and distribution, wages, prices, and the quality of goods, with a view to protecting the weak from the strong and ensuring the necessities of life to all.

Nuremberg was a center of arts and crafts rather than of larger-scale industry or finance. Its streets were still medievally tortuous, and shaded by overhanging upper stories or balconies; its red-tiled roofs, high-peaked gables, and oriel windows made a picturesque confusion against its rural background and turgid stream. The people were not as affluent here as in Augsburg, but they were jolly and *gemütlich,* and loved to disport themselves in such festivities as their annual carnival of mask, costume, and dance. Here Hans Sachs and the Meistersingers sang their lusty airs; here Albrecht Dürer raised German painting and engraving to their zenith; here the best goldsmiths and silversmiths north of the Alps made costly vases, church vessels, statuettes; here the metalworkers fashioned a thousand plant, animal, and human forms in bronze, or wrought iron into handsome railings, gates, or screens; here the woodcutters took joy in their frolicsome forms. The churches of the cities became repositories and museums of art, for every guild or corporation or prosperous family commissioned some work of pious beauty for the shrine of a patron saint. It was characteristic of Nuremberg that the most famous of her merchants, Willibald Pirkheimer, was also an enthusiastic humanist, a patron of the arts, a devoted friend of Dürer.

The voyages of Columbus and Da Gama, the Turkish control of the Aegean, and Maximilian's wars with Venice disturbed the trade between Germany and Italy. More and more German exports and imports moved on the great rivers to the Baltic, the North Sea, and the Atlantic; wealth and power passed from Augsburg and Nuremberg to Cologne, Bremen, Hamburg, and Antwerp. The Fuggers and Welsers furthered this trend by making Antwerp a chief center of their operations. The northward movement of German money and commerce divorced northern Germany from the Italian economy, and made it strong enough to protect Luther from emperor and pope. Partly for opposite reasons southern Germany remained Catholic.

Religion

By and large, Catholicism flourished in fifteenth-century Germany. The overwhelming majority of the people were strictly orthodox, and—between their sins and cups—sternly pious. The German family was almost a church, where the mother served as catechist and the father as priest; prayer was punctual, and books of family devotion were in every home. Several monastic orders had returned to the observance of their rule and performed many works of practical benevolence.

The complaints against the German clergy were chiefly against the prelates, and on the score of their wealth and worldliness. Some bishops and abbots had to organize the administration and economy of great areas that had come into possession of the Church; though mitred or tonsured, they were in practice feudal seigneurs; they behaved like men of the world, and it was alleged that some of them rode to provincial or federal diets with their concubines in their trains. A learned Catholic prelate and historian, Johannes Janssen, has summed up, perhaps too severely, the abuses of the German Church on the eve of the Reformation.

> The contrast of pious love and worldly greed, of godly renunciation and godless self-seeking, made itself apparent in the ranks of the clergy as well as in other classes of society. By too many among the ministers of God and religion preaching and the care of souls were altogether neglected. Avarice, the besetting sin of the age, showed itself among the clergy of all orders and degrees, in their anxiety to increase to the utmost all clerical rents and incomes, taxes and perquisites.

The German Church was the richest in Christendom. It was reckoned that nearly a third of the whole landed property of the country was in the hands of the Church—which made it all the more reprehensible for the ecclesiastical authorities to be always seeking to augment their possessions. In many towns the church buildings and institutions covered the greater part of the community.

In 1457, Martin Meyer, chancellor to Archbishop Dietrich of Mainz, addressed to Cardinal Piccolomini an angry summary of the wrongs that Germans felt they suffered from the Roman Curia:

> The election of prelates is frequently postponed without cause, and benefices and dignities of all kinds are reserved for the cardinals and papal secretaries; Cardinal Piccolomini himself has been granted a general reservation in an unusual and unheard of form in three German provinces. Expectancies without number are conferred, annates and other taxes are collected harshly, and no delay is granted, and it is also known that more has been exacted than the sums due. Bishoprics have been bestowed not on the most worthy, but on the highest bidder. For the sake of amassing money, new indulgences have daily been published, and war tithes imposed, without consulting the German prelates. Lawsuits that ought to have been dealt with at home have been hastily transferred to the Apostolic tribunal. The Germans have been treated as if they were rich and stupid barbarians, and drained of their money by a thousand cunning devices. . . . For many years Germany has lain in the dust, bemoaning her

poverty and her sad fate. *But now her nobles have awakened as from sleep; now they have resolved to shake off the yoke, and to win back their ancient freedom.*

Among the people, anticlericalism went hand in hand with piety. "A revolutionary spirit of hatred for the Church and the clergy," writes the honest Pastor, "had taken hold of the masses in various parts of Germany. . . . The cry of 'Death to the priests!' which had long been whispered in secret, was now the watchword of the day."

So keen was this popular hostility that the Inquisition, then rising in Spain, hardly dared condemn anyone in Germany. Violent pamphlets rained assaults not so much upon the German Church as upon the Roman See. Some monks and priests joined in the attack and stirred up their congregations against the luxury of the higher clergy. Pilgrims returning from the jubilee of 1500 brought to Germany lurid—often exaggerated—stories of immoral popes, papal poisonings, cardinals' roisterings, and a general paganism and venality. Many Germans vowed that, as their ancestors had broken the power of Rome in 476, they or their children would crush that tyranny again; others recalled the humiliation of the Emperor Henry IV by Pope Gregory VII at Canossa, and thought the time had come for revenge. In 1521 the papal nuncio Aleander, warning Leo X of an imminent uprising against the Church, said that five years earlier he had heard from many Germans that they were only waiting for "some fool" to open his mouth against Rome.

A thousand factors and influences—ecclesiastical, intellectual, emotional, economic, political, and moral—were coming together, after centuries of obstruction and suppression, in a whirlwind that would throw Europe into the greatest upheaval since the barbarian conquest of Rome. The weakening of the papacy by the Avignon exile and the Papal Schism; the breakdown of monastic discipline and clerical celibacy; the luxury of prelates, the corruption of the Curia, the worldly activities of the popes; the morals of Alexander VI, the wars of Julius II, the careless gaiety of Leo X; the relic-mongering and peddling of indulgences; the triumph of Islam over Christendom in the Crusades and the Turkish wars; the spreading acquaintance with non-Christian faiths; the influx of Arabic science and philosophy; the collapse of

Scholasticism in the irrationalism of Scotus and the skepticism of Ockham; the failure of the conciliar movement to effect reform; the discovery of pagan antiquity and of America; the invention of printing; the extension of literacy and education; the translation and reading of the Bible; the newly realized contrast between the poverty and simplicity of the Apostles and the ceremonious opulence of the Church; the rising wealth and economic independence of Germany and England; the growth of a middle class resentful of ecclesiastical restrictions and claims; the protests against the flow of money to Rome; the secularization of law and government; the intensification of nationalism and the strengthening of monarchies; the nationalistic influence of vernacular languages and literatures; the fermenting legacies of the Waldenses, Wyclif, and Huss; the mystic demand for a less ritualistic, more personal and inward and direct religion—all these were now united in a torrent of forces that would crack the crust of medieval custom, loosen all standards and bonds, shatter Europe into nations and sects, sweep away more and more the supports and comforts of traditional beliefs— and perhaps mark the beginning of the end for the dominance of Christianity in the mental and moral life of West European man.

ᵐᵐᵐ

THE REFORMATION II (1517–55): LUTHER AND THE COMMUNISTS

TETZEL

On March 15, 1517, Pope Leo X promulgated the most famous of all indulgence offerings. Catholics then accepted the doctrine that Christ had given Peter—and Peter had transmitted to all succeeding popes—the power to absolve a confessing penitent from the guilt of his sins—but not from the penances attached to them; if any of these penances remained unpaid at death, they would have to be paid for by suffering in purgatory, which a merciful God had established as a temporary and escapable hell.

Meanwhile the saints by their sufferings, and Christ by his death, had earned a treasury of merits, from which the pope might draw to cancel a part of a sinner's due period of purgatorial torture if some earthly penitent would perform penances, or good works, or contribute gifts, prescribed by the Church. The substitution of a money fine for punishment was readily accepted by the faithful because it had long been an established custom in medieval courts.

The indulgence offered by Leo X was for contributing to the expense of completing the great basilica which Pope Julius II had begun, and had almost forgotten in the ecstasies of war. Leo appointed Albrecht of Brandenberg, the young archbishop of Mainz, to manage the distribution of this indulgence in Magdeburg, Halberstadt, and Mainz. Albrecht chose as his principal purveyor Johann Tetzel, a Dominican friar famous for his ability to raise money. Tetzel set forth, usually with the approval of the local clergy, and offered the following indulgence:

> May our Lord Jesus Christ have mercy on thee, and absolve thee by the merits of His most holy Passion. And I, by His authority, and that of the blessed Apostles Peter and Paul, and of the most holy Pope, granted and committed to me in these parts, do absolve thee, first from all ecclesiastical censures, . . . and then from all thy sins, transgressions and excesses, however enormous they may be, even such as are reserved for the cognizance of the Holy See; and as far as the keys of the Holy Church extend, I remit to you all punishment which you deserve in purgatory on their account, and I restore you to the holy sacraments of the Church . . . and to that innocence and purity which you possessed at baptism; so that when you die the gates of punishment shall be shut, and the gates of the paradise of delight shall be opened; and if you shall not die at present, this grace shall remain in full force when you are at the point of death. In the name of the Father, of the Son, and of the Holy Ghost.

The Catholic historian Pastor wrote of this:

> There is no doubt that Tetzel did, according to what he considered his authoritative instructions, proclaim a Christian doctrine that nothing but an offering of money was required to gain the indulgence for the dead, without there being any question of contrition or confession. He also taught, in accordance with the opinion then held, that an indulgence could be applied to any given soul with unfailing effect. Starting from this assumption, there is no doubt that his doctrine was virtually that of the drastic proverb: "As soon as money in the coffer rings, the soul from purgatory's fire springs." The papal bull of indulgence gave no sanction whatever to this proposition. It was a vague Scholastic opinion . . . not any doctrine of the Church.

Tetzel might have escaped history had he not approached too closely to the lands of Frederick the Wise, elector of Saxony. Moved by reluctance to let the coin of Saxony emigrate, and perhaps by reports of

Tetzel's hyperboles, Frederick forbade the preaching of the 1517 indulgence in his territory. But Tetzel came so close to the frontier that people in Wittenberg crossed the border to obtain the indulgence. Several purchasers brought these "papal letters" to Martin Luther, professor of theology in the University of Wittenberg, and asked him to attest their efficacy. He refused. The refusal came to Tetzel's ears; he denounced Luther and became immortal.

LUTHER GROWING (1483–1517)

The man who was to have more influence upon subsequent history than anyone but Copernicus and Columbus was born in Eisleben, Germany, to a peasant-then-miner named Hans Luther and his wife Margarethe. Frightened by a theology of terror and punishment, they brought up their children with such rigor of word and rod that the "severe and harsh life I led with them," recalled Luther, "was the reason that I afterward took refuge in the cloister and became a monk." Parents and children believed in angels, witches, and demons roaming in the air, and in a God who condemned the larger part of his human creations to an everlasting hell. Martin met his tribulations with a vigor of body and will that molded his rough features and kept him undefeated to his death.

At school in Mansfeld there were more rods and catechism. Martin was flogged (we are told) fifteen times in a day for misdeclining a noun. At fourteen he was transferred to the School of St. George at Eisenach, and had three relatively happy years in the comfortable home of Frau Cotta. He never forgot her remark that there was nothing on earth more precious than the love of a good woman. In this atmosphere he developed the natural charms of youth—health, cheerfulness, sociability, frankness. He sang well and played the lute.

In 1501 his prospering father sent him to the University of Erfurt. There he learned a little Greek and less Hebrew, and read the more reputable Latin classics. He found Scholasticism so disagreeable that he complimented a friend on "not having to learn the dung" that was offered as philosophy. In 1505 he received the degree of master of arts. His father sent him, as a graduation present, an expensive edition of the

Corpus iuris civilis and rejoiced when his son began to study law. But after two months Martin threw aside his law books as shedding no light on the problems that haunted him.

Vigorous to the edge of sensuality, visibly framed for a life of normal instincts, and yet so infused at home and school with the conviction that man is by nature sinful, and that sin offends an omnipotent and punishing God, he had never been able to reconcile his natural impulses with his acquired beliefs. The God who had been taught to him inspired more terror than love; and Jesus was not only the "gentle Jesus meek and mild" of the Beatitudes, but also the Christ of the Last Judgment, threatening sinners with everlasting fire. One day, caught in a storm of thunder and lightning and longing for protective cover, he made a vow to St. Anne that if he survived he would become a monk.

Surviving, he applied for acceptance as a novice by the Augustinian Eremites, the strictest of the twenty cloisters in Erfurt. Received, he performed the lowliest duties with a proud humility. He froze in an unheated cubicle, recited prayers in hypnotic repetition, fasted, and scourged himself in the hope of exorcising the devils that seemed to inhabit his body. In 1506 he took irrevocable vows, and in 1507 he was ordained a priest.

His fellow friars, fearing for his sanity, gave him a Latin Bible, and urged him to read it unquestioningly. But in St. Paul's Epistle to the Romans (1:17) he came upon a passage that added to his wonderment: "The just shall live by faith." And in St. Augustine he found the disturbing thought that God, before the creation, had chosen some souls for salvation and paradise, others for eternal damnation, and that the elect had won salvation only through the merits earned by the sufferings of Christ. These ideas—election by God for salvation, and salvation not through one's own good works but through faith in the merits earned for man by Christ—became the basic tenets of Luther's theology, and that of his followers.

In 1505 he was transferred to a monastery in Wittenberg, was given the post of instructor in logic and physics in the university, and then the chair of philosophy and theology. When reports were brought to him of Tetzel's way with indulgences, he felt that the time had come to speak out about the merchandising of religion. Rapidly he composed in Latin ninety-five theses, which he entitled *Disputation for Clarification of the Power of Indulgences.* On October 11, 1517, he affixed a copy of these theses to the main door of the Castle Church of Wittenberg. The practice of announcing theses—and offering to defend them against all challengers—had long been established in medieval universities, and the door that Luther chose had regularly been employed as an academic billboard. He prefixed to the theses an amiable invitation:

> Out of love for the faith, and the desire to bring it to light, the following propositions will be discussed at Wittenberg under the chairmanship of the Reverend Father Martin Luther, Master of Arts and Sacred Theology, and Lecturer in Ordinary on the same at that place. Wherefore he requests that those who are unable to be present and debate orally with us may do so by letter.

With characteristic audacity he sent a copy of the theses to Archbishop Albrecht of Mainz; and to make sure that they would be widely read, he had a German translation circulated among the people. Cautiously, perhaps unwittingly, he had begun the German Reformation.

REFORMATION AS REVOLUTION

The theses became the private talk of literate Germany. The pent-up anticlericalism of generations had found a voice. The sale of indulgences declined. But there were strong denunciations of Luther: one by the vice-chancellor of the University of Ingolstadt, another by Jakob van Hoogstraten of Cologne—who proposed that Luther should be burned at the stake. Luther defended his view in a Latin brochure entitled *Resolutiones* (April 1518), of which he sent copies to the local bishop and the pope. But to Leo X privately he professed an unwonted humility:

> Most blessed Father, I offer myself prostrate at the feet of your Holiness, with all that I am and have. Quicken, slay, call, recall, approve, reprove, as may seem to you good. I will acknowledge your voice as the voice of Christ, residing and speaking in you. If I have deserved death I will not refuse to die.

However, Leo's councilors warned him that the *Resolutiones* affirmed the superiority of an ecumenical council (of all bishops) over the pope, spoke slightingly of relics and pilgrimages, and rejected all additions made by the popes in the last three centuries to the theory and practice of indulgences. To allow such views to spread was to endanger ecclesiastical discipline and papal revenues. Leo, who had at first brushed aside Luther's ideas as a passing ferment among theoreticians, now took the matter in hand and summoned the monk to Rome (July 7, 1518).

Fearful of being kept a hostage or prisoner in Rome, Luther wrote to Georg Spalatin, chaplain to Frederick, elector of Saxony, suggesting that German princes should protect their citizens from extradition to Italy. Frederick agreed, and Emperor Maximilian advised him to "take good care of that monk." Leo compromised by bidding Luther present himself at Augsburg before Cardinal Cajetan to answer charges of indiscipline and heresy.

Luther went (October 12, 1518), but found no theologian to argue with, only a stern literalist: the cardinal informed the rebel that the Church, as a matter of ecclesiastical order, could not allow a monk to violate his vow of unquestioning obedience by publishing views long since condemned by the Church. Cajetan demanded that Luther should publicly retract his heresies and pledge himself never again to disturb the peace of Christendom. Luther refused, and returned to his cell in Wittenberg.

Cajetan asked Frederick to send the rebel to Rome; the elector refused. On November 9, Leo issued a bull repudiating many of the extreme claims that had been made for indulgences. On November 18, Luther published an appeal from the judgment of the pope to that of a general council. Leo sent a young Saxon nobleman in minor orders to make another attempt to win Luther to submission. When they met (January 3, 1719), Luther was so charmed by the youth that he wrote a friendly letter to Tetzel (who was soon to die); and on March 3 he sent Leo a letter of complete submission. The pope made a friendly reply (March 19), invited him to come to Rome, and offered him money for the journey. But on March 17, Luther had written to Spalatin, probably in humor: "I am at a loss to know whether the Pope is Antichrist or his apostle." He remained in Germany.

Public opinion there increasingly acclaimed him. Many of the university students were his warm defenders. Important men hardly known to Luther, like Dürer the artist and Pirkheimer the respected merchant, both of Nuremberg, proclaimed their support. Ulrich von Hutten, the rebel poet, lauded him, and called upon Frederick and all other German rulers to appropriate all monastic wealth and put to German uses the money that was usually sent to Rome.

So encouraged, Luther published, in the spring of 1520, an *Epitome* which met the absolutes of dogma with the ecstasies of attack:

> If Rome thus believes and teaches with the knowledge of popes and cardinals (which I hope is not the case), then in these writings I freely declare that the true Antichrist is sitting in the temple of God and is reigning in Rome—that empurpled Babylon—and that the Roman Curia is the Synagogue of Satan. . . . If the fury of the Romanists thus goes on, there will be no remedy left except that the emperors, kings and princes, girt about with force and arms, should attack these pests of the world, and settle the matter no longer by words but by the sword. . . . If we strike thieves with the gallows, robbers with the sword, heretics with fire, why do we not much more attack in arms these masters of perdition, these cardinals, these popes, and all this sink of the Roman Sodom which has without end corrupted the Church of God, and wash our hands in their blood?

In a bull of June 15, 1520, Leo X condemned forty-one statements by Luther, ordered the public burning of the writings containing them, and bade him come to Rome and make a public recantation. After sixty days of further refusal, Luther was to be cut off from all Christendom by excommunication, he was to be shunned as a heretic by all the faithful, and all secular authorities were to banish him from their dominions or deliver him to Rome.

Luther countered this by a declaration almost without precedent in history. He found someone to publish, not in Latin but in German, *An Open Letter to the Christian Nobility of the German Nation Concerning the Reform of the Christian Estate*. There was as yet no German nation, there were only German principalities, each independent, with its own customs, laws, army, and supportive pride; Luther overrode these boundaries and spoke to all Germans, if only through their rulers, who, in Luther's view, were letting precious revenues slip through their frontiers into hostile Italy.

> Some have estimated that every year more than 300,000 gulden find their way from Germany to Italy. . . . *We have come to the heart of the matter.* . . . How comes it that we Germans must put up with such robbery and such extortion of our property at the hands of the pope? . . . If we justly hang thieves and behead robbers, why should we let Roman avarice go free? For he is the greatest thief and robber that has come or can come into the world, and all in the holy name of Christ and St. Peter! Who can longer endure it or keep silence?

Luther proceeded to detail his religious program. The German clergy should establish a national church, under the leadership of the archbishop of Mainz; mendicant orders should be reduced; priests should marry; pilgrimages, masses for the dead, and holy days (except Sunday) should be abolished. All canon law (which divorced clerical offenses from secular legislation) should be discarded. The German Church should be reconciled with the Hussites of Bohemia. "We should vanquish heretics with books, not burning." "The Pope is the true Antichrist," and "thou, O pope, art not the most holy of men, but the most sinful. Oh, that God from heaven would soon destroy thy throne, and sink it in the abyss of hell!"

Cautious men considered the *Open Letter* rash and intemperate; many Germans hailed it as among the most heroic deeds in history. The presses of Wittenberg were kept busy meeting demands for new printings of the *Open Letter*. Germany, like England, was ripe for an appeal to nationalism; there was as yet no Germany on the map, but there were Germans, newly conscious of themselves as a people. As Huss had stressed his Bohemian patriotism, as Henry VIII would reject not Catholic doctrine, but papal power over England, so Luther now planted his standard of revolt not in theological deserts, but in the rich soil of the German national spirit. Wherever Protestantism won, nationalism carried the flag.

Despite Luther's uncompromising defiance, a papal agent sought him out and persuaded him to send Leo a letter disclaiming any intent to attack him personally and presenting temperately the case for reform. He expressed his respect for the pope as an individual, but condemned without compromise the corruption of the papacy in the past, and of the papal Curia in the present:

> Thy reputation, and the fame of thy blameless life . . . are too well known and too high to be assailed. . . . But thy See, which is called the Roman Curia, and of which neither thou nor any man can deny that it is more corrupt than any Babylon or Sodom ever was— . . . that See I have truly despised. . . . The Roman Church has become the most licentious den of thieves, the most shameless of all brothels, the kingdom of sin, death, and hell. . . . I have always grieved, most excellent Leo, that thou hast been made pope in these times, for thou wert worthy of better days. . . .
>
> Do not listen, therefore, dear Leo, to those sirens who make thee out to be no mere man but a demigod. . . . Thou art a servant of servants. . . . They err who exalt thee above the Church universal. They err who ascribe to thee the right of interpreting Scripture, for under cover of thy name they seek to set up their own wickedness in the Church; and, alas, through them, Satan has already made much headway under thy predecessors. In short, believe none who exalt thee, believe those who humble thee.

Meanwhile papal agents were spreading Leo's bull of excommunication throughout Germany. In some cities they arranged public burnings of Luther's books. Retaliating, Luther led some of Wittenberg University's pupils in burning a copy of the bull, along with canonical decretals and volumes of Catholic theology. The students joyfully collected additional volumes and with them kept the fires burning till late afternoon. On December 11, Luther proclaimed that no one could be saved unless he renounced rule by the papacy. The monk had excommunicated the pope.

THE DIET OF WORMS (1521)

Leo now sought secular help for the challenged Church by asking Charles V—who at nineteen had become head of the Holy Roman Empire in 1519—to summon a diet of German princes and prelates to examine Luther's conduct and publications as a threat not only to the Catholic Church but also to the basic social order of European civilization.

The situation that now confronted the pope, the German princes, and the young emperor involved some of the basic problems of government and history: How far does a government depend upon psychological factors for the maintenance of its rule, and how far do psychological factors depend upon economic conditions and political power? Were the authority and efficacy of a ruler dependent upon the aid of religion in maintaining social order, public obedience, and governmental prestige? And could a government acquire or preserve power by securing control of religious institutions and revenues? Those German princes who protected Luther against the Catholic Church gambled on their ability to organize and use the religious beliefs of their people independently of the Roman papacy; and Leo gambled on the unlikeliness that German rulers would use this opportunity to free themselves from papal power over the German Church and its growing revenues.

Of course it was a life-and-death gamble for Luther. He had challenged the most powerful institution in Europe—a Church weak in physical weapons, but strong in representing the religious foundations of West European civilization. He had attacked almost every aspect of the Catholic Church and had nothing to protect him but a few German princes uncertain of their power and support.

Only the generality of the people supported him, and with an intoxicating ardor. A papal legate reported:

All Germany is up in arms against Rome. All the world is clamoring for a council that shall meet on German soil. Papal bulls of excommunication are laughed at. Numbers of people have ceased to receive the sacraments of penance. . . . Martin is pictured with a halo above his head. The people kiss these pictures. Such a quantity has been sold that I am unable to obtain one. . . . I cannot go out in the streets but the Germans put their hands to their swords and gnash their teeth at me. I hope the Pope will give me a plenary indulgence and look after my brothers and sisters if anything happens to me.

The Diet of Worms assembled on January 27, 1521: the leading nobles and clergy of Germany, the representatives of the free cities, and agents of the emperor and the pope. Charles sent Luther an invitation to come and testify concerning the charges made against him, and offered him a safe-conduct from Wittenberg to Worms and return, adding, "You need fear no violence or molestation." Luther's friends advised him not to go, reminding him of Huss's fate at Constance. Luther went, saying, "Though there are as many devils in Worms as there are tiles on the roofs, I will go." The streets of Worms filled to see the famous heretic; 2,000 people gathered around his carriage; even the emperor was cast into the shade.

On April 17, in monastic garb, Luther appeared before the Diet and its presiding emperor. He was confronted by a collection of his works and was asked would he reject all heresies contained therein. For a while his courage failed; he asked for time to consider; Charles granted him a day. On April 18 he faced the court again, and agreed to recant any passage in his books that could be proved contrary to Scripture. Johann Eck, representing the archbishop of Trier, challenged him in Latin:

> Martin, your plea to be heard from Scripture is the one always made by heretics. You do nothing but renew the errors of Wyclif and Huss. . . . How can you assume that you are the only one to understand the sense of Scripture? Would you put your judgment above that of so many famous men and claim that you know more than all of them? You have no right to call into question the most holy orthodox faith, instituted by Christ the perfect Lawgiver, proclaimed throughout the world by the Apostles, sealed by the red blood of martyrs, confirmed by the sacred councils, and defined by the Church, . . . and which we are forbidden by the Pope and the Emperor to discuss, lest there be no end to debate. I ask you, Martin—answer candidly and without distinction—do you or do you not repudiate your books and the errors which they contain?

Luther made his historic reply in German:

> Since your Majesty and your lordships desire a simple reply, I will answer without distinctions. . . . Unless I am convicted by the testi-

mony of Sacred Scripture or by evident Reason (I do not accept the authority of popes and councils, for they have contradicted each other), my conscience is captive to the word of God. I cannot and I will not recant anything, for to go against my conscience is neither right nor safe. God help me. Amen.*

Eck countered that no error could be proved in the doctrinal decrees of the councils. Luther answered that he was prepared to prove such errors, but the emperor intervened peremptorily: "It is enough; since he has denied councils we wish to hear no more." Luther returned to his lodging.

On April 19, having waited two days for Luther to repent, Charles called the leading princes to his chamber and read to them a declaration of intent:

A single friar who goes counter to all the Christianity of a thousand years must be wrong. . . . I will have no more to do with Luther. He may return under his safe-conduct, but without preaching or making any tumult. I will proceed against him as a notorious heretic, and trust you to declare yourselves as you promised me.

Four electors agreed; Frederick of Saxony and Ludwig of the Palatinate abstained. On April 26, Luther began his return to Wittenberg. Leo X sent orders that the safeguard should be respected. Nevertheless, Elector Frederick, fearing that the Imperial police might arrest Luther after the expiration of his safe-conduct on May 6, arranged, with Luther's consent, to have him live for a while in quiet seclusion and rural disguise in the remote castle of Wartburg on a mountaintop a mile from Eisenach. Charles made no effort to arrest him, and on February 19, 1522, Luther returned to Wittenburg University, where he proceeded to expound a theology which is still in essentials the faith of Lutheran churches everywhere. Meanwhile he found himself faced with a different but related revolution as basic as his own.

* We cannot fully authenticate the famous words engraved on the majestic *Denkmal* (Memorial) at Worms: *Stehe Ich, Ich kann nicht anders*—"Here I stand; I can do no other." The words do not occur in the transcript of Luther's reply as given in the records of the Diet; they make their first appearance in the earliest printed version of his speech.

THE SOCIAL REVOLT (1522–36)

The Peasants' War

The apparent success of Luther's rebellion against the Roman Church encouraged uprisings of monks and priests against celibacy, poverty, and submission to an alien and authoritarian power. The hardships that had already spurred a dozen rural outbreaks still agitated the peasant mind, and with new intensity now that Luther had defied the Church, berated the princes, broken the dams of discipline and awe, made every man a priest, and proclaimed the freedom of the Christian man. The increasing circulation of the New Testament was a blow to political as well as religious authority: it exposed the worldliness of the clergy, the communism of the Apostles, the sympathy of Christ for the poor and oppressed. In these respects it was for the radicals of this age a veritable *Communist Manifesto.*

In 1521 a pamphlet by Johannes Eberlin demanded universal male suffrage, the subordination of every ruler and official to popularly elected councils, the abolition of all capitalistic organizations, a return to medieval price-fixing for bread and wine, and the education of all children in Latin, Greek, Hebrew, astronomy, and medicine.

In 1522 a pamphlet entitled *The Needs of the German Nation* called for the removal of "all tolls, duties, passports, and fines," the limitation of business organizations to a capital of 10,000 gulden, the exclusion of the clergy from civil government, the confiscation of monastic wealth, and the distribution of the proceeds among the poor. Preachers mingled Protestant evangelism with utopian aspirations. One revealed that heaven was open to peasants but closed to nobles and clergymen; another counseled the peasants to give no more money to priests or monks; Münzer, Carlstadt, and Hubmaier advised their hearers that "farmers, miners, and corn-threshers understand the Gospel better, and can teach it better, than a whole village . . . of abbots and priests . . . or doctors of divinity"; Carlstadt added, "and better than Luther."

Thomas Münzer's career caught all the excitement of the time. He invited the princes to lead the people in a communistic revolt against clergy and capitalists. When the princes did not rise to the opportunity, he called upon the people to overthrow them, too, and "to establish a refined society such as was contemplated by Plato." "All things

are in common," he wrote, "and should be distributed as occasion re-
quires, according to the several necessities of all. . . . Any prince,
count, or baron who, after being earnestly reminded of this truth, shall
be unwilling to accept it, is to be beheaded or hanged." Münzer organized workers and peasants into an army, and had heavy artillery cast
for it in a monastery. "Forward!" was his call; "forward while the fire is
hot! Let your swords be ever warm with blood!" On August 24, 1524,
Hans Müller, acting on a suggestion from Münzer, gathered about him
some Stühlingen peasants and bound them into an "Evangelical Brotherhood" pledged to emancipate farmers throughout Germany. By the
end of 1524 there were some 30,000 peasants in arms in southern Germany, refusing to pay taxes, church tithes, or feudal dues, and sworn to
emancipation or death. At Menningen their delegates (March 1525)
drew up "Twelve Articles" that set half of Germany on fire:

> To the Christian reader peace, and the grace of God through Christ.
> . . . It has been the custom hitherto for men to hold us as their prop-
> erty, and this is pitiable, seeing that Christ has redeemed and bought
> us all with the precious shedding of his blood. . . . To our chosen and
> appointed rulers (appointed for us by God) we are willingly obedient
> in all proper and Christian matters, and have no doubt that, as true
> and real Christians, they will gladly release us from serfdom, or show
> us in the Gospel that we are serfs. . . .
> We have a heavy grievance because of the services which are in-
> creased from day to day. . . .
> We are aggrieved because some have appropriated to themselves
> meadows out of the common fields, which once belonged to the
> community. . . .
> If one or more of the articles here set forth . . . can be shown by
> the word of God to be improper, we will recede from it if this is ex-
> plained to us with arguments from Scripture. . . .

The peasant leaders, encouraged by Luther's semirevolutionary pro-
nouncements, sent him a copy of the Articles and asked for his support.
He replied with a pamphlet printed in April 1525, *Ermahnung zum
Frieden* (Admonition to Peace). He applauded the peasants' offer to
submit to correction by Scripture. He noted the charges, already cur-

rent, that his speeches and writings had stirred revolt; he denied his responsibility and referred to his inculcation of civil obedience. But he
did not withdraw his criticism of the master class:

> We have no one on earth to thank for this mischievous rebellion ex-
> cept you, princes and lords, and especially you blind bishops and mad
> priests and monks, whose hearts are hardened against the Holy
> Gospel, though you know that it is true. . . . In your temporal gov-
> ernment you do nothing but flay your subjects, in order that you may
> lead a life of splendor and pride and the poor common people can bear
> it no longer. . . . Since you are the cause of this wrath of God, it will
> undoubtedly come upon you if you do not mend your ways in
> time. . . . The peasants are mustering, and this must result in the
> ruin, destruction, and desolation of Germany by cruel murder and
> bloodshed, unless God be moved by our repentance to prevent it.

He advised the princes and lords to recognize the justice of many of
the articles and urged a policy of kindly consideration. To the peasants
he addressed a frank admission of the wrongs done to them, but
pleaded with them to refrain from violence and revenge; a resort to violence, he predicted, would leave them worse off than before. He foresaw that a violent revolt would bring discredit upon the movement for
religious reform and that he would be blamed for everything. He advised the peasants to obey the authorities and, in a reckless moment,
asked them to interpret the "freedom of the Christian man" as a spiritual liberty, consistent with serfdom, even with slavery:

> Did not Abraham and other patriarchs and prophets use slaves?
> Read what St. Paul teaches about servants, who at that time were all
> slaves. Therefore your third article is dead against the Gospel. . . .
> This article would make all men equal . . . and that is impossible.
> For a worldly kingdom cannot stand unless there is in it an inequal-
> ity of persons, so that some are free, some imprisoned, some lords,
> some subjects.

The peasant leaders mourned Luther as a traitor and advanced their
revolt. Some of them took literally the dream of equality: the nobles

were to dismantle their castles and live like peasants or burghers; they were no longer to ride on horseback, for that raised them above their fellowmen. Pastors were to be servants, not masters, of their congregations, and were to be expelled if they did not adhere strictly and only to the Scriptures. Town workers denounced the monopoly of offices by the rich, the embezzlement of public funds by corrupt officials, the repeated rise in prices while wages lagged behind. Some leaders of the revolt proposed that all Church property should be confiscated to secular needs, that all transport tolls and tariffs should be removed, and that there should be, throughout the Empire, one coinage and one system of weights and measures.

In the spring of 1525 the revolt flared up in a dozen scattered localities. At Heilbronn, Rothenburg, and Würzburg a commune of labor representatives captured the municipal administration. At Frankfurt-am-Main the victorious commune announced that it would thereafter be council, burgomaster, pope, and emperor all in one. At Rothenburg the priests were driven from the cathedral, religious images were demolished, a chapel was destroyed, and clerical wine cellars were emptied with triumphant gaiety. Nearly the whole duchy of Franconia joined the uprising. Many lords and bishops, unprepared to resist, swore to accept the reforms demanded of them; several at once freed their serfs.

Many of the lower clergy, hostile to the hierarchy, supported the revolt. At Leipheim on the Danube some 3,000 peasants, led by a priest, captured the town, drank all discoverable wine, pillaged the church, smashed the organ, made themselves leggings from sacerdotal vestments, and paid mock homage to one of their number, robed as a priest and seated on the altar. An army of mercenaries hired by the Swabian League and led by General Georg von Truchsess, laid siege to the town and frightened the undisciplined rebels into surrender. Five leaders were beheaded; the rest were spared, but the League's troops burned many peasant cottages.

On Good Friday, April 15, 1525, three rebel contingents under Metzler, Geyer, and Rohrbach, laid siege to Weinsberg (near Heilbronn), where ruling Count Ludwig von Helfenstein was especially hated for his severities. A delegation of peasants approached the walls and asked for a parley; the count and his knights made a sudden sortie and massacred the delegation. On Easter Sunday the attackers broke through the walls and cut down the 40 men at arms who resisted. The count, his wife (daughter of the late Emperor Maximilian), and sixteen knights were taken prisoner. Rohrbach ordered the seventeen men to run the gauntlet between rows of peasants armed with pikes. The count offered all his fortune in ransom; it was refused as a temporizing expedient. The countess, prostrate and delirious, begged for her husband's life. Rohrbach bade two men hold her up so that she could witness the orgy of revenge. As the count walked to his death amid a volley of daggers and pikes, the peasants recalled to him his own brutalities. "You thrust my brother into a dungeon," one cried, "because he did not bare his head as you passed by." "You harnessed us like oxen to the yoke," shouted others, "you caused the hands of my father to be cut off because he killed a hare on his own field. . . . Your horses, dogs, and huntsmen have trodden down my crops. . . . You have wrung the last penny out of us." During the next half-hour the sixteen knights were similarly sent to rest. The countess was allowed to retire to a convent.

In nearly every section of Germany peasant bands ran riot. Monasteries were sacked, or were compelled to pay high ransoms. At Mainz, Archbishop Albrecht fled before the storm, but his deputy saved the see by signing the Twelve Articles and paying a ransom of 15,000 guilders. On April 11 the townsfolk of Bamberg renounced the bishop's sovereignty, pillaged and burned his castle, and plundered the houses of the orthodox. In Alsace the revolt spread so rapidly that by April's end every orthodox or rich landlord was in terror of his life. On April 28 an army of 10,000 peasants attacked Zabern, seat of the bishop of Strasbourg, and despoiled the monastery, took the town, forced every fourth man to join them, renounced all payment of tithes, and demanded that thereafter all officials except the emperor should be elected by popular suffrage and be subject to recall. At Freiburg-im-Breisgau the peasants looted castles and monasteries and forced the city to join the Evangelical Brotherhood. In that same month of May a peasant band drove the bishop of Würzburg out of his palace and feasted on his stores. In Neustadt in the Palatinate, Elector Ludwig, surrounded by 8,000 armed peasants, invited their leaders to dinner and cheerfully complied with their demands. "There," said a contemporary, "one saw villeins and their lord sit, eat, and drink together. He had, it seemed, one heart to them, and they to him."

Amid this torrent of events, Luther issued from the Wittenberg press, in May 1525, the pamphlet "Against the Robbing and Murdering Hordes of Peasants." Its vehemence startled prince and peasant, prelate and humanist, alike. Shocked by the excesses of the infuriated rebels, dreading a possible overturn of all law and government in Germany, and stung by charges that his own teachings had loosed the flood, he now ranged himself unreservedly on the side of law and order:

> Any man against whom sedition can be proved is outside the law of God and the Empire, so that the first who can slay him is doing right and well. . . . For rebellion brings with it a land full of murder and bloodshed, makes widows and orphans, and turns everything upside down. . . . Therefore let everyone who can, smite, slay, and stab, secretly or openly, remembering that nothing can be more poisonous, hurtful, or devilish than a rebel. It is just when one must kill a mad dog. . . .

He rejected the supposed scriptural warrant for communism:

> The Gospel does not make goods common, except in the case of those who do of their own free will what the Apostles and disciples did in Acts IV. They did not demand, as do our insane peasants . . . that the goods of others—of a Pilate or a Herod—should be common, but only their own goods. Our peasants, however, would have other men's goods common, and keep their own goods for themselves. Fine there! I think there is not a devil left in hell; they have all gone into the peasants.

To Catholic rulers he offered his forgiveness if they smote the rebels without trial. To Protestant rulers he recommended prayer, contrition, and negotiation, but if the peasants should remain obdurate, then swiftly grasp the sword. For a prince or lord must remember in this case that he is God's minister and the servant of His wrath (Romans 13), to whom the sword is committed for use upon such fellows:

If he can punish and does not—even though the punishment consist in the taking of life and the shedding of blood—then he is guilty of all the murder and the evil which these fellows commit. . . . The rulers, then, should go on unconcerned, and with a good conscience lay about them as long as their hearts still beat. . . . If anyone think this too hard, let him remember that rebellion is intolerable, and that the destruction of the world is to be expected every hour.

It was Luther's misfortune that this call to war reached its readers just about the time that the propertied classes were beginning to subdue the revolt; and the Reformer received undue credit for the terrorism of the suppression. Elector Frederick died May 5, 1525, leaving to his successor counsels of moderation. But Elector John felt that his brother had been unwisely lenient. He joined his forces with those of Duke Henry of Brunswick and Philip I, landgrave of Hesse, and together they moved against Munzer's encampment outside of Munchausen. The opposed armies were matched only in number—each some 8,000 strong; but the ducal troops were mostly trained soldiers, while the peasants were indifferently armed. The first barrage of the prince's cannon slaughtered hundreds, and the terrified rebels fled into the town of Frankenhausen (May 15). The victor followed them, and massacred 5,000. Three hundred peasants were condemned to death; their women begged mercy for them; it was granted on condition that they beat out the brains of two priests who had encouraged the revolt; it was so done while the victorious dukes looked on. Munzer was captured, was tortured into confessing the error of his ways, and was beheaded.

Meanwhile, Georg von Truchsess, leading another princely force, captured the town of Böblingen, and from its walls bombarded a rebel camp outside (May 11). Those peasants who survived the cannonade were cut down by cavalry. Turning next to Weinsburg, Truchsess burned it to the ground, and slowly roasted Jäcklein Rohrbach, who had directed the "Massacre of Weinsberg." Truchsess proceeded to recapture Würzburg, and beheaded eighty-one chosen rebels as a warning to the rest. One of the survivors was the rebel knight Gotz von Berlichingen, whose legend provided Goethe with the inspiration for an early play.

The revolt in Alsace was crushed by the slaughter of from 1,000 to 6,000 peasants in Lipstein and Zabern. By May 27 some 20,000 peasants had been killed in Alsace alone; the air of some towns was fetid with the stench of the dead. Margraf Casimir had some of his surrendering peasants beheaded, some hanged; in milder cases he chopped off hands or gouged out eyes. Saner princes intervened to reduce the ferocity of the retaliation. "If all the rebels are killed," one noble warned, "where shall we get peasants to provide for us?"

The losses of German life and property in the Peasants' War were to be exceeded only in the Thirty Years' War. Of peasants alone some 130,000 died in battle or in expiation. Truchsess' hired executioner boasted that he had killed 1,200 condemned with his own hand. The peasants had destroyed hundreds of castles and monasteries. Hundreds of villages and towns had been depopulated or ruined, or impoverished by huge indemnities.

Over 50,000 homeless peasants roamed the highways or hid in the woods. Widows and orphans were legion, but charity was heartless or penniless. Concessions were made to peasants in Austria, Baden, and Hesse; elsewhere serfdom was strengthened, and would continue, east of the Elbe, till 1800. Intellectual developments were aborted, censorship of publications increased, under Catholic and Protestant authorities alike. Humanism wilted in the fire. The Renaissance joy in life, literature, and art gave way to theology, pietism, and meditations on death.

The peasants never forgave Luther. They felt that the new religion had sanctified their cause, had aroused them to hope and action, and had deserted them in the hour of decision. Some of them, in angry despair, became cynical atheists. Many of them, or their children, returned to the Catholic fold. Some of them followed the radicals whom Luther had denounced, and heard in the New Testament a summons to communism.

Anabaptist Communism

The most radical of the new sects took the name of Anabaptists (*Wiedertaufer*—"Again Baptizers"), from their insistence that baptism, if received in infancy, should be repeated in maturity or, still better, that it should be deferred, as by John the Baptist, till the recipient could knowingly and voluntarily make his profession of the Christian faith.

They condemned all use of force, especially by governments. They rejected military service on the ground that it is always sinful to take human life. They refused to swear oaths, not excepting oaths of allegiance to prince or emperor. Their usual salutation was "The peace of the Lord be with you"—an echo of the Jewish and Moslem greeting, and a forerunner of the Quaker mode.

While Luther, Zwingli, Calvin, and Knox agreed with the popes on the necessity of religious uniformity, the Anabaptists practiced religious toleration, and one of them, Balthasar Hubmaier, wrote the first clear defense of it known to us (1524). They shunned public office and all resort to litigation. They were Tolstoian anarchists three centuries before Tolstoi. Some of them proclaimed a community of goods; some, if we may credit possibly hostile chroniclers, proposed a community of wives. In general, however, the sect rejected any compulsory sharing of goods, and comforted themselves with the hope that in the coming kingdom of heaven communism would be automatic and universal. They lived in the confident expectation of the Second Coming of Christ, who would establish the Kingdom of Heaven on earth, in which the elect would live in a terrestrial paradise without laws or marriage and abounding in all good things for all.

The Anabaptists appeared first in Switzerland about 1521, but Zwingli, who had become dominant in Zürich, made life so uncomfortable for them that they migrated to Germany, where Luther seemed to have prepared for them by breaking the dams of custom and discipline, making "every man a priest," and proclaiming the freedom of the Christian man. In Augsburg they made rapid headway among the textile workers; in Tirol many miners, contrasting their poverty with the wealth of the Fuggers and Hochstetters who owned the mines, took up Anabaptism when the peasants' revolt collapsed; in Strasbourg the sect grew unhindered for a while because pugnacity was absorbed in the conflict between Protestants and Catholics. But a pamphlet of 1528 warned the authorities that "he who teaches that all things are to be in common" has naught else in mind than to excite the poor against the rich, the subjects against the rulers ordained by God. In that year Charles V issued a mandate making rebaptism a capital crime.

The Diet of Speyer (1529) ratified the emperor's edict and ordered that Anabaptists everywhere were to be killed like wild beasts as soon as taken, without judge or trial. By 1530, said the contemporary Sebastian Frank, 2,000 Anabaptists had been put to death.

Despite these killings the sect increased, and moved from place to place in Germany. In Prussia and Württemberg some nobles welcomed them as peaceful and industrious farmers. In Saxony, says an early Lutheran historian, the valley of the river Werra was filled with them, and in Erfurt they claimed to have sent three hundred missionaries to convert the dying world.

In Austerlitz, Hans Hut and his followers established a communistic center and maintained it for almost a century. The nobles who owned the land protected them as enriching the estate by their conscientious toil. Farming was communal: materials for agriculture or handicrafts were bought and allotted by communal officers; part of the proceeds was paid to the landlord as rent, the rest distributed according to need. The social unit was not the family but a *Haushabe,* or household, containing 400 to 2,000 people, with a common kitchen, a common laundry, a school, a hospital, and a brewery. Children, after weaning, were brought up in common, but monogamy remained. In the Thirty Years' War, by an imperial edict of 1622, this communistic society was suppressed; its members accepted Catholicism or were banished.

In the Netherlands, Melchior Hofmann, a Swabian tanner, preached the Anabaptist gospel with some success. At Leyden his pupil Jan Matthys concluded that the advent of the new Jerusalem could no longer be patiently awaited, but must be achieved at once, and, if necessary, by force. He sent out through Holland twelve apostles to announce the glad tidings. The ablest of them was a young tailor, Jan Beuckelszoon, known to history as John of Leyden, and in Meyerbeer's opera as *Le Prophète.* Without formal education, he had a keen mind, a vivid imagination, a handsome presence, a ready tongue, and a resolute will. In 1533, at twenty-four, he accepted an invitation to come to the aid of the Anabaptists who had risen to control in Münster, the rich and populous capital of Westphalia.

Arriving there on January 13, 1534, he found the city besieged by a

Catholic force under Bishop Franz von Waldeck. He joined in the resolute resistance and soon rose to almost absolute leadership of the executive Committee of Public Safety (April 5, 1534). New elections were held; the Anabaptists won control of the committee and established communism as a war economy. Inspired by religious faith and John's eloquence, the citizens accepted a "socialist theocracy" in the hope that they were realizing the New Jerusalem visioned by the Apocalypse.

John and his aides, perhaps to give some helpful authority to their precarious rule, clothed themselves in the splendid garments left behind by wealthy exiles. According to a hostile witness, they decreed that "all possessions must be in common," but apparently few obeyed. Three "deacons" were appointed to supply the necessities of the poor; and to supply these charities the remaining well-to-do were persuaded or compelled to yield up their superfluity. Land available for cultivation within the city was assigned to each household according to its size. One edict confirmed the traditional dominion of the husband over the wife.

Public morals were regulated by strict laws. Dances, games, and religious plays were encouraged, under supervision, but drunkenness and gambling were severely punished. Prostitution was banned; fornication and adultery were made capital crimes. An excess of women, caused by the flight of many men, moved the leaders to decree, on the basis of biblical precedents, that unattached women should become "companions of wives"—in effect, concubines. John himself took several.

Though many Anabaptists in Germany and Holland repudiated the resort of their Münster brethren to force, many more applauded the revolution. Cologne, Trier, Amsterdam, and Leyden murmured with Anabaptist prayers for its success. On March 28, echoing the Münster uprising, an Anabaptist band captured and fortified a monastery in West Friedland. Confronted with this spreading revolt, the conservative forces of the Empire, Protestant as well as Catholic, mobilized to suppress Anabaptism everywhere. Luther, who in 1528 had recommended lenience with the new heretics, advised in 1530 "the use of the sword" against them as "Blasphemers" and revolutionists. City after city sent money or men to Bishop von Waldeck and his troops; and a

Diet of Worms (April 4, 1535) ordered a tax on all Germany to finance
the attack on Münster. The bishop was now able to encircle the city and
shut off all its supplies.

Facing famine and deteriorating morale, King John announced that
all who wished might leave the city. Many women and children, and
some men, seized the opportunity. The men were imprisoned or killed
by the bishop's soldiers; the women were spared for diverse services.
One of the émigrés saved his life by agreeing to show the besiegers an
undefended part of the town walls. Under his guidance a force of lands-
knechts scaled them and opened a gate (June 24); soon several troops
poured into the city. Starvation had so far done its work that only 800
of the besieged could still bear arms. They barricaded themselves in the
marketplace; then they surrendered on a promise of safe-conduct to
leave Münster; when they yielded up their arms, they were massacred
en masse. Houses were searched, and 400 hidden survivors were slain.
John of Leyden and two of his aides were bound to stakes; every part of
their bodies was clawed with red-hot pincers until "nearly all who were
standing in the market place were sickened by the stench." At last daggers were driven into their hearts.

The bishop regained his city and augmented his former power; hereafter all actions of the civil authorities were to be subject to episcopal
veto. Catholicism was triumphantly restored. Throughout the Empire
the Anabaptists, fearing for their lives, repudiated every member
guilty of using force; nevertheless many pacifist heretics were executed.
Luther and Melanchthon advised Philip of Hesse to put to death all adherents of the sects. The Anabaptists accepted the lesson, postponed
communism to the millennium, and resigned themselves to sober,
pious, peaceful living tolerable by the state.

Menno Simons, a Catholic priest converted to Anabaptism, gave to
his Dutch and German followers such skillful guidance that the "Mennonites" survived all tribulations and formed successful agricultural
communities in Holland, Russia, and America. There is no clear affili-
ation between the Continental Anabaptists and the English Quakers or
the American Baptists, but the Quaker rejection of war and oaths, and
the Baptist insistence on adult baptism, probably stem from the same
traditions of creed and conduct that in Switzerland, Germany, and

Holland took Anabaptist forms. One branch of the Anabaptists migrated in 1719 from Germany to Pennsylvania, and settled in or near Germantown. In eastern Pennsylvania the "Amish" Mennonites (named from a seventeenth-century leader, Jakob Amen) still officially reject razors, buttons, railroads, automobiles, motion pictures, newspapers, and tractors; but their farms are among the tidiest and most prosperous in America.

The theology that supported the Anabaptists through hardship, poverty, and martyrdom hardly accords with our transient philosophies, but they, too, in their sincerity, devotion, and friendliness, enriched our heritage, and redeemed our tarnished humanity.

THE REFORMATION TRIUMPHANT (1525-55)

If the Reformation succeeded in Germany it was probably because Emperor Charles V and Popes Leo X, Adrian VI, and Clement VII were absorbed in a competition for supremacy in Christendom, and the German princes thought that the revenues of German piety could be put to better uses by them than by Rome. While Italy and France were busy with war, the Germans sloughed off the costly demands of the Church, and, one by one, the electors consented to sovereignty.

Erasmus looked on in astonishment and grief while Europe tore itself apart with theology and war. He had supported the earlier phases of Luther's rebellion, but stood aloof when it threatened the breakdown of the Catholic Church as a pillar of social order in Europe. He acknowledged his share in opening a path for Luther, his *Praise of Folly* was at that moment circulating by the thousands throughout Europe, making fun of monks and theologians and giving point to Luther's blunt fulminations.

When the Catholics charged him with laying the egg that Luther was hatching, he admitted, "Yes, but the egg that I laid was a hen, whereas Luther has hatched a game cock." He feared that the division of Christianity into hostile camps would put Europe back a century (as it would do to Germany in the following century).

When Luther appealed to him for his continued friendship (March 18, 1519) he replied by cautioning Luther not to let loose the dogs of war; meanwhile he wrote to Elector Frederick asking him to protect the rebel. And, like any poor scholar, he remembered his papal pensions and English sinecures, and held his peace.

In any case the withdrawal of German principalities from the Roman communion proceeded at a rising pace. In 1546, Luther died at the age of sixty-three, after many ailments and much suffering. His gospel was carried on quietly by Melanchthon, and protected by electors whose power increased as that of the Catholic emperor was yearly reduced by expensive wars, rising cares, and the diseases of senility. In 1555, at the Diet of Augsburg, Charles V yielded to most of the demands of the German electors, who were left free to choose their own religion and to make it obligatory among their subjects. There was no pretense of religious toleration; the right of private judgment, which the Reformation had upheld in the ecstasy of revolt, was now abandoned, if only because it had led to such a diversity of warring creeds as threatened the mind of Europe. However, the discontented rebel was free to migrate to a principality whose official cult best fitted his own.

Or such a citizen might break all national barriers and seek in Switzerland his choice of Reform faiths between Zwingli in Zurich and Calvin in Geneva; or he might cross the sea to worship with Scottish Calvinism under John Knox, or with Anglican Catholicism under Henry VIII.

Only in the secret heresies of a few humanists in Germany, or in the quiet skepticism of a few Italians and Englishmen, had mental freedom survived amid the absolutisms of dogma.

Chapter Twenty

ᙁᙁᙁ

THE CATHOLIC
REFORMATION (1517–63)

CATHOLIC REFORMERS

Many Italians mourned the deterioration of the Church in moral leadership and doctrinal reform. In Venice, hub of Italy's trade with non-Christian states, skepticism flourished and criticism of the clergy was popular; Cardinal Caraffa reported to Pope Clement VII (1532) that very few Venetian males ever went to confession; and Clement himself described the "Lutheran heresy" as widely spread among both clergy and laity in Italy. Renée, daughter of Louis XII and wife of Ercole d'Este, ruler of Ferrara, was a confirmed Protestant, and received Calvin there. In Modena, Lucca, and Rome the learned academies included many heretics, some of them far more skeptical than Luther.

But, of course, it was impossible for Italy to go Protestant. The common people there, though anticlerical, were religious even when they did not go to church. They loved the time-hallowed ceremonies, the helping or consoling saints, the seldom-questioned creed that lifted their lives from the poverty of their homes to the sublimity of the greatest drama ever conceived—the redemption of fallen man by the death of his God.

The wealth of the papacy was an Italian heirloom and vested interest; any Italian who proposed to end that tribute-receiving organization seemed to most Italians to be verging on lunacy. The upper classes quarreled with the papacy as a political power over central Italy, but they cherished Catholicism as a vital aid to social order and peaceful government. They realized that the glory of Italian art had been bound up with the Church through the inspiration of her legends and the support of her gold. Catholicism itself had become an art; its sensuous elements had submerged the ascetic and the theological: stained glass, incense, music, architecture, sculpture, painting, even drama—these were all in the Church and of her, and in their marvelous ensemble they seemed inseparable from her. The artists and the scholars of Italy did not have to be converted from Catholicism, for they had converted Catholicism to scholarship and art.

Hundreds, thousands, of scholars and artists were supported by bishops, cardinals, and the popes; many humanists, some polite skeptics, had risen to high positions in the Church. Italy loved attainable beauty too much to despoil itself over unattainable truths. And had those fanatical Teutons, or that sour popelet in Geneva, or that ruthless ruler on the throne of England, found the truth? What depressing nonsense those reformers were shouting—just when the intellectual classes in Italy had quite forgotten hell and damnation!

Consequently the Italian argument was all for reform within the Church. And, indeed, loyal churchmen had for centuries admitted—proclaimed—the need for ecclesiastical reform. The outbreak and progress of the Reformation gave new urgency to the need and the demand. "A vast torrent of abuse in hundreds and thousands of pamphlets and caricatures poured down upon the clergy." The sack of Rome touched the conscience and income of terrified cardinals and populace; a hundred priests pronounced the calamity a warning from God. Bishop Stafileo, preaching in 1528 before the Rota (a judiciary branch of the Curia) explained, almost in Protestant terms, why God had struck the capital of Christendom: "Because all flesh has become corrupt, we are citizens not of the holy city of Rome, but of Babylon, the city of corruption." As Luther had said.

Early in the pontificate of Paul III, the renowned jurist Giovan Battista Caccia presented to him a treatise on the reformation of the Church. "I see," said the preamble, "that our Holy Mother Church has been so changed that she seems to have no tokens of her evangelical character, and no trace can be found in her of humility, temperance, continence, and Apostolic strength." Paul showed his own mood by accepting the dedication of this work. On November 20, 1534, he appointed Cardinals Piccolomini, Sanseverino, and Cesi to draw up a program of moral renovation for the Church; and on January 15, 1535, he ordered strict enforcement of Leo X's reform bulls of 1513. Enmeshed in papal and Imperial politics, endangered by the advance of the Turks, and unwilling, in these crises, to disturb the structure or functioning of the Curia by radical changes, Paul deferred active reform; but the men whom he raised to the cardinalate were almost all known for integrity and devotion.

The movement for internal reform triumphed when its leader, Caraffa, became Paul IV (1555). Monks absent from their monasteries without official sanction and clear necessity were commanded to return at once. On the night of August 22, 1558, the pope ordered all the gates of Rome closed, and all vagrant monks arrested; similar procedures were followed throughout the Papal States, and some offenders were sent to the galleys. Monasteries were no longer to be assigned to support absentee officials with their revenue. Bishops and abbots not actually serving the Curia in a fixed office were required to return to their posts or forfeit their income. The holding of plural benefices was prohibited. All departments of the Curia were bidden to eliminate any suspicion of simony in appointments to clerical positions. Rome now assumed an uncongenial air of external piety and morality. In Italy—less vividly beyond it—the Church had reformed her clergy and her morals while leaving her doctrines deliberately intact.

ST. TERESA

Unique among the monastic reformers was Teresa of Avila in Spain. Her father was a Castilian Knight of Avila, proud of his moral rectitude and his loyalty to the Church; each night he read to his family from the lives of the saints; her mother was an invalid who eased her pain with chivalric romances.

Teresa's childhood imagination vacillated between romantic love and saintly martyrdom. Admirers came when her beauty bloomed; she fell in love with one of them; her father sent her to a nunnery. There she developed a form of epilepsy whose repeated attacks left her physically exhausted. Her father removed her from the convent and sent her to live with her half-sister in the country. On the way an uncle gave her a volume of St. Jerome. Its vivid letters described the terrors of hell and represented the flirtations of the sexes as a parade to eternal damnation. Teresa read anxiously. In 1534 she returned to Avila and there entered the Carmelite Convent of the Incarnation.

For a time she was happy in the soothing routine of repeated masses, collective prayers, and cleansing confessions. Her romantic imaginings were transformed into religious ecstasies; when she took the Sacrament, she felt the consecrated wafer as veritably Christ on her tongue and then in her blood.

In the growing intensity of her religious feelings she was more and more disturbed by the lax discipline of the convent. The nuns lived not in cells but in comfortable rooms; they ate well despite weekly fasts; they adorned their persons with necklaces, bracelets, and rings; they received visitors in the parlor and enjoyed extended vacations outside the convent walls.

Teresa's seizures continued, and worsened into brief but painful paralysis, and at last confined her to her bed. She resolved to refuse all medical treatment and to rely entirely upon prayer. For three years she suffered and prayed. Then, one morning in 1540, she woke to find herself no longer paralyzed. She rose and walked, and daily joined more actively in the conventual regimen. Her recovery was acclaimed as a miracle, and she believed it so. Her visions continued, but now took the form of religious ecstasies. In one it seemed to her that "an exceedingly beautiful angel thrust a long dart of gold," tipped with fire, "through my heart several times, so that it reached my very entrails. So real was the pain that I was forced to moan aloud, yet it was so surpassingly sweet that I would not wish to be delivered from it. No delight of life can give more content. As the angel withdrew the dart he left me all burning with a great love of God." This and other passages in St. Teresa's writings lend themselves to psychoanalytic interpretations, but no one can doubt the high sincerity of the saint. She was convinced that she saw God and that the most recondite problems were made clear to her in these visions.

Fortified by them, Teresa, in her fifty-eighth year, decided to reform the order of the Carmelite nuns. She organized a new convent, to which she removed such nuns and novices as would accept a regimen of absolute poverty. The original Carmelites had worn coarse sackcloth, had gone always barefoot, had eaten frugally and fasted frequently. Teresa required of her Discalced (shoeless) Carmelites approximately the same rule not as an end in itself, but as a symbol of humility and rejection of this tempting world. A thousand obstacles were raised; the townsmen of Avila denounced the plan as threatening to end all communication between the nuns and their relatives.

The provincial of the order refused permission for the experiment. Teresa appealed to Pope Pius V and won his consent. She found four nuns to join her, and the new convent of St. Joseph was consecrated in 1562 on a narrow street in Avila. The sisters wore sandals of rope, slept on straw, ate no meat, and remained strictly within their house.

Teresa's rule was loving, cheerful, and firm. The convent was closed to the lay world; the windows were covered with cloth; the tiled floor served as beds, tables, and chairs. A revolving disk was built in the wall; whatever food was placed in it by the unseen people was gratefully accepted, but the nuns were not allowed to beg. They eked out their sustenance by spinning and needlework; the products were placed outside the convent gate; any buyer might take what he liked and leave whatever he wished in return. Despite these austerities new members came; and one of them was the most beautiful and courted woman in Avila.

The general of the Carmelites was so impressed that he asked Teresa to establish similar houses elsewhere in Spain. In 1567, taking a few nuns with her, she traveled in a rude cart over seventy miles of rough roads to establish a Discalced Carmelite nunnery at Medina del Campo. The only house available to her was an abandoned and dilapidated building with crumbling walls and leaking roof; but when the townspeople saw the nuns trying to live in it, carpenters and roofers came, unasked and unpaid, to make repairs and simple furniture.

Amid her travels and tribulations, Teresa wrote famous manuals of mystical devotion. In one of them she revealed the return of her physical ailments. "It seems as though many swollen rivers were rushing, within my brain, over a precipice; and then again, hardly drowned by the noise of the water, are voices of birds singing and whistling. I weary my brain and worsen my headaches." Her attacks returned, and her stomach found it hard to retain food. Even so, she passed painfully from one to another of the nunneries she had founded, examining, improving, inspiring. At Malaga she was seized with a paralytic fit; she recovered, went to Toledo, and had another seizure; again recovered, she went on to Segovia, Valladolid, and Burgos to Alba de Tormes. There a hemorrhage of the lungs forced her to stop. She accepted death cheerfully, confident that she was leaving a world of pain and evil for the everlasting friendship of Christ.

Meanwhile a more famous saint had come out of Spain to reform the Church and move the world.

IGNATIUS LOYOLA

He was born in the castle of Loyola in the Basque province of Guipuzcoa in 1491. He was brought up to be a soldier and showed no interest in religion. His reading was almost confined to romances of chivalry. He fell in love with the new queen of Spain, Germaine de Foix; he chose her as his "Queen of Hearts" and dreamed of winning a lace handkerchief from her hand for victory in a tournament.

In his autobiography he confessed that he had engaged in less lofty amours as the usual consolation of a soldier's life. When the French attacked Pamplona, he fought eagerly in its defense; he suffered severe injury to his right leg, and incompetent surgery left it permanently shorter than its mate. During a long convalescence in the family castle he asked for books; the only ones available were a *Life of Christ* and *Flos sanctorum,* recalling and adorning the sufferings of the saints. He resolved to equal them in bravery; as soon as his leg healed, he would lead a Christian army against Islam. In him, as in St. Dominic, the intensity of Spanish faith made religion no quiet devotion but total dedication in a holy war.

He had read that the Holy Grail had once been hidden in a castle of Montserrat in the province of Barcelona. There, said the most famous of all romances, Amadis had kept a full night's vigil before an image of the Virgin to prepare himself for knighthood. As soon as Ignatius could travel, he mounted a mule and set out for the distant shrine. Arrived in Montserrat, he cleansed his soul with three days of confession and penance, gave his costly raiment to a beggar, and donned a pilgrim's robe of coarse cloth.

He spent the night of March 24–25, 1522, alone, we are told, in the chapel of a Benedictine monastery, kneeling or standing before the altar of the Mother of God. He pledged himself to perpetual chastity and poverty. The next morning he received the Eucharist, gave his mule to the monks, and set out on limping foot for Jerusalem.

He sailed from Barcelona in February 1523. He stayed two weeks in Rome, escaping before its pagan spirit could bend him from sanctity. On July 14 he took a ship from Venice to Jaffa. He suffered a host of calamities before reaching Palestine, but his visions sustained him. Jerusalem itself was a tribulation: the Turks who controlled it allowed Christian visitors, but no proselytizing, and when he proposed to convert the Moslems, the Franciscan provincial who had been charged by the pope to keep the peace bade the saint return to Europe. In March 1524 he was back in Barcelona.

Perhaps he felt now that, though he was master of his body, he was the slave of his imaginings. He resolved to chasten his mind with education. Though now thirty-three, he joined schoolboys in studying Latin. But the itch to teach is stronger than the will to learn. Soon Ignatius, as he was scholastically called, began to preach to a circle of pious but charming women. Their lovers denounced him as a spoilsport and beat him brutally.

Disappointed with Spain, he set out for Paris, always on foot and in pilgrim garb, but now driving before him a donkey loaded with books. At Paris he lived in the poorhouse and begged in the streets for his food and tuition. He entered the Collège de Montaigu, where his sallow, haggard face, starved body, unkempt beard, and aged clothing made him a focus of unsympathetic eyes; but he pursued his purposes with such absorbed intensity that some students began to revere him as a saint. Under his lead they engaged in spiritual exercises of prayer, penance, and contemplation. In 1529 he transferred to the Collège de Ste. Barbe, and there, too, he gathered disciples. His two roommates came by different routes to believe in his sanctity. Pierre Favre—Peter Faber—had suffered severely from fears superstitious or real, and under their influence he had vowed perpetual chastity. The other roommate, Francis Xavier, came from Pamplona, where Loyola had soldiered. He had a long line of distinguished ancestors; he was handsome, rich, proud, a gay blade who knew the taverns of Paris and their girls. Yet he was clever in his studies; he already had a master's degree, and was aiming at a doctorate. One day he saw a man whose face was pocked with syphilis; it gave him pause. Once, when Francis was expounding his ambition to shine in the world, Ignatius quoted to him the Gospel: "What is a man profited if he gain the whole world and lose his own soul?" Xavier could not forget that question. He began to join Loyola and Faber in their spiritual exercises.

They scourged themselves, fasted, slept in thin shirts on the floor of an unheated room, and stood barefoot and almost naked in the snow to harden and yet subdue their bodies. Ignatius modeled these exercises on an old Benedictine form, but he poured into that mold a fervor of feeling and imagination that made his little book a moving force in modern history.

Their call to lifelong devotion found nine students at Paris ready to accept it. He proposed that in due time they should go together to Palestine and live there a life as nearly as possible like Christ's. On August 15, 1534, Loyola, Faber, Xavier, and seven others, in a little chapel in Montmartre, took the vows of chastity and poverty, and pledged themselves, after two years of further study, to go and live in the Holy Land. In the winter of 1536–37 they walked through France, over the Alps, and across Italy to Venice, where they hoped to find passage to Jaffa. But Venice was at war with the Turks; the trip was impossible. Loyola and his disciples agreed that if, after a year's wait, Palestine should still be closed to them, they would offer themselves to the pope for any service that he might assign to them. Faber secured permission for all of them to be ordained priests. In the fall of 1537, Loyola, Faber, and Laynez set out from Venice for Rome to ask papal approval of their plans. They walked all the way, begged their food, and lived mostly on bread and water. But they sang songs happily as they went along, as if they knew that out of their small number would grow a powerful and brilliant organization.

They were well received by Pope Paul III, were dissuaded from going to Palestine, and reorganized themselves into the Compañia de Jesus as soldiers enlisted for life in a war against unbelief and all other forces making for the dissolution of the Church. As new candidates were received into the Company, it became desirable to define its principles and its rule. The role of obedience was added to those of chastity and poverty; the "general" chosen by them was to be obeyed only next to the pope.

A fourth vow was taken to "serve the Roman Pontiff as God's vicar on earth," and "to execute immediately without hesitation or excuse all that the reigning pontiff or his successors may enjoin upon them for the benefit of souls or for the propagation of the faith" anywhere in the world. In 1539, Loyola asked Cardinal Contarini to submit these articles of organization to Pope Paul III. The pope overcame all opposition and, by a bull of September 27, 1540, formally established what the bull called the Societas Jesu.

On April 17, 1541, Ignatius was elected general of the new order. For several days thereafter he washed dishes and discharged the humblest offices. Between 1547 and 1552 he drew up the Constitutions, which, with minor changes, are the Jesuit rule today. From his small, bare room he guided with severe authority and great skill the movements of his little army in every quarter of Europe and in other quarters of the globe. The task of governing the expanding Society, and of establishing and administering two colleges and several charitable foundations, proved too much for his temper as he aged; and though kind to the weak he became cruelly harsh to his close subordinates. He was severest on himself. He made many a meal from a handful of nuts, a piece of bread, and a cup of water. When he died (1556), many Romans felt that a sharp wind had ceased to blow, and some of his followers mingled relief with their grief. Men could not realize, so soon, that this indomitable Spaniard was one of the most influential men in modern history.

By the time of his death there were a hundred Jesuit colleges. Through education, diplomacy, and devotion, through fervor directed by discipline, through coordination of purposes and reach. Through skillful variation of means, the Jesuits in 1536 turned back the Protestant tide and recaptured much of Germany, most of Hungary and Bohemia, and all of Christian Poland for the Church. Rarely has so small a group achieved so much so rapidly. Year by year its prestige and influence grew, until, within twenty years of its formal establishment, it was recognized as the most brilliant product of the Catholic Reformation.

When at last the Church dared to summon a general council to quiet its theological strife and heal its wounds, it was to a handful of Je-

suits—to their learning, loyalty, discretion, resourcefulness, and eloquence—that the popes entrusted the defense of their own challenged
authority and the undiminished preservation of the ancient faith.

THE COUNCIL OF TRENT (1545–63)

A thousand voices, long before Luther, had called for a council to reform the Church. Luther appealed from the pope to a free and general
council; Charles V demanded such a council in the hope of getting the
Protestant problem off his hands, and perhaps of disciplining Clement
VII. That harried pope could find a hundred reasons for postponing a
council until he should be beyond its reach. Paul III had all of
Clement's fears, but more courage.

In 1536 he proclaimed a general council to meet at Mantua on May
23, 1537, and he invited the Protestants to attend. He assumed that all
participants would accept the conclusions of the conference; but the
Protestants, who would be in a minority there, could hardly accept
such an obligation. Luther advised against attending, and the congress
of Protestants at Schmalkalden returned the pope's invitation un-
opened. After many negotiations and delays Paul agreed to have the
council meet at Trent, at the foot of the Alps, on November 1, 1542.
Charles V, hoping to persuade the Protestants to attend, asked for a
postponement, and it was not till December 13, 1545, that the "Nineteenth Ecumenical Council of the Christian Church" began its active
sessions.

Four cardinals, four archbishops, twenty bishops, five generals of
monastic orders, some abbots, and a few theologians made up the assembly. Whereas at the Councils of Constance and Basel, priests,
princes, and certain laymen, as well as prelates, could vote, here only
the cardinals, bishops, generals, and abbots could vote, and the vote
was by individuals; hence the Italian bishops—most of them indebted
to the papacy—dominated the assembly with their numerical majority. "Congregations" sitting in Rome under the supervision of the pope
prepared the issues which alone might be submitted for debate. Since
the Council claimed to be guided by the Holy Ghost, a French delegate
remarked that the third person of the Trinity regularly came to Trent in
the courier's bag from Rome.

In May 1546, Paul sent two Jesuits, Laynez and Salmeron, to help his legates in matters of theology and papal defense; later they were joined by Peter Canisius and Claude Le Jay. The unequaled erudition of the Jesuits gave them paramount influence in the debates, and their unbending orthodoxy guided the Council to declare war against the ideas of the Reformation rather than seek reconciliation and unity. It was apparently the judgment of the majority that no concessions to the Protestants would heal the schism; that Protestants were already so numerous and diverse that no compromise could satisfy some without offending others; that any substantial alteration of traditional dogmas would weaken the whole doctrinal structure and stability of Catholicism; that the admission of priestly powers in the laity would undermine the moral authority of the priesthood and the Church; that authority was indispensable to social order; and that a theology frankly founded on faith would stultify itself by submitting to the vagaries of individual reasoning.

Consequently the fourth session of the Council (April 1546) reaffirmed every item of the Nicene Creed, claimed equal authority for Church tradition and Scripture, gave the Church the sole right to interpret and expound the Bible, and declared the Latin Vulgate of Jerome to be the definitive translation and text. Thomas Aquinas was named as the authoritative exponent of orthodox theology, and his *Summa theologica* was placed on an altar only below the Bible and the Decretals. Catholicism as a religion of infallible authority dates in practice from the Council of Trent, and took form as an uncompromising response to the challenge of Protestantism, rationalism, and private judgment. The "Gentlemen's Agreement" of the Renaissance Church with the intellectual classes came to an end.

The thirteenth session of the Council (October 1551) reaffirmed the Catholic doctrine of transubstantiation: the priest, in consecrating the bread and wine of the Eucharist, actually changes each of them into the body and blood of Christ. Thereafter it seemed useless to hear the Protestants, but Charles insisted on it. The duke of Württemberg, Elector Maurice of Saxony, and some southern German towns chose members for a Protestant delegation, and Melanchthon drew up a statement of Lutheran doctrine to be submitted to the Council. On January 24, 1552, the Protestant deputies addressed the assembly.

They proposed that the decrees of the Councils of Constance and Basel on the superior authority of the councils over the popes should be confirmed, that the members of the present body should be released from their vows of fealty to the pope (who was now Julius III); that all decisions hitherto reached by the Council should be annulled; and that fresh discussion of the issue should be held by an enlarged synod in which the Protestants would be adequately represented. Julius III forbade consideration of these proposals.

Military developments supervened upon theology. In January 1552, the king of France signed an alliance with the German Protestants; in March, Maurice of Saxony led a Protestant army against Innsbruck; Charles V fled, and no force could prevent Maurice, if he wished, from capturing Trent and swallowing the Council. The bishops one by one disappeared, and on April 28 the Council of Trent was formally suspended. By the Treaty of Passau (August 2) King Ferdinand of Germany conceded religious freedom to the militarily victorious Protestants. They took no further interest in the Council.

After diverse delays the seventeenth session of the Council convened on January 18, 1562. At Ferdinand's request a safe-conduct was offered to any Protestant delegate who might care to attend; none came. In the end the papal authority was not lessened but enlarged, and every bishop was required to take an oath of complete obedience to the pope. This basic matter settled, the Council quickly dispatched its remaining business. Clerical marriage was forbidden, and severe penalties were decreed against priestly concubinage. Many minor reforms were enacted to improve the morals and discipline of the clergy. The powers of the Curia were curbed. Rules were laid down for the reform of Church music and art; nude figures were to be sufficiently covered to avoid stimulating the sensual imagination. Purgatory, indulgences, and the invocation of the saints were defended and redefined.

The Council frankly recognized the abuses that had sparked Luther's rebellion; one decree read: "In granting indulgences . . . the Council decrees that all criminal gain therewith connected shall be entirely done away with, as a source of grievous abuse among Christian people." Pope and emperor having agreed that the Council had now reached an end of its duties and usefulness, it was finally dissolved on December 4,

1563, amid the happy declamations of wearied delegates. The course of the Church had been fixed for centuries.

The Catholic or "Counter" Reformation succeeded in its major purposes. Men continued, in Catholic and Protestant countries, to lie and steal, seduce maidens and sell offices, kill and make war. But the morals of the clergy improved, and the wild freedom of Renaissance Italy was tamed to a decent conformity with the pretensions of mankind.

Prostitution, which had been a major industry in Renaissance Rome and Venice, now hid its head; chastity became fashionable. The joyous character of Renaissance Italy faded; Italian women lost some of the allure and exhilaration that had come from pre-Reformation freedom; a conscious morality produced an almost puritan age in Italy. Monasticism revived.

Ecclesiastical reforms were substantial and lasting. Though the papal monarchy was exalted as against the episcopal aristocracy of the councils, this was in the spirit of the times, when aristocracies everywhere, except in Germany, were losing power to the kings. The popes were now morally superior to the bishops, and the discipline required for ecclesiastical reform could be better effected by a centralized than by a divided authority. The popes ended their nepotism and cured the Curia of its costly procrastinations and flagrant venality.

The administration of the Church, according to non-Catholic students of the matter, became a model of efficiency and integrity. The dark confessional box was introduced (1547) and made obligatory (1614); the priest was no longer tempted by the occasional beauty of his penitents. Indulgence pedlars disappeared. Instead of retreating before the advance of Protestantism and free thought, the Catholic Church set out to recapture the mind of youth and the allegiance of power.

The spirit of the Jesuits—confident, positive, energetic, and disciplined—became the spirit of the militant Church.

Chapter Twenty-one

SHAKESPEARE AND BACON

PERSPECTIVE

The Age of Elizabeth I in England was the Renaissance (Shake-speare), the Reformation (Elizabeth), and the Enlightenment (Bacon) united in an explosive concentration of genius and history.

A hundred factors contributed to the complex result: the liberation of England from external control of her religious and intellectual life; forty-five years of political stability and development under a judicious queen and her self-effacing councillors; the appropriation of ecclesiastical wealth for the educational, political, and economic life of England; the growth of agriculture, industry, navigation, commerce, and finance in a nation bursting with liberated inventiveness and energy; the defeat of the Spanish Armada in 1588; the resultant mastery of the North Atlantic; the easier access to a North America inviting investment and enterprise; the spread of education, the multiplication of schools and colleges, the widening acquaintance of Englishmen and Englishwomen with Italian, French, and Spanish civilization, literature, and art.

These and other developments raised the mind and spirit of a sturdy, stoic, and enterprising people to heights unrivaled before or since on

[t]his fortress built by nature for herself
Against infection and the hand of war,

This happy breed of men, this little world,
This precious stone set in the silver sea. . . .
This blessed plot, this earth, this realm, this England.

So sang her most famous son (*Richard II* 3.2).

One problem England had not solved: how to restore peace of mind and worship after a religious revolution that had left England divided into a dozen faiths or with no religious belief at all, and inviting the moral chaos that comes with the shedding of once-feared and -honored gods who had served as guardians of order and peace. Catholics and Protestants, Puritans and Epicureans, agnostics and atheists, competed with one another in an arena wider than ever since the coming of Christianity to the isle.

Raleigh and Marlowe made little effort to conceal their atheism; Raleigh was beheaded after repeated pardons and offenses; Marlowe died in a tavern brawl. Many Londoners, especially at the court, were agnostics, but kept it secret except in their inner circles. Shakespeare mourned his loss of faith as reducing human life to an unforgivable succession of pains and griefs culminating in the transformation of even the most virtuous soul into a defeated dream. His resentment of this defeat of theology by biology darkened some of his greatest plays into the bitterest indictment of human life in English literature.

THE PESSIMISM OF SHAKESPEARE

In 1582, Shakespeare, eighteen years old, submitted to a "shotgun" marriage with Anne Hathaway, twenty-five, both of Stratford-on-Avon. Six months later she gave him a daughter, Susanna; and in 1585, twins, Hamnet and Judith. Probably toward the end of that year he left wife and children; then we lose track of him till we find him, age twenty-eight, in London, doing well as an actor and already writing plays; his *Richard III* (1593) astonished Marlowe and other predecessors with its depth of analysis, intensity of feeling, and brilliant flashes of happy phrase; the lusty youths of the capital were shouting, "A horse! a horse! my kingdom for a horse!" Yet it was in that hectic and disillusioning environment that Shakespeare—perhaps to win a gift from a titled dedicatee—wrote his narrative poems—*Venus and Adonis*

and *The Ravishment of Lucrece,* and, in Petrarchan style, 154 sonnets that
hovered between homosexual and heterosexual love.

All the illuminees of the English-speaking world are familiar with
the themes and delights of the thirty-seven plays that Shakespeare
wrote, in part or in whole, but perhaps too little wonder has been expressed at the almost brutal cynicism that sometimes cries out in one
play after another. Amid the happy splendor of their style there cries
out an almost cynical note of anguish, even in the lighthearted comedies; so, in *As You Like It* (1600), "Monsieur Melancholy Jacques" re-
minds us that the only certainty in life is death:

> *And so from hour to hour we ripe and ripe,*
> *And then from hour to hour we rot and rot,*
> *And thereby hangs a tale.* (2.7)

In *Hamlet* (1601) a brutal crime embitters the highly refined son of the
victim to find a graveyard as the end of all greatness: "To what base uses
we must return, Horatio; why may not imagination trace the noble
dust of Alexander till he find it stopping a bung-hole?" (5.1). The
world, in Hamlet's view, "is an unweeded garden that grows to seed;
things rank and gross in nature Possess it merely" (1.2). In *Othello*
(1604), Iago stands for evil, falsehood, and treachery, and triumphantly
survives; Desdemona is goodness, honesty, and fidelity, and is murdered.

The murderer in *Macbeth* judges life mercilessly:

> *Out, out, brief candle!*
> *Life's but a walking shadow, a poor player*
> *That struts and frets his hour upon the stage,*
> *And then is heard no more; it is a tale*
> *Told by an idiot, full of sound and fury,*
> *Signifying nothing.* (5.5)

Could there be any bitterer judgment on life? Yes. Consider Timon
of Athens, once an Athenian millionaire surrounded by flattering, receptive friends. When he loses his money and sees his friends vanish

overnight, he kicks the dust of civilization from his feet and retires to a forest solitude, where, he hopes, he "shall find the unkindest beasts more kinder than mankind." He wishes Alcibiades were a dog, "that I might love thee something." He lives on roots; digs, finds gold. Friends appear again; he drives them off with lashing scorn; but when prostitutes come, he gives them gold, on condition they will infect as many men as possible with venereal disease:

> *Consumption sow*
> *In hollow bones of man; strike their sharp shins,*
> *And mar men's spurring {marriages}. Crack the*
> *Lawyer's voice,*
> *That he may never more false title plead,*
> *And sound his quillets {quibbles} shrilly; hoar the flamen {priest}*
> *That scolds against the quality of flesh,*
> *And not believes himself; down with the nose,*
> *Down with it flat; take the bridge quite away. . . .*
> *And let the unscarr'd braggarts of the war*
> *Derive some pain from you; plague all*
> *That your activity may defeat and quell*
> *The source of all erection. There's more gold;*
> *Do you damn others, and let this damn you. (Timon of Athens 4.3)*

In an ecstasy of hatred he bids nature cease breeding men, and hopes that vicious beasts may multiply to wipe out the human race. The excesses of this misanthropy make it seem unreal; we cannot believe that Shakespeare felt this ridiculous superiority to sinful men, this cowardly incapacity to stomach life. Such a *reductio ad nauseam* suggests that the disease was purging itself, and that Shakespeare would soon smile again.

In the culminating plays there is a hesitant recognition that, amid the evils of this world, there are blessings and delights, amid the villains many heroes and some saints—for every Iago a Desdemona, for every Goneril a Cordelia, for every Edmund an Edgar or a Kent; even in *Hamlet* a fresh wind blows from Horatio's faithfulness and Ophelia's wistful tenderness. After the tired actor and playwright leaves the consuming chaos and crowded loneliness of London for the green fields and family love of his Stratford home, he will recapture the strong man's love of life.

RECONCILIATION

"He was wont," said John Aubrey (1626–97), "to go to his native country once a year." In 1597 he bought for 60 pounds "New Place," the second-largest house in Stratford, but he continued to live in London. His father died in 1601, leaving him two houses in Stratford. A year later the prospering playwright bought, near Stratford, 127 acres of land. In 1605 he bought for 440 pounds a share in the ecclesiastical tithes of Stratford and three other communities. While he was writing his greatest plays, he was known in Stratford as a successful business-man, frequently engaged in litigation about his investments.

His son Hamnet had died in 1596. In 1607 his daughter Susanna married a prominent Stratford physician, and a year later she made the poet a grandfather. He had now new ties to draw him homeward. About 1610 he left London and the stage, and moved into New Place. Apparently it was there that he composed *Cymbeline* (1609), *The Winter's Tale* (1610), and *The Tempest* (1611). The last shows him still master of his dramatic skills and his poetic flare. Here is Miranda, who at the outset reveals her nature when, seeing a shipwreck from the shore, she cries out, "Oh, I have suffered with those that I saw suffer!" And here is Prospero, the kindly old magician, surrendering the wand of his art, and bidding his airy world a fond goodbye. We hear Shakespeare in Prospero's farewell to his art:

> *Our revels now are ended, These our actors,*
> *As I foretold you, were all spirits,*
> *And are melted into thin air, into thin air,*
> *And, like the baseless fabric of this vision,*
> *The cloud-capped towers, the gorgeous palaces,*
> *The solemn temples, the great globe itself,*
> *Yea, all which it inherits, shall dissolve,*
> *And, like this insubstantial pageant faded,*
> *Leave not a rack behind. We are such stuff*

As dreams are made on, and our little life
Is rounded with a sleep.

But this is not now the dominant mood; on the contrary the play is Shakespeare relaxing, talking of brooks and flowers, singing songs like "Full fathom five," and "Where the bee sucks there suck I." And, despite all cautious demurrers, it is the aging poet who speaks through Prospero's farewell:

> *. . . Graves at my command*
> *Have waked their sleepers, oped, and let 'em forth*
> *By my so potent art. But this rough magic*
> *I here abjure. . . . I'll break my staff,*
> *Bury it certain fathoms in the earth,*
> *And deeper than did ever plummet sound*
> *I'll drown my book.*

And perhaps it is Shakespeare again, rejoiced by his daughter and his grandchild, who cries out, through Miranda:

> *O wonder!*
> *How many goodly natures are there here!*
> *How beauteous mankind is! O brave new world*
> *That hath such people in it!*

But now, having learned to love life, he had to prepare for death. Edgar had told Gloucester in *King Lear*:

> *Men must endure their going hence,*
> *Even as their coming hither;*
> *Ripeness is all.* (5.2)

Maturity, not eternity, should be our goal. On March 25, 1616, Shakespeare made his will. In April, according to John Wall, vicar (1661–81) of Stratford Church, "Shakespeare, Drayton, and Ben Jonson had a merry party, and, it seems, drank hard, for Shakespeare died of a fever there contracted." Death came on April 23, 1616. The body was buried under the chancel of the Stratford Church. Nearby, on the floor, graven on a stone bearing no name, is an epitaph which local tradition ascribes to Shakespeare:

> Good friends, for Jesus sake forbear
> To dig the dust enclosed here.
> Blese be ye man yt (that) spares thes stones
> And curst be he yt moves my bones.

BACON, ESSEX, AND ELIZABETH

How different from Shakespeare was Francis Bacon—emotion subordinated to intellect, defeat overcome by hope, the vicissitudes of life submerged in the largest vision of the coming triumph of the human mind. Did ever such optimism survive so devastating a defeat?

He had every advantage, and earned an apparently mortal defeat. He was born (1561) in the very aura of the court—at York House, official residence of the lord keeper of the Great Seal, who was his father, Sir Nicholas Bacon: Queen Elizabeth called the boy "the young Lord Keeper." His frail constitution drove him from sports to study; his agile mind took to knowledge hungrily; soon his erudition was among the wonders of those spacious times. After three years at Cambridge he was sent to France with the English ambassador to let him learn the ways of state. While he was there, his father died, before buying the supportive property that he had intended for Francis, who was a younger son; and the youth, suddenly reduced to meager means, returned to London to study law at Gray's Inn.

Being a nephew of William Cecil, lord treasurer of the realm, he appealed to him for some political place; after four years of waiting, he sent him a whimsical reminder that "the objection of my years will wear away with the length of my suit"—he should have known that wit hinders political advancement. Nevertheless, in that year 1584, still but twenty-three, he was elected to Parliament.

The earl of Essex relished the keenness of Bacon's mind and invited his advice. The young sage counseled the young noble to seem, if he could not be, modest; to moderate his expenditures, and to regard his popularity with the populace as a barrier to the queen. He himself was hardly modest, as witness his further appeal to Cecil (1591):

> I wax now somewhat ancient; one-and-thirty years is a great deal of sand in the hourglass. . . . The meanness of my estate doth some- what move me. . . . I confess that I have as vast contemplative ends as I have moderate civil ends; for I have taken all knowledge to be my province. . . . This, whether it be curiosity, or vainglory, or nature . . . is so fixed in my mind as it cannot be removed.

Edward Coke, technically more fit for the office in mind—attorney general—was chosen instead.

Despite Bacon's advice, Essex joined the war party and planned to make himself head of an army. His dashing bravery at Cádiz made him too popular for the Privy Council's taste; failure in the Azores and his undiminished pride, extravagance, and sharp tongue alienated the court and irritated the queen. When she flatly rejected his recommen- dation of Sir George Carew for office in Ireland, he turned his back on her with a gesture of contempt. Furious, she boxed his ears and cried, "Go to the Devil!" He grasped his sword and shouted at her, "This is an outrage that I will not put up with. I would not have put up with it from your father's hands." He rushed in anger from the room, and all the court expected him to be banished to the Tower (1598). Instead— perhaps to get rid of him—she appointed him lord deputy to Ireland.

Bacon had cautioned him to avoid that ungrateful task of counter- ing a faith by an army, but Essex wanted an army. On March 27, 1599, he left for Dublin amid the acclamation of the populace, the misgiv- ings of his friends, and the satisfaction of his enemies. Six months later, having failed in his mission, he hurried back to England without per- mission of the government, rushed unannounced into the queen's dressing room, and tried to explain his failure. She listened wrathfully and had him committed to the Lord Keeper (Bacon's father) at York House until the charges against him could be heard.

The people of London murmured, for they were ignorant of his fail- ure and recalled his victories. The Privy Council ordered a semipublic trial, and commissioned Bacon—as a lawyer pledged to defend the queen—to draw up a statement of the charges against Essex. He asked to be excused; the council insisted. He drew up as moderate an indictment as possible.

Essex acknowledged its truth and offered full submission. He was suspended from all his offices, and was told to remain in his home till the queen should be pleased to free him (June 5, 1600). Bacon pleaded for him, and on August 26 Essex was restored to liberty.

In his own Essex House he continued to search for power. One of his intimates was Shakespeare's patron Henry Wriothesley, earl of Southampton. Essex sent him to Ireland to propose that Mountjoy, now lord deputy there, should return to England with the English army and help Essex to capture the government. Mountjoy refused. Early in 1601, Essex wrote to James VI of Scotland, asking his aid and promising to support him as successor to Elizabeth; James sent him a letter of moderate encouragement. Wild rumors spread through the excited capital: that Robert Cecil was planning to make the Spanish infanta queen of England; that Essex was to be immured in the Tower; that Raleigh had vowed to kill him. Perhaps to force Essex to show his hand, the younger Essex induced the queen to bid Essex come and attend the Privy Council. His friends warned him that this was a ruse to seize him. One friend, Sir Gilly Merric, paid the Chamberlain's Company to stage, that same evening in Southwark, Shakespeare's *Richard II,* which showed a sovereign justly deposed.

The next morning (February 7, 1601) some three hundred of Essex's supporters, fervent and armed, gathered in the courtyard of his home. When the lord keeper and three other dignitaries came to ask the cause of this illegal assembly, the crowd locked them up and swept the hesitant earl with them to London and revolution. He had hoped that the people would rise to his cause, but preachers bade them stay indoors, and they obeyed. The forces of the government routed the rebels. Essex was captured and lodged in the Tower.

He was quickly brought to trial on a charge of treason. The council bade Bacon help Coke in preparing and presenting the government's case. His refusal would have ruined his political career; his consent ruined his posthumous reputation. When Coke faltered in presenting the indictment, Bacon rose and stated the case with convincing clarity.

Essex confessed his guilt and named his accomplices. Five of these were arrested and beheaded.

Legend told how Essex sent the queen a ring once given him by her with a promise to come to his aid if he should ever return it in his hour of need. If sent, it seems never to have reached her. On February 25, 1601, at thirty-five, Essex went gallantly to the fate that was the seal of his character. For a year the Tower displayed the severed and decaying head.

THE MAGIC FADES (1601–3)

The sight of that head, or the knowledge that it was staring down upon her night and day, must have shared in the somber mood of Elizabeth's final years. She sat alone for hours in pensive melancholy. She maintained the amusements of her court and made at times a pretense of gaiety, but her health was gone and her heart was dead. England had ceased to love her; it felt that she had outlived herself and should make room for younger royalty. The last of her parliaments rebelled more vigorously than any before against her infringements of parliamentary freedom, her persecution of Puritans, her gift of monopolies to her favorites. To everyone's surprise, the queen yielded on the last point and promised to end the abuse. All the members of the Commons went to thank her, and they knelt as she gave what proved to be her last address to them, her wistful "Golden Speech" (November 30, 1601):

> There is no jewel, be it of never so rich a price, which I prefer before . . . your love. For I do esteem it more than any treasure. . . . And though God has raised us high, yet this I count the glory of my crown, that I have reigned with your loves.

She bade them rise, and then continued:

> To be a king and wear a crown is a thing more glorious to them that see it than it is pleasant to them that bear it. . . . For my own part, were it not for conscience' sake to discharge the duty that God hath laid upon me, and to maintain his glory, and keep you in safety, in

mine own disposition I should be willing to resign the place I hold
to any other, and glad to be freed of the glory with the labors, for it is
not my desire to live or to reign longer than my life and reign shall
be for your good. And though you have had and may have many
mightier and wiser princes sitting in this seat, yet you never had, nor
shall have, any love you better.

Rumors moved across Europe that she was dying of cancer. But she
was dying of too much life. Her frame could no longer bear the joys and
sorrows, the blows and burden of the relentless years. In March 1603,
having exposed herself too boldly to the winter cold, she caught a fever.
Through three weeks it consumed her. She spent them mostly in a
chair, or reclining on cushions. She would have no doctors, but she
asked for music. Finally she was persuaded to take to her bed.

Archbishop John Whitgift expressed a hope for her longer life; she
rebuked him. He knelt beside her bed and prayed. When he thought it
was enough, he tried to rise, but she bade him continue; and again,
when "the old man's knees were weary," she motioned to him to pray
some more. He was released only when, late at night, she fell asleep.
She never woke.

She was no saint or sage, but a woman of temper and passion, lustily
in love with life. Not all of her subjects could, as Shakespeare thought,
"eat in safety, under their own vines, what they had planted, and sing
the merry songs of peace"; the Puritans, and to a considerable degree
the Catholics, bore some persecution and disabilities. The wisdom of
her rule was partly that of her aides. The vacillations of her mind
proved often fortunate, perhaps by the chance of change; sometimes
they brought such weakness of policy that the internal troubles of her
enemies had to help her survive. But survive she did, and she prospered
by fair means or devious.

She found England exhausted and despised, and left it rich and powerful; and the sinews of learning and literature grew strong in the
breadth of her understanding and the wealth of her people. She continued the despotism of her father, but moderated it with humanity and
charm.

Denied husband and child, she mothered England, loved it devot-
edly, and used herself up in serving it. Wise in her choice of councillors,

and helped by their counsel, she was the greatest ruler that England has ever had.

THE RISE AND FALL OF FRANCIS BACON
(1603–21)

On the peaceful accession of James VI of Scotland to be James I of England, Francis Bacon, in a letter of adulation in the manner of the time, suggested himself to the king as fit and due for a governmental post. He had already served in Parliament for nineteen years, winning repute for wide learning, constructive thought, clear and striking speech.

Periodically he sent to the king "memories" eloquent with prudent advice: how to improve mutual understanding between Commons and Lords, to unite the parliaments of England and Scotland, to end persecution for religious diversity, to pacify Ireland by conciliating its Catholics, to give greater freedom to Catholics in England without opening the door to papal claims, and to find a compromise between Anglicans and Puritans. "To carry out this program," in the judgment of the historian who most thoroughly studied the politics of this period, "would have been to avert the evils of the next half-century." James put the proposals aside as too much in advance of public opinion, and contented himself by including Bacon in the three hundred knighthoods that were distributed in 1603. Sir Francis had to cool his heels.

Nevertheless his skill as a lawyer slowly raised him to affluence. By 1607 he estimated his wealth at 24,155 pounds. On his luxurious estate at Gorhambury, manned with select and expensive servants, and alert secretaries like Thomas Hobbes, he could enjoy the beauty and comfort that he loved too well. He nursed his health by gardening and built amid his gardens a costly retreat for his scholastic privacy. He wrote like a philosopher and lived like a prince. He saw no reason why reason should be penniless, or why Solomon should not be king.

He did not fall far short. In 1607, James, valuing him at last, made him solicitor general; in 1613, attorney general; in 1616, a member of the Privy Council; in 1617 lord keeper of the Great Seal; in 1618 chancellor. New dignities were added to grace his powers: in 1618 he was created First Baron Verulam; in January 1621, Viscount St. Albans. When James went to Scotland, he left his chancellor to rule England. Bacon "gave audience in great state to ambassadors," and lived in such splendor at Gorhambury that it "seemed as if the court were there, and not in Whitehall or St. James."

All was won save honor. In the pursuit of position, Bacon had occasionally sacrificed principle. As attorney general he used his influence to secure judicial verdicts desired by the king. As keeper of the seal he defended and protected the most oppressive monopolies. As judge he accepted substantial gifts from persons suing in his court. All this was in the loose custom of the age: public officials were poorly paid, and they recompensed themselves with "gifts" from those whom they aided. James confessed, "If I were . . . to punish those who take bribes I should soon have not a single subject left"; and James himself took bribes.

The Parliament that assembled in January 1621 was in angry revolt against the king. It hated Bacon as James' best advocate, who had ruled that monopolies were legal. If it could not yet depose the king, it could impeach his minister. In February it named a committee to inquire into the courts of justice. In March the committee reported that it had found many irregularities, especially in the conduct of the lord chancellor. Twenty-three specific cases of corruption were charged against him. He appealed to the king to save him, predicting that "those who now strike at the Chancellor will soon strike at the Crown." James advised him to acknowledge the charges and so set an example deterrent to further venality in office. On April 22, Bacon sent in his confession to the House of Lords. He admitted taking gifts from litigants, as other judges did; he denied that his decisions had been thereby influenced—in several cases he had ruled against the giver.

The Lords condemned him to pay a fine of 40,000 pounds; to be imprisoned in the Tower during the king's pleasure; to be forever incapable of holding any public office in the Commonwealth; never to sit in Parliament nor come within the verge of the Court. He was taken to the Tower on May 31, but was released within four days by order of the king, who also remitted the ruinous fine. The chastened chancellor retired to Gorhambury and tried to live more simply. In cipher, on paper left by Bacon at his death, his first biographer, Rawley, found the famous statement, "I was the justest judge that was in England these fifty years. But it was the justest censure in Parliament that was these 200 years."

The effects of the indictment were good. It lessened corruption in office, and it set a precedent for the responsibility of the king's ministers to Parliament. It turned Francis Bacon back from politics, where he had been a liberal in views and a reactionary in practice, to his alternative pursuit of science and philosophy, where he would "ring the bell that called the wits together," and would proclaim, in majestic prose, the revolt and promise of reason.

THE GREAT RENEWAL

Philosophy had long been Bacon's refuge from affairs, if not his secret love and happiest aptitude. He had already, in 1605, published *The Proficience and Advancement of Learning*, but that now seemed to him rather a prospectus than a performance. In 1609 he had written to the bishop of Ely, "If God give me leave to write a just and perfect volume of philosophy, . . . " and in 1610 to Isaac Casaubon, "to bring about the better ordering of man's life . . . by the help of sound and true contemplations—this is the thing I aim at."

During those harrassed years of office he had conceived—with a rash assumption of abundant days—a magisterial plan for the renovation of science and philosophy, and seven months before his fall he had announced the plan in a Latin work addressed to all Europe, boldly entitled *Instauratio magna* (The Great Renewal). The title page itself was a challenge: it showed a vessel passing full sail through the Pillars of Hercules into the Atlantic; and where a medieval motto had set between these pillars the warning *Ne plus ultra* (Go no further beyond), Bacon wrote, *"Multi pertransibunt, et augebitur slientia"* ("Many will pass through, and knowledge will be increased").

Finding that "in what is now done in the matter of science there is only a whirling round about, and perpetual agitation, ending where it begins," he concluded, "there was but one course left: . . . to try the whole thing anew upon a better plan, and to commence a total reconstruction of sciences, [practical] arts, and all human knowledge raised upon the proper foundation."

He dedicated the entire project to James I, with apologies for "having stolen from your affairs so much time as was required for this work," but hoping that the result would "go to the memory of your name and the honor of your age"—which it did. James was a man of considerable learning and goodwill; if he could be persuaded to finance the plan, what progress might not be made?

As Roger Bacon, in 1268, had sent to Pope Clement IV his *Opus majus,* seeking aid for a proposed expansion of knowledge, so now his namesake appealed to his sovereign to undertake, as a "royal work," the organization of scientific research and the philosophical unification of the results for the material and moral benefit of mankind. He reminded James of the "philosopher kings"—Nerva, Trajan, Hadrian, Antoninus Pius, and Marcus Aurelius—who had given good government to the Roman Empire for a century (A.D. 96–180).

In an imperial prospectus—*Distributio operis*—he offered a plan of the enterprise. First, he would attempt a new classification of existing or desirable sciences and divide among them the problems and areas of research; this he accomplished in *The Advancement of Learning,* which he translated and expanded in *De augmentis scientiarum* (1623) to reach an international audience. Second, he would examine the shortcomings of contemporary logic and seek a "more perfect use of human reason" than that which Aristotle had formulated in his logical treatises collectively known as the *Organon;* this Bacon did in his *Novum organum* (1620). Third, he would begin a "natural history" of the "phenomena of the universe"—astronomy, physics, biology. Fourth, he would enlist, in a "Ladder of the Intellect," examples of scientific inquiry according to his new method. Fifth, as "Forerunners," he would describe "such things as I myself have discovered."

And sixth, he would begin to expound that philosophy which, from sciences so pursued, would be developed and certified. "The completion, however, of the last part, is . . . both above my strength and beyond my hope." To us who now flounder and gasp in the ocean of knowledge and specialties, Bacon's program seems majestically vain; but knowledge was not then so immense and minute, and the brilliance of the parts performed forgives the presumption of the whole. When he told Cecil, "I have taken all knowledge to be my province," he did not mean that he could embrace all knowledge in detail, but only that he proposed to survey the sciences "as from a rock," with a view to their coordination and encouragement. William Harvey said of Bacon that he "wrote philosophy like a lord chancellor"; yes, and planned it like a general.

We feel the range and sharpness of Bacon's mind as we follow him in *The Advancement of Learning*. He offers his ideas with unwonted modesty, as "not much better than that noise . . . which musicians make while they are tuning their instruments." He calls for the multiplication and support of colleges, libraries, laboratories, biological gardens, museums of science and industry; for the better payment of teachers and researchers, for ampler funds to finance scientific experiments, for better intercommunication, cooperation, and division of labor among the universities of Europe. He does not lose his perspective in the worship of science; he defends a general and liberal education, including literature and philosophy, as promoting a wise judgment of ends to accompany the scientific improvement of means.

Many of his demands have been met by the sciences—for better clinical records, for the prolongation of life by the development of preventive medicine, for the careful examination of "psychical phenomena," and for the development of social psychology. He even anticipated our contemporary studies in the technique of success.

The second and boldest part of the Great Renewal was an attempt to formulate a new method of science. Aristotle had recognized, and occasionally practiced, induction, but the predominant mode of his logic was deduction, and its ideal was the syllogism. Bacon felt that the old *Organon* had kept science stagnant by its stress on theoretical thought rather than practical observation. His *Novum organum* proposed a new organ and system of scientific procedure: the inductive study of nature itself through experience and experiment. Though this book, too, was left incomplete, it is, with all its imperfections, the most brilliant production in English philosophy, the first clear call for an Age of Reason.

It was written in Latin, but in such lucid and pithy sentences that half of it radiates epigrams. The very first lines compacted a philosophy, announcing the inductive revolution, foreshadowing the Industrial Revolution, and giving an empirical impetus to Hobbes, Locke, and John Stuart Mill:

Man, being the servant and interpreter of Nature, can do and understand so much, and so much only, as he has observed, in fact or in
thought, of the course of Nature; beyond this he neither knows anything nor can do anything. . . . Human knowledge and human
power meet in one, for where the course is not known, the effect cannot be produced. Nature, to be commanded, must be obeyed.

And as Descartes, seventeen years later, in his *Discourse on Method,*
would propose to begin philosophy by doubting everything, so Bacon
here demands "an expurgation of the intellect" as the first step in the
Great Renewal:

Human knowledge as we have it is a mere medley and ill-digested
mass, made up of much credulity and much accident, and also of the
childish notions which are at first imbibed.

Therefore we must, at the start, clear our minds of all preconcep-
tions, prejudices, assumptions, and theories. We must turn away even
from Plato and Aristotle, we must sweep out of our thought the
"idols," or time illusions and fallacies, born of our personal idiosyn-
crasies of judgment or the traditional beliefs and dogmas of our group;
we must banish all logical tricks of wishful thinking, all verbal absurdities of obscure thought. We must put behind us all those majestic de-
ductive systems which proposed to draw a thousand eternal verities out
of a few axioms and principles.

There is no magic hat in science; everything taken from the hat in
works must first be put into it by observation or experiment. And not
by mere casual observation, nor by "simple enumeration" of data, but
by "experience . . . sought by experiment." Thereupon Bacon, so often
belittled as ignoring the true method of science, proceeds to describe
the actual method of modern science:

The true method of experience first lights the candle [by hypothesis]
and then by means of the candle shows the way, commencing as it
does with experience duly ordered, . . . and from it educing axioms
["first fruits," provisional conclusions], and from established axioms
again new experiments. . . . Experiment itself shall judge.

However, Bacon was wary of hypotheses; these were too often suggested by tradition, prejudice, or desire—"idols"; he distrusted any procedure in which hypothesis, consciously or not, would select from experience confirmatory data and gloss over, or be blind to, contrary evidence.

The ultimate aim, Bacon felt, should be to apply the method of science to the rigorous analysis and resolute remolding of human character. He urges a study of instincts and emotions, which bear the same relation to the human mind as wind to the sea. Here the fault lies not merely in the seeking of knowledge, but in its transmission. Man could be remade by an enlightened education if we were willing to draw first-rate minds into pedagogy by giving them adequate remuneration and honor. Bacon admires the Jesuits as educators. The confident chancellor concludes: "I stake all on the victory of art over Nature in the race."

A STATESMAN'S PHILOSOPHY

Here, we feel, is a powerful mind—a man, one in a century, at home equally in philosophy and government. It would be interesting to know what the philosopher thought in politics, and what the politician thought in philosophy.

Not that he had any system in philosophy, or left any exposition of his thought, except in logic. We must gather his views from incidental remarks and literary fragments, including his *Essays* (1597, 1612, 1625). With the vanity inherent in authorship, he wrote, in dedicating these to Buckingham, "I do conceive . . . [the] volume may last as long as books last"—but indeed it may. In his formal letters his style is labored and involved so that his wife confessed, "I do not understand his enigmatical folded writing"; in the *Essays* he concealed still more intense labor, disciplined his pen to clarity, and achieved such compact force of expression that very few pages in English prose can match them for significant matter pressed with luminous similes into perfect form. It is as if Tacitus had taken to philosophy and condescended to be clear.

His wisdom is worldly. He leaves metaphysics to the mystical or the rash; even his vaulting ambition rarely leaped from the fragment to the whole. Sometimes, however, he seems to plunge into a determinist materialism: "In nature nothing really exists besides indivisible bodies performing . . . according to a fixed law"; and "inquiries into nature have the best result when they begin with physics and end in mathematics"; but "nature" here may mean only the external world.

He preferred the skeptical pre-Socratic philosophers to Plato and Aristotle, and he praised the materialist Democritus. But he accepted a sharp distinction between body and soul, and anticipated Bergson's chiding of the intellect as a "constitutional materialist": "The human understanding is infected by the sight of what takes place in the mechanical arts, . . . and so imagines that something similar goes on in the universal nature of things."

He rejected in advance the mechanistic biology of Descartes. With careful ambivalence he "seasons" his philosophy with religion "as with salt. I had rather believe all the fables in the [Golden] Legend, and the Talmud, and the Alcoran, than that this universal frame is without a mind."

He puts atheism in its place in a famous passage twice repeated. He analyzes the causes of atheism as . . . "divisions in religion, if they be many; for any one main division addeth zeal to both sides, but many divisions introduce atheism. Another is scandal of priests. And lastly, learned times, specially with peace and prosperity; for troubles and adversities do more bend men's minds to religion."

He lays it down as a rule that "all knowledge is to be limited by religion." According to Rawley, his chaplain, he "repaired frequently, when his health would permit him, to the services of the church . . . and died in the true faith established in the Church of England." Nevertheless, like his great predecessor William of Ockham, he availed himself of the distinction between theological and philosophical truth: faith might hold to beliefs for which science and philosophy could find no evidence, but philosophy should depend only on reason, and science should seek purely secular explanations in terms of physical cause and effect.

Despite his zest for knowledge, Bacon subordinates it to morality; there would be no gain to humanity if the extension of knowledge brought no gain in benevolence. "Of all virtues and dignities of the mind, goodness is the greatest." However, his usual enthusiasm subsides when he speaks of the Christian virtues. Virtue should be practiced in moderation, for the wicked may take advantage of the indiscreetly good. A little dissimulation is necessary to success, if not to civilization. Love is a madness, and marriage is a noose. "He that hath wife and children hath given hostages to fortune, for they are impediments to great enterprises." He agreed with the popes about clerical celibacy: "A single life doth well with churchmen, for charity will hardly water the ground when it must first fill a pool." Friendship is better than love, and married men make unsteady friends.

His political philosophy faced conditions rather than theories. He said a good word for Machiavelli, and frankly accepted the principle that states are not bound by the moral code taught to their citizens. Like Nietzsche he felt that a good war halloweth any cause. In any case "a just and honorable war is the true exercise" to keep a nation in trim. "For empire and greatness it is of most importance that a nation profess arms as their principal honor, study, and occupation." "In the youth of a state arms flourish; in the middle age of a state, learning; and then both of them together for a time; in the declining age of a state, mercantile acts and merchants."

He warned against the concentration of wealth as a chief cause of sedition and revolt. Of these

the first remedy or prevention is to remove by all means possible that material cause . . . which is want and poverty. . . . To which purpose serveth the opening and well-balancing of trade, the cherishing of manufactures; the banishing of idleness; the repression of waste and excess by sumptuary laws, . . . the regulating of prices of things vendible. . . . Above all things good policy is to be used that the treasuries and monies in a state be not gathered into a few hands. . . . Money is like mulch, not good except it be spread.

Bacon smiles at "the philosophers" who "make imaginary laws for imaginary commonwealths; their discourses are as the stars, which give little light because they are so high." Nevertheless in *The New Atlantis* (1624) he described fondly an imaginary island whose people lived happily under laws made for them by a late King Salomon. Instead of a Parliament, a "Salomon's House": an aggregation of observatories, laboratories, libraries, zoological and botanical gardens—manned by scientists, economists, technicians, physicians, psychologists, and philosophers, chosen (as in Plato's *Republic*) by equal tests after equal educational opportunity, and then (without elections) governing the state, or rather ruling nature in the interest of man. "The end of our Foundation," one of these rulers explains to barbarians from Europe, "is the knowledge of causes and secret motions of things, and the enlarging of the bounds of Human Empire, to the effecting of all things possible."

Already, in this South Pacific enchantment, the Salomonic wizards have invented microscopes, telescopes, self-winding clocks, submarines, automobiles, and airplanes; they have discovered anesthetics, hypnosis, and ways of grafting plants, generating new species, and transmitting music to distant places. In Salomon's House government and science are bound together, and all the tools and organization of research that Bacon had begged James I to provide are there part of the equipment of the state. The island is economically independent; it avoids foreign trade as a snare to war; it imports knowledge rather than goods. So the humbled philosopher replaces the proud statesman, and the same man who had advised an occasional war as a social tonic now, in his closing years, dreams of a magic paradise of peace.

THE CHANTICLEER OF REASON

He was not, as Pope thought, "the wisest, brightest, meanest of mankind." Montaigne was wiser, Voltaire brighter, Henry VIII meaner; and Bacon's enemies called him kindly, helpful, and quick to forgive. He was self-seeking to the point of servility, and proud enough to anger the gods, but we share these faults sufficiently to pardon his humanity for the light that he shed. His egotism was the wind in his sails. To see ourselves as others see us would be crippling.

He was not a scientist, but a philosopher of science. His range of observation was immense, but his field of speculation was too vast to allow him much time for special investigations; he attempted some, with little result. He fell far behind the progress of contemporary science. He rejected the Copernican astronomy, but gave good reasons for doing so. He ignored Kepler, Galileo, and Napier. He often noted, in *The New Atlantis,* but still underrated, the role of imagination, hypothesis, and deduction in scientific research. His proposal for a patient collection of facts worked well in astronomy, where the stellar observations and records of thousands of students gave Copernicus inductive material for revolutionary deductions, but it bore small resemblance to the actual methods that in his time discovered the laws of planetary motion, the satellites of Jupiter, the magnetism of the earth, and the circulation of the blood.

He did not claim to have discovered induction. He was not the first to "overthrow Aristotle"; men like Roger Bacon and Petrus Ramus had been doing this for centuries past. And the Aristotle whom they deposed was not (as Francis Bacon sometimes realized) the Greek who had often used and praised induction or experiment, but the transmogrified *ille philosophus* of the Arabs and the Scholastics. He was not the first to emphasize knowledge as the road to power; Roger Bacon had done it, and Campanella had said, with Baconian pithiness, *Tantum possumus quantum scimus*—"Our power is proportioned to our knowledge."

Perhaps the statesman stressed unduly the utilitarian ends of science; yet he recognized the value of "pure" as compared with "applied" science—of "light" as distinct from "fruits." He urged a study of ends as well as means, and foresaw that a century of inventions might create greater problems than it solved if it left human nature unchanged. He might have discovered in his own moral laxity the abyss created by the progress of knowledge beyond the discipline of character.

What remains after all these hindsight deductions? This: that Francis Bacon was the most powerful and influential intellect of his time. Of course Shakespeare stood above him in imagination and literary art, in subtlety of perception and thought; but Bacon's mind ranged over the universe like a searchlight peering and prying curiously into every nook and secret of space. All the exhilarating and expanding enthusiasms of the Renaissance were in him, all the excitement and pride of Columbus sailing madly into a new world. Hear the joyful cry of Cock Robin announcing the dawn:

> Thus have I concluded the portion of learning touching Civil Knowledge, and with civil knowledge have concluded Human Philosophy, and, with human knowledge, Philosophy in General. And being now at some pause, looking back in that I have passed through, this writing seemeth to me, as far as a man can judge of his

own work, not much better than that noise or sound which musicians make while they are tuning their instruments; which is nothing pleasant to hear, but yet is a cause why the music is sweeter
afterwards. So have I been content to tune the instruments of the
muses that they may play that have better hands. And surely, when I
set before me the condition of these times, in which learning hath
made her third visitation or circuit, in all the qualities thereof, as the
excellence and vivacity of the wits of this age; the noble helps and
lights which we have by the travails of ancient writers; the art of
printing, which communicateth books to men of all fortunes; the
openness of the world by navigation, which hath disclosed multi-
tudes of experiments, and a mass of natural history, . . . I cannot but
be raised to this persuasion, that this third period of time will far
surpass that of the Grecian and Roman learning. . . . As for my
labors, if any, if any man shall please himself or others in the repre-
hension of them, they shall make that ancient and patient request,
Verbere sed audi ("Strike me if you will, only hear me"); let men rep-
rehend them, so they observe and weight them.

Men would not listen to him at first; in England, France, and Germany they preferred to carry the competition of faiths to the arbitra-
ment of arms; but when their fury had cooled, those who were not
fettered with certainties organized themselves in the spirit of Bacon for
the enlargement of man's empire not over men but over the conditions
and hindrances of human life.

When Englishmen founded the Royal Society of London for Improving Natural Knowledge (1660), it was Francis Bacon who was
honored as its inspiration, and Salomon's House in *The New Atlantis*
probably pointed its goal. Leibniz hailed Bacon as the regenerator of
philosophy. And when the *philosophes* of the Enlightenment put together their world-shaking *Encyclopédie* (1751), they dedicated it to
Francis Bacon.

"If," said Diderot in the prospectus, "we have come to it successfully,
we shall owe most of it to the Chancellor Bacon, who proposed the plan
of a universal dictionary of sciences and arts at a time when, so to speak,
neither arts nor sciences existed. That extraordinary genius, at a time
when it was impossible to write a history of what was known, wrote

one of what it was necessary to learn." And d'Alembert, in an ecstasy of enthusiasm, called Bacon "the greatest, the most universal and the most eloquent of philosophers." When the Enlightenment had burst into the French Revolution, the Convention had the works of Bacon published at the expense of the state. The tenor and career of British thought from Hobbes to Spencer—excepting Berkeley and Hume and the English Hegelians—followed Bacon's line.

So we may place Francis Bacon at the head of the Age of Reason. He was not, like some of his successors, an idolator of reason; he distrusted all cogitations unchecked by actual experience, and all conclusions tainted with desire. "The human understanding is no dry light, but receives an infusion from the will and affections; whence proceed sciences which may be called 'sciences as one would.' For what man had rather were true he more readily believes." Nor did he, like the *philosophes* of the eighteenth century, propose reason as an enemy of religion, or as a substitute for it; he made room for both of them in philosophy and life. But he repudiated the reliance upon traditions and authorities; he required natural and rational explanations instead of emotional presumptions, supernatural interventions, and popular mythology.

He raised a banner for all the sciences, and drew to it the most eager minds of the succeeding centuries. Whether he willed it or not, the enterprise that he called for—the comprehensive organization of scientific research, the ecumenical expansion and dissemination of knowledge—contained in itself the seeds of the profoundest drama of modern times: Christianity, Catholic or Protestant, fighting for its life against the spread and power of science and philosophy. That drama had now spoken its prologue to the world.

INDEX

ABOUT THE AUTHOR

Will Durant (1885–1981) was awarded the Pulitzer Prize (1968) and the Medal of Freedom (1977). He spent over fifty years writing his critically acclaimed eleven-volume *Story of Civilization* (the later volumes written in conjunction with his wife Ariel). His book *The Story of Philosophy* (1926) is credited as the "work that launched Simon and Schuster" as a major publishing force and is credited with introducing more people to the subject of philosophy than any other book. Throughout his life Durant was passionate in his quest to bring philosophy out of the ivory towers of academia and into the lives of the common man and woman. A champion of human rights issues such as the brotherhood of man and social reform long before such issues were popular, Durant, through his writings, continues to entertain and educate readers the world over, inspiring millions of people to lead lives of greater perspective, understanding, and forgiveness.

This book is also available on audio tape and CD format, read by Will and Ariel Durant. If you would like more information on this and other products featuring Will Durant's life-enhancing philosophy, we encourage you to visit the web site at *www.willdurant.com*.